P9-AGK-108

# DATE DUE

| MY 98 | | | |
|---|---|---|---|
| | | | |
| MY 28'98 | | | |
| MY 7'99 | | | |
| JY 27'99 | | | |
| AP 3'02 | | | |
| | | | |
| | | | |
| | | | |
| | | | |
| | | | |
| | | | |
| | | | |
| | | | |
| | | | |
| | | | |
| | | | |
| | | | |

DEMCO 38-296

# EDITH WHARTON

R

# EDITH WHARTON
## *Art and Allusion*

Helen Killoran

*The University of Alabama Press*

Tuscaloosa and London

Riverside Community College
Library
JUL '97 4800 Magnolia Avenue
Riverside, California 92506

Copyright © 1996
The University of Alabama Press
Tuscaloosa, Alabama 35487-0380

PS 3545 .H16 Z687 1996

Killoran, Helen, 1941-

Edith Wharton

:a

ets the minimum
d for Information
rary Materials,

The picture on the frontispiece shows Edith Wharton in April 1923 as she was being awarded an honorary doctorate by Yale University. AP/ Wide World Photos.

**Library of Congress Cataloging-in-Publication Data**

Killoran, Helen, 1941–
    Edith Wharton : art and allusion / Helen Killoran.
        p.  cm.
    Includes bibliographical references (p. 207) and index.
    ISBN 0-8173-0766-4 (alk. paper)
    1. Wharton, Edith, 1862–1937—Technique.  2. Women and literature—
United States—History—20th century.  3. Allusions in literature.
4. Fiction—Technique.  I. Title.
PS3545.H16Z687  1996
813'.52—dc20                                                      95-8519
                                                                              CIP

British Library Cataloguing-in-Publication Data available

*To my father, Thomas Hanley Killoran,*
*and the memory of my mother,*
*Geraldine Watt Killoran, with love*

# Contents

# Illustrations

# Preface

THIS BOOK CLAIMS that Edith Wharton's techniques of literary allusion are in large part new and meaningful, its writing having been preceded by a thorough study of known techniques of literary allusion. Possibly the best source for a quick survey is Alex Preminger, ed., *The Encyclopedia of Poetry and Poetics* (Princeton: Princeton University Press, 1965). Allusion studies reached a peak in the mid-1970s, fortified by a thorough compilation of works by Carmela Perri. (See Bibliography.) Thereafter interest lagged, although a few books have since appeared, among them David Cowart, *Thomas Pynchon: The Art of Allusion* (Carbondale: Southern Illinois University Press, 1980); Beverly Schlock, *Continuing Presences: Virginia Woolf and the Use of Literary Allusion* (University Park: Pennsylvania State University Press, 1979); Edwin Stein, *Wordsworth's Art of Allusion* (University Park: Pennsylvania State University Press, 1988); and Michael Wheeler, *The Art of Allusion in Victorian Fiction* (London: Macmillan, 1979). In addition, there exist two well-known theoretical studies, Harold Bloom's *A Map of Misreading* (New York: Oxford University Press, 1975) and John Hollander's *The Figure of Echo: A Mode of Allusion in Milton and After* (Berkeley: University of California Press, 1981).

A fault in some (but certainly not all) of the various studies is that terms for allusion, such as "subjunctive," "gnomic," "assimilative" or "paradigmatic," convey little information and create unnecessary difficulty. In an attempt to avoid this problem, I have used the most descriptive existing terms for familiar literary allusions and have tried, when inventing designations, to make them as self-explanatory as possible.

A second background source for this book was a study of Edith Wharton's reading and library. My master list of approximately three thousand titles came from direct references by Edith Wharton in her published and unpublished letters and other writing and from the occasionally inaccurate Maggs Brothers booksellers' list of the contents of her library. My information cannot be completely verified, however, for unfortunately the anonymous owner of Edith Wharton's library ignores scholars' requests for permission to examine the books.

Great help and moral support was provided by many friends and colleagues. While acknowledging their indispensability, I feel obliged to confine printed thanks to those who, at some point in the development of the book, read and commented on portions of it: Ross Posnock, Richard J. Dunn, and Mark Patterson of the University of Washington, Seattle; Adeline Tintner of New York City; Alan Price of Pennsylvania State University, Hazleton; Lawrence I. Berkove of Michigan State University, Dearborn; Clare Colquitt of San Diego State University; and Alan Gribben of Auburn University, Montgomery.

Ohio University—Lancaster has generously provided grants to help defray the costs of permissions. Finally, I wish to thank the University of Alabama Press, especially Nicole Mitchell and Marcia Brubeck, for their editorial patience and precision.

## Permissions

### *Printed Material*

Quotations from *The Writing of Fiction, Ghosts,* "A Cycle of Reviewing," "The Great American Novel," and *Twilight Sleep* reprinted by permission of the estate and the Watkins/Loomis Agency.

Quotations from *In Morocco* by Edith Wharton reprinted with permission of Scribner's, an imprint of Simon & Schuster from *In Morocco* by Edith Wharton. Copyright 1919, 1920 Charles Scribner's Sons; and with permission of the estate and the Watkins/Loomis Agency.

Quotations from *The Age of Innocence* reprinted with the permission of Scribner's, an imprint of Simon and Schuster from *The Age of Innocence* by Edith Wharton. Copyright 1920 D. Appleton and Company; copyright renewed 1948 William R. Tyler; and with permission of the estate and the Watkins/Loomis Agency.

Quotations from *The Glimpses of the Moon* reprinted with the permission of Scribner's, an imprint of Simon and Schuster from *The Glimpses of the Moon* by Edith Wharton. Copyright 1922 D. Appleton and Company; copyright renewed 1949 William R. Tyler; and with permission of the estate and the Watkins/Loomis Agency.

Quotations from *The Mother's Recompense* reprinted with the permission of Scribner's, an imprint of Simon and Schuster from *The Mother's Recompense* by Edith Wharton. Copyright 1925 D. Appleton and Company; copyright renewed 1952 William R. Tyler; and with permission of the estate and the Watkins/Loomis Agency.

Quotations from *The Children* reprinted with the permission of Scribner's, an imprint of Simon and Schuster from *The Children* by Edith Wharton. Copyright 1928 Pictorial Review Company and D. Appleton and Company; copyright renewed (c) 1952 William R. Tyler; and with permission of the estate and the Watkins/Loomis Agency.

Quotations from *Hudson River Bracketed* reprinted with the permission of Scribner's, an imprint of Simon and Schuster from *Hudson River Bracketed* by Edith Wharton. Copyright 1929 D. Appleton & Company; copyright renewed (c) 1957 William R. Tyler; and with permission of the estate and the Watkins/Loomis Agency.

Quotations from *The Gods Arrive* reprinted with the permission of Scribner's, an imprint of Simon and Schuster from *The Gods Arrive* by Edith Wharton. Copyright 1932 D. Appleton & Company; copyright renewed (c) 1960 William R. Tyler; and with permission of the estate and the Watkins/Loomis Agency.

Quotations from Edith Wharton works at the Beinecke Rare Book and Manuscript Library reprinted with permission of the library and Yale University.

*Frontispiece*

Edith Wharton, Yale University, April 1923. AP/Wide World Photos.

*Paintings*

Antonio Correggio, *Venus, Satyr and Cupid*, Musée du Louvre, Cliché des Musées Nationaux—Paris. © Photo R. M. N.

Jean Fragonard, *The Music Lesson*, Musée du Louvre, Cliché des Musées Nationaux—Paris. © Photo R. M. N.

Pablo Picasso, *Gertrude Stein*, New York, The Metropolitan Museum of Art, Bequest of Gertrude Stein, 1946 (47.106).

Nicholas Poussin, *The Inspiration of the Poet*, Musée du Louvre, Cliché des Musées Nationaux—Paris. © Photo R. M. N.

Sir Joshua Reynolds, *The Age of Innocence*, The Tate Gallery, London.

Sir Joshua Reynolds, *Joanna Leigh, Mrs. R. B. Lloyd,* Private Collection, London.

Theodore van Rijsselberghe, *The Reef,* The Kröller-Müller Foundation, Amsterdam.

Theodore Rousseau, *Le Givré,* Walters Art Gallery, Baltimore.

John Singer Sargent, *Bedouin Camp,* circa 1905–06. Watercolor on paper 25.4 × 35.7 (10 × 14 1/16) The Brooklyn Museum 09.811. Purchased by special subscription.

John Singer Sargent, *Robert Louis Stevenson,* 1887, Oil on canvas, 51 × 61.8 cm. (20 1/16 × 24 5/16 i.), 1931.472. Bequest of Mr. and Mrs. Charles Phelps Taft; Taft Museum, Cincinnati, Ohio.

John Vanderlyn, *Ariadne Asleep on the Island of Naxos,* Courtesy of the Pennsylvania Academy of the Fine Arts, Philadelphia. Gift of Mrs. Sarah Harrison (The Joseph Harrison, Jr. Collection).

# Abbreviations

Standard editions of Wharton's works are indicated as follows:

| | |
|---|---|
| AI | *The Age of Innocence* |
| BG | *A Backward Glance* |
| CC | *The Custom of the Country* |
| CH | *The Children* |
| EF | *Ethan Frome* |
| GS | *Ghosts* |
| HM | *The House of Mirth* |
| HRB | *Hudson River Bracketed* |
| GM | *The Glimpses of the Moon* |
| GA | *The Gods Arrive* |
| IB | *Italian Backgrounds* |
| MC | *In Morocco* |
| MR | *The Mother's Recompense* |
| RF | *The Reef* |
| SR | *Summer* |
| TW | *Twilight Sleep* |
| WF | *The Writing of Fiction* |

EDITH WHARTON

# Introduction
## The Sphinx and the Furies

THIS BOOK DESCRIBES how Edith Wharton developed new types of literary allusion that she used as a code, or a cipher containing a message. The following chapters identify the allusions and consider the ways in which allusions to books and art reveal unexpected themes in Wharton's novels. I show how the novels' themes develop into a complex pattern and how that densely woven pattern unveils a personal mythology based on overarching allusions to Greek myths of the Sphinx, the Furies, and the dual-horned "horse," the Dilemma. This mythology in turn reveals personal concerns associated with experiences Edith Wharton preferred not to discuss openly. The messages derive from these concerns.

If Edith Wharton could, she might well react to this study as Nick Lansing of *The Glimpses of the Moon* responds to Susy Lansing's literary critical taste. He "consoled himself by remembering that *Wilhelm Meister* has survived many weighty volumes on aesthetics."[1] Although New Americanists frequently consider studies of literary aesthetics hopelessly unsophisticated in the intricacies of indeterminate discourse, in Edith Wharton's letters, in *A Backward Glance*, and in her novels, she insisted on her aesthetic sensitivity.[2] Aesthetics is a "classic" subject having roots in Aristotle. The topic interests me, and others, and like Goethe's *Wilhelm Meister*, Edith Wharton's work will survive our curiosity.

After careful reading of the chapters describing Wharton's layered allusions, an expert who shares my interest in aesthetics suggested in the kindest way that I must be "much cleverer than Wharton," implying that since Wharton couldn't have accomplished such a massive undertaking, some of the ideas must be mine. I wish I could accept such extravagant credit. My formal training, though reputable, made me, like Lily Bart, a bit too much of a specialist—an "Americanist" with little background, as yet, in the vast riches of the continent, ancient and modern. Wharton would probably have said I am a model product of the progressive American education she so severely criticizes in *Hudson River Bracketed*.[3] The multitudes of books and paintings of which I had never heard until Edith Wharton taught me, like Vance Weston, to find a library, read the books, and examine the paintings, would fill a volume—as in fact it does: this one.

While working with Edith Wharton's allusions, I began to notice not only her unmarked, unattributed allusions, such as the phrase "backward glance"[4] taken from Whitman's memoirs for use as a title for her own but also, woven into her prose, what I came to call "one-word clues." These numerous "clues" might—indeed *should*—raise an alert reader's antennae to the possibility of less than rigorous scholarship. Yet formal logic underlies all my work. One premise is that words have meaning; another is that in literary art every word is important. Gradually, I've come to notice single words that are unusual in a novel's individual style, rhythm, and tone. An example of one I have not yet explained occurs in *Ethan Frome*,[5] a novel written in a plain style to reflect the limited vocabulary and educational simplicity of the New England people that it depicts. Suddenly, and just once, the author uses the word "ebullition" to describe Ethan Frome's reaction to Mattie (*EF* 141). The word is too sophisticated for Ethan. A second look shows that the word is spoken by the narrator, a well-educated engineer, but the vocabulary is lofty coming even from him. And what is the function of "astrolabe" in *The Mother's Recompense*?[6] Are these Edith Wharton's errors? Possibly. But so far I have found that such words usually indicate an "intraauthorial" allusion or a "thematic" allusion. The question becomes, for example: when the word "hamlet" occurs, referring to a small New England town in *Summer*,[7] should I suspect an allusion to Shakespeare? In my work on Edith Wharton the answer is "yes" until I can rule it out.

"Ebullition" and "astrolabe" remain in question, but in *The Age of Innocence*,[8] after finding a direct reference to Edgar Allan Poe, a theme of live burial, and numerous associated words like "abyss" and "vortex," along with echoes of Gissing's novel *The Whirlpool*, the best explanation of the puzzle dictated that Wharton's unexpected use of the word "maelstrom" was—to adopt another Whartonian word—a "signpost," a one-word clue or allusion, in this case to Edgar Allan Poe's short story, "The Descent into the Maelstrom," in which the narrator and his ship are sucked into a whirlpool. While I have not paused in my arguments to explain every one-word clue, reasoning similar to that behind Poe lies behind all such single-word hints. The attempt is to follow the inductive and deductive methods of the author who once called herself the "high priestess of reason" and who claims in *A Backward Glance* that she raised herself on her brother's college text, "Coppée's Elements of Logic" (*BG* 71).

In a recent parody, John Hitt, in the persona of "Nicolitto Machiavelli," advises "Lorenzo the Insignificant" that "if you should write a book (you had better not), be sure that it is unreadable; otherwise you will be called 'brilliant' and forfeit all respect."[9] While there is not much chance that he is right, Edith Wharton risks clarity. I attempt to follow where she leads.

Among the many characteristics that make these allusions new is that they require investigations into the *content* of allusions, not just into their names or designations. Long hours locating the sources of the allusions were followed by even longer periods spent poring over the books themselves, and I have tried to be led only by Edith Wharton's allusions in context. When doubts are possible, I introduce conditionals.

Perhaps the ultimate double twist of irony is that in Edith Wharton's "hieroglyphic world," the "real thing" *is* said and done (*AI* 45) but often goes unrecognized by the characters. The hieroglyphic world appears to allude subtly to Horace Walpole's *Hieroglyphic Tales,* six political satires in the genre of fables that focus on elaborate distortions of logic.[10] According to one such tale, "A New Arabian Nights Entertainment," "naturalists hold that all things are conceived in an egg"; therefore, "the goats of Hirgonqúu might be oviparous" (109). Ellen Olenska's comments on the archaeological fragments in the Cesnola collection contrast with Archer's vision of the "Arabian Night" marvels of future technology (*AI* 284). The second tale, "The King and His Three Daughters," reverberates to "The Three Princesses" in Washington Irving's *The Alhambra* (*AI* 146), the function of which I discuss in Chapter 4, on *The Age of Innocence*. Most of the tales describe children neglected or allowed too much license. In the third tale, "The Dice Box," which recalls the allusion to goddesses playing at dice in *The Reef,* a five-year-old princess is placed on a throne to rule as ruthlessly as Undine does in *The Custom of the Country* and to escape fate in the same type of "fury." Wharton appears to allude to the fourth tale, "The Peach in Brandy" in *The Mother's Recompense,* when Mrs. Minity's daughter in Bridgeport sends her "brandy-peaches" (*MR* 20, 265). In tale 5, "Mi Li: A Chinese Fairy Tale," Mi Li's tutor is deaf and dumb and therefore uses sign language "in recompence" [*sic*]. Tale 6, "A True Love Story," a fable that features a spoiled, neglected "child" who runs sexually wild like a dog while his mother gambles at bridge, recalls the image of Effie Leath "flying down one of the long alleys at the head of her pack."[11] Perhaps these apparent allusions represent only a string of coincidences, but the chances that they are random diminish with each new similarity.

The tale of "Mi Li" also includes a subtle allusion to Oedipus and the Sphinx: "He had been too well educated to put the question to his godmother, for he knew when she uttered an oracle, that it was with intention to perplex, not to inform; which has made people so fond of consulting all those who do not give an explicit answer, such as prophets, lawyers, and any body you meet on the road, who, if you ask the way, reply by desiring to know whence you came" (126).

Some readers may well feel that one or another phrase analyzed here as a literary allusion is a mere cliché. The first question to ask is whether the phrase was a cliché at the time it was written. Even if so, not to begin by assuming that even a cliché is present for a reason badly underestimates the quest for technical perfection that irritated some of Edith Wharton's editors. My work indicates that Wharton did nothing casually and rarely made mistakes. Consider the possibility that in *A Backward Glance* she becomes Robin Goodfellow, Puck, intending to mislead hapless critics like night wanderers away from her secrets, partly from a need for privacy and partly from a tendency toward pure intellectual mischief. In that case, we do well to note her anecdote about the time she published a short story in French only to have Henry James admonish her witheringly: "I do congratulate you, my dear, on the way in which you've picked up every old worn-out literary phrase that's been lying about the streets of Paris for the last twenty years, and managed to pack them all into those few pages." He later added to a friend, "A very creditable episode in her career. *But she must never do it again*" (BG 183–84). The story in question is probably "Les Metteurs en Scène" ("The Stage Managers"), published in 1908 when Wharton was at the height of her allusive creativity, so her "worn-out phrases" may well deserve reexamination as literary allusions.[12]

Many clichés have their source in literature, such as "all's well that ends well" used in *The Mother's Recompense* (MR 266). An old joke comes to mind, the gag about the man who refused to read Shakespeare's plays because they are full of clichés. Wharton seems deliberately to have resorted to the appearance of using them in the course of simplifying the surface of her fiction. So whether a reader judges a particular novel a success or a failure, it is mistaken to assume that Wharton's late work, especially, is not literary art but simply the kind of slick magazine fiction in which clichés are common. Still, it *is* possible that Wharton accidentally included some clichés, that I have made unwarranted literary associations after the fact, or that Wharton made unconscious connections. Yet everything about her use of art and allusion seems so well organized that I can only present these ideas in a spirit of openness to the inquiry of others.

The thesis that nearly every allusion is intentional is based on the vast knowledge of books that made it possible for Wharton to become an aesthetic pioneer. She read prolifically and quickly on many subjects in English, French, German, and Italian. In three days in March 1906, for instance, she completed four volumes of history, each between four and five hundred pages long.[13] If Percy Lubbock can be trusted on the subject, she retained what she read.[14] She was not only well read but well educated in all facets of literature, literary criticism, travel, social and natural sciences, history, philosophy, and the fine arts, including painting, sculpture, and music, and applied arts, especially architecture, interior design, and landscape gardening.

Her knowledge of art was remarkable. Wharton constantly traveled Europe, and the purpose of much of her "motoring" was to study art and architecture.[15] Sometimes she traveled with the great but temperamental Italian Renaissance art historian Bernard Berenson, with whom she enjoyed a thirty-year friendship. Like Henry James, in some of his letters Berenson complained that Edith dragged him through art museums all over Europe at a terrible pace. (Like James, Berenson was slow and methodical.)[16] Berenson would swear to his wife, Mary, that he would never venture on such a jaunt again, but he always did. Wharton's unrelenting grilling of "B.B." on painting and related subjects essentially shows her being chased by Furies of aesthetic interests that, according to *A Backward Glance,* began in childhood (*BG* 29).

In an early travel book, *Italian Backgrounds* (1905), Wharton describes discovering a mislabeled group of terra cotta figures of the Della Robbia school. She had photographs taken and sent them to a reputable academic who confirmed her attribution.[17] Her work constituted a genuine contribution to art historical scholarship. The lengthy list of allusions to artists and sculptors in her work also reflects her knowledge and reading in art history. In fact, half her library, some fifteen hundred titles on art and architecture, was lost when, after Wharton's heir, William R. Tyler, had stored them in London, they were destroyed in Hitler's blitz.[18]

The time and place at which Edith Wharton personally viewed a particular painting to which she alludes is mentioned here when possible, but on the basis of her travels and intellectual friendships with Berenson and other artists and art historians, and her constant, active scholarship, I suspect that while most of the time she had seen them in person, some of those now destroyed fifteen hundred volumes might have served her just as well.

Wharton's study of art and literature became the basis for original techniques of literary allusion, some of which function like symbols or flex like the elaborate "conceits" of seventeenth-century metaphysical poetry. Most fascinating, they work together to form a code. Using the dilemma of contrasting demands by the Sphinx and the Furies as a centering theme, this book defines Wharton's techniques and discusses how literary allusions usually lead to fresh readings of ten novels. From the themes commonly highlighted, this study infers a social message and a human message.

At first I did not suspect what I am now beginning to believe, that Edith Wharton's writing can be studied not only as a continuing series but as a unit that follows a Balzacian plan formulated perhaps around 1898. If the idea of a lifelong plan had occurred to me initially, I would have omitted nothing. But every book must start and stop somewhere between two covers, so I have decided to examine only full-length, complete novels, beginning with Edith Wharton's first success, *The House of Mirth* (1905), and ending with her last complete work, *The Gods Arrive* (1932). (The only exceptions are *The Fruit of the Tree,* which I intended to study with the shorter "New England" novels, and *A Son at the Front,* which I mentally classed with the war writings.) In their techniques, themes, and mythology, the novels contain the code to the "hieroglyphic world" at which *The Age of Innocence* hints and a mythological world mentioned in *A Backward Glance*.

When Edith was five or six years old, a certain Mr. Bedlow came to dine every Sunday evening. As a little girl, she says, "I was allowed to perch on his knee while he 'told me mythology'. . . . The domestic dramas of the Olympians roused all my creative energy. . . . I felt more at home with the gods and goddesses of Olympus who behaved so much like the ladies and gentlemen who came to dine . . . and about whom I was forever weaving stories of my own" (*BG* 33).

Wharton's Olympian story world includes, but certainly does not limit itself to, the tales behind the allusions to the Sphinx and the Furies that recur in these novels. A favorite character in Greek mythology was a monster called the Sphinx that had the body of a lion and the head of a woman. Incestuous offspring of the half-serpent Echidna and her dog-son, Orthus, she killed everyone who failed to answer her riddle. In Sophocles' *Oedipus Rex*, Oedipus encounters the Sphinx but answers her riddle correctly, so he escapes, though ironically his freedom results in fulfillment of the very Delphic prophecies he was attempting to flee: he kills his father and marries his mother.

Another character, Chronus (Time), wanted to murder his father, Uranus, but could not, since Uranus was immortal. Instead, Chronus castrated him. Uranus's testicular blood dripped onto the earth, where it conceived three daughters, goddesses known as the Eumenides or Furies, whose mission was to avenge familial crimes. (The Furies are sometimes loosely known as Fate, a practice I shall continue, although there are some differences in the background legends.) In Aeschylus's tragedy *The Eumenides* (part of the *Orestia* trilogy), Orestes was pursued by the Furies for the murder of his mother, Clytemnestra. He sought protection and justice from the goddess Athena who, among other things, was the inventor of musical instruments, symbols for techniques of poetry and literature. In a trial before Athena, Orestes was vindicated and the Furies pacified.

In Greek legend, any character could be the prey of the Furies, but in Wharton's writing they tend to pursue artists or women (although George Darrow is caught by one in *The Reef*). Lily Bart found that "there were two selves in her, the one she had always known and a new abhorrent being to which it found itself chained. She had once picked up, in a house where she was staying, a translation of the *Eumenides*, and her imagination had been seized by the high terror of the scene where Orestes, in the cave of the oracle, finds his implacable huntresses asleep and snatches an hour's repose. Yes, the Furies might sometimes sleep, but they were there, always there. . . . " (Wharton's ellipses).[19] In *The Children*, the nanny, Miss Scope, confides to Martin Boyne that she fears to tell him more about the children's luck "for fear of the

Fates overhearing."[20] An interesting variation in *The Custom of the Country* is that rather than being pursued, Undine is the pursuer, a goddess before whose "storms of destructive fury" her timid parents cower (*CC* 357). In *Twilight Sleep* nineteen-year-old Nona feels she is a first aid station for her irresponsible parents: "Fate seemed to have put her, Nona, at the very point where all their lives intersected";[21] at this same point the Wyants and the Manfords misunderstand each other's social codes (*TW* 257, 258, 315). There, between the Fates and the codes, the territories of the Sphinx and the Furies meet. During one dark period for the author Vance Weston of *Hudson River Bracketed,* "old memories of pain fed their parasitic growth on new ones, and dead agonies woke and grew rosy when the Furies called. . . . " (*HRB* 400, Wharton's ellipses). Yet when he must write, he is in a "fury" to begin (*HRB* 409). Like his creator, he makes an art of pain, an idea at the core of Wharton's messages.

Occasionally Edith Wharton drops hints of mysteries symbolized by the Sphinx. In the introduction to *Ethan Frome* she remarks that most of the meaning is beneath the "granite outcroppings" (*EF* v). "The real stuff is way down, not on the surface," says Vance in *Hudson River Bracketed* (*HRB* 320). R. W. B. Lewis noticed Wharton's subterranean puzzle when he mentioned that in her "love diary," "Edith had taken to employing a private literary code—quotations from poetry and fiction—as a way of hinting to herself about her most private feelings."[22]

This code extends to the novels but is less evident in them because as time progressed, even as she was increasing the complexity of her allusive techniques, Wharton was making a conscious effort to simplify her prose. She wanted to keep it accessible to the general public. In "A Cycle of Reviewing" she remarks that years of writing experience "subdued my natural tendency to 'put things' pointedly, and I became conscious—and happily conscious—of having reduced my style to a more even and unnoticeable texture."[23]

Part of the reason was that although she had inherited wealth and used some of her writing income for luxuries, Wharton also depended on it for personal charities, including war orphans and, in later years, pensions for elderly servants and relatives. So even as the Furies nagged her to create "literature," she wished to sell her work to a general readership for both financial and educational reasons, and to do so she needed to write novels easily accessible to the average American.

In spite of her "unnoticeable texture," Wharton says she expects her readers to meet her halfway.[24] She knew that her general audience was not well enough educated to meet her halfway, however, as is clear from her career-long criticism of American reading and education in, for instance, "The Vice of Reading" (1901), "The Recovery" (1908), "The Legend" (1910), "Xingu" (1916), and *Hudson River Bracketed* (1929). Consequently, her relation to her audience was a paradox, a dilemma, the explanation of which is part of the

"Sphinx and Furies" analogy. This analogy is itself paradoxical, since even as the Sphinx keeps the author's riddles, secrets, and messages, her relentless Furies drive her to reveal them. Hence Wharton's cryptic code.

The advice Wharton gives young authors about audience in *The Writing of Fiction* represents an ideal to which she herself could not altogether adhere, yet it shows how the Sphinx side of the conflict eventually prevailed. The writer, she says, "will never do his best till he ceases altogether to think of his readers (and his editor and publisher) and begins to write, not for himself, but for the other self with whom the creative artist is always in mysterious correspondence, and who, happily, has an *objective* existence somewhere, and will some day receive the *message* sent to him, though the sender may never know it" (italics mine) (Lewis 396).

Over time, Wharton hinted more and more boldly about her Sphinx-like riddles. In some places literary allusions are slipped in unmarked by quotes or italics, and unattributed to their authors (that is, "unmarked, unattributed" literary allusions). But gradually, as years passed, allusions became marked and attributed more and more often. Most of her work includes allusions to allusions, to the Furies, the Sphinx, to riddles, puzzles, codes, mazes, labyrinths, and messages sent but either unreceived or misunderstood. For instance, there is urgency in Halo's voice as she leaves a message for Vance: " 'Don't mention my name. . . . Just say it's somebody with a message—*somebody with a message*,' she repeated, trying with her sharp italics to bore the fact into the youth's brain" (*HRB* 82). That message is incorrectly delivered. And like Wharton's audience, Vance, a developing but badly undereducated author, was ignorant of "allusions to people and books, associations of ideas, images and metaphors," that would have given an "electric shock to his imagination" and made him "want to linger and question" (*HRB* 97). Furthermore, Wharton pointedly emphasizes Vance's ignorance of the mythology around the oracle at Delphi, whom Oedipus consults before meeting the Sphinx.

In spite of the conflicts between the concepts of the Sphinx and the Furies, and between Wharton's need to direct—in fact, I believe, to *teach*—her vast store of art and literature to an audience inclined to underestimate her, Wharton herself became a subtle Fury who pursued readers tenaciously, prodding us to notice the code, solve the riddle, understand its half-hidden messages. But Sphinx-like, she refused to discuss them openly. Whether even Henry James knew she was attempting to bury messages in allusions is questionable, although his response to *The Reef,* discussed in Chapter 2, suggests that he suspected. In any event, Lapsley's comment that *Summer* was called "Hot Ethan" by Wharton's intimates indicates that she must have discussed her work, at least in general, with members of her inner circle.[25]

By the time Wharton wrote *Hudson River Bracketed* and *The Gods Arrive,* the Furies had evolved from Lily Bart's symbols of nagging fear and guilt into an emblem of a driven, voracious intellectual appetite. Though they had not lost their capacity to feed on the author's pain, the ravening Furies gorge most on art, literature, and history. Edith Wharton translated that driving energy and intellectual appetite—for demonstrably the Furies were a salient part of herself—into experiments with literary allusion. Then she waited.

While Wharton watched with evident detachment, her brilliant techniques of literary allusion eluded even educated readers. She must have felt frustrated when people failed to recognize her, like Henry James, as a serious literary artist (rather than merely a best-selling writer).

A detail that emerged incidentally in this study is that occasionally the Sphinx alludes to the works of "The Master" but much as she alludes to other authors and artists. Undoubtedly hearing those echoes without understanding their purpose prompted reviewers and critics to level those infamous charges of miniature Jamesianism. Even so, Wharton hid her code when the public came too close to it, going so far as to apologize and change her "error" of "mistakenly" substituting part of the burial ceremony for the wedding service in *The Age of Innocence,* a novel so full of "clusters" of "thematic allusions" to burial that a mistake seems unlikely.[26] On the other hand, the very fact that her techniques went unnoticed made it possible for Wharton to write about issues that in her era were unmentionable in print. It was, after all, a time when Halo's unremorseful unwed pregnancy could nearly prevent the publication of *The Gods Arrive* in the 1930s (Lewis 502).

In these and other respects, then, Wharton found herself on the horns of yet another mythological creature, the Dilemma, symbol of equally unpleasant alternatives. Things she had learned from experience urgently needed to be expressed, but she could not say them directly and expect to be published. In addition, the extremes represented by the Sphinx and the Furies were paradoxical. While the Sphinx is timeless and passive, the Furies, active in the present, are also described by Aeschylus alternately as the "goddesses of destiny" (l. 962) and the "mind of the past" (l. 838).[27] Wharton solved her dilemma by incorporating complex allusions beneath an artfully glossy surface.

Drawing on the words of past authors to form the present of her work while hoping to influence future Vance Westons, Edith Wharton created a composite literary world where past, present, and future form parts of the same Emersonian primordial whole. For instance, the recurring symbol of the bridge emerges prominently at the end of *The Mother's Recompense,* a story about dilemmas, when Kate Clephane decides to live in Sphinx-like silence on the Riviera.

Wharton believed that the "thousand and one bits of the past . . . give meaning and continuity to the present."[28] Perhaps only when "the thousand and one bits" of the puzzle are reconstructed can the Furies be calmed and the more peaceful Sphinx predominate. When Vance becomes aware of allusions, he feels they "free him to move backward through this mysterious past which was so much newer . . . than any present" (*HRB* 118). And he "felt that he needed some kind of tuition to prepare him for the library. The Past was too big, too complicated, too aloof to surrender its secrets so lightly" (*HRB* 119).

While Wharton's struggle with the simultaneous urges to reveal and disguise never completely ended, in the later novels the Furies do seem largely replaced by that silent, smiling enigma with powerful secrets. "Each of us have our Sphinx," Halo remarks in *Hudson River Bracketed* (*HRB* 175), and one of her own secrets she "wears like a jewel" (*HRB* 464).

Ultimately, through literary allusion Edith Wharton attempted and largely succeeded in achieving a psychological, literary, and cultural reconciliation, a bridge between Sphinx and Furies, horns of the Dilemma, generations, and expatriate and resident Americans. That "bridge" has larger implications regarding her position in American literature. Recalling that, though she was a generation older, she was writing at the same time as heavily allusive, difficult-to-read modernists like T. S. Eliot, Ezra Pound, James Joyce, and Virginia Woolf, readers can suddenly understand her seeming curmudgeonly scorn for these writers. *She* had used allusions first, and had arguably used them better, still managing to keep her literature democratically accessible to the housewife and the "man with the dinner pail."[29] Even so, Wharton was not a modernist in the sense in which that term is usually understood. She believed in cultural continuity and advancement rather than "wip[ing] out the past" (*HRB* 258), demolishing tradition and starting over, despite the fact that such cycles have been an American pattern since the Puritans. But her goal of putting together the thousand and one pieces of a puzzling tradition, illustrated by Lily Bart's waking "each morning with an obliterated past" (*HM* 476), was partially similar to that of the modernists, who also wished to reassemble post–World War I cultural fragments. They, on the other hand, preferred a new epistemology. But Wharton's effort to invent a code of literature and an art of the past to be pieced together by that unknown "objective presence" in the future created a technical bridge spanning the literary historical gap between Henry James and various modernists.

Revealing Edith Wharton's secrets involves recognizing that she concealed them using techniques of literary and art allusion, from which she devised a code used in new ways that requires rereadings of familiar novels. The rereadings disclose strongly interwoven themes on the basis of which the nature of Edith Wharton's Furies can be inferred. These themes include logical and philosophical paradoxes, along with suicide, poison, pain, reason, physical and psychological child neglect, and the importance of every kind of education. In any given novel one or two of these will be major themes, the others present but subordinate. In either case, the entire project demands comprehension of the astonishing extent of Edith Wharton's intellect and the depth of her reading and knowledge, all of which were necessary to the construction of this allusive code. Her nonrepetitious reiteration of themes in turn reinforces an underlying assumption that Edith Wharton was in her way as great a literary artist as any other author of her era, male or female.

The categorical organization of the allusions is mine, not necessarily Wharton's, and in that sense arbitrary. Yet Wharton herself supplied some of my terms, like "branching," "umbrella," and "layered," by using the images as she did. "Layered allusions" take their name from a line in *Hudson River Bracketed* (a similar line occurs in her story, "Mr. Jones"): "The white stretch of illumination / . . . was filled with layer upon layer of delicately drawn motionless leaves" (*HRB* 93). Indeed, I was tempted to redesignate the "structural allusions" that appear fully developed in *The House of Mirth* as "architectural allusions," so often does Wharton use the word "architecture" in letters about that novel, but I retained the term "structural" to avoid confusion when the subject of architecture itself arises as it does, for instance, in *Hudson River Bracketed*.

Remarkably, Wharton's most complex methods of allusion can be identified as early as *The House of Mirth* and *The Reef*. Nevertheless, the sophistication and originality of each type developed as Edith Wharton accrued experience. The structure of this book is chronological to reflect this increasing complexity. Each chapter defines its terms, demonstrates at least one new technique, and builds on those that precede it.

Chapter 1 shows how Edith Wharton experimented with "thematic" and "structural" (architectural) allusions in *The House of Mirth* (1905). Chapter 2 focuses primarily on "clustered" thematic allusions in *The Reef* (1912). Chapter 3 demonstrates how *The Custom of the Country* (1913) uses "mythic" allusion to imbue history-starved America with a further mythology, and Chapter 4 describes "branching thematic" allusions in *The Age of Innocence* (1920). Chapter 5 demonstrates "layered art allusions" and "autoliterary allusions" in *The Glimpses of the Moon* (1922). Chapter 6 discusses the "umbrella" allusion of *The Mother's Recompense* (1925), Chapter 7 reveals a "generic allusion" in *Twilight Sleep* (1927), and Chapter 8 "metaphysical allusions" in *The Children* (1928). Finally, "layered" and "reverberating" allusions are explained in Chapters 9 and 10 on *Hudson River Bracketed* (1929) and its sequel, *The Gods Arrive* (1932).

Chapter 11, the conclusion, discusses "messages," showing how themes that emerge from these readings of the novels are in concord with the themes of the Sphinx and the Furies. It further discusses my claim that Edith Wharton's writing can be studied not only as a continuing series but as a unit that follows a plan possibly based on a career-long umbrella allusion to Ralph Waldo Emerson's poem "The Sphinx," in which "the universal dame" spoke "through a thousand voices."[30]

Impossible as it is to master all "thousand" allusive voices, the conclusion endeavors to decipher the riddle of Edith Wharton's Sphinx and makes inferences about the Furies that drove her to continue hinting at it, working at it, and encoding it. In brief, the Furies of Aeschylus, "afflicted, [had] borne what can not be borne" (ll. 790–91). Some critics now believe that as a child Edith Wharton, too, had "borne what cannot be borne"—psychological Furies caused by incest.[31] She not only survived but emerged with a "constant heart . . . / faithful in the paths of truth," as she says in her poem "The Eumenides" (1909).[32] Her statement that her little girl "life" was "safe" and "guarded" seems more and more untrustworthy in the light of accumulating evidence (*BG* 7). And even though her initial efforts to grapple with what is ultimately an insidious crime against identity were apparently futile, the author who had been psychologically orphaned by parental abuse and neglect, who worked so hard for orphans of the Great War, learned to convert the resulting pain into social benefit as well as into fine—many would say great—literature. Somehow she seems to have remained hopeful that Americans would eventually recognize her literary contributions and the messages that warn us—never more appropriately than now—to allow children, all children, their "age of innocence."

# 1 | *The House of Mirth*
Structural and Thematic Allusions

IN *The House of Mirth* Edith Wharton's early experiments in the use of literary allusion converge upon structural allusions almost all of which are used thematically.[1] "Structural allusions" are simply literary allusions used as an architectural skeleton upon which to hang all or parts of the plot.[2] Some of the structural allusions are supported architecturally by several types of "thematic allusions"—allusions that reflect one or more of the novel's themes. Many thematic allusions, especially those to nature, sleep, and deities, occur in *The House of Mirth,* and even though these early experiments seem limited in relation to the brilliant and original accomplishments of the later novels, they are thoroughly polished.

The themes that emerge from the allusions sometimes agree with general critical perception, such as the idea of woman as art object, sometimes not, such as the idea of Lawrence Selden as a well-meaning but ineffectual Prince Charming.[3] Either way, Edith Wharton's accomplishments in *The House of Mirth* appear original *for the novel* (as opposed to poetry), if not for allusion itself, a factor that should contribute to an upward reevaluation of her work. Furthermore, discovery of this experimentation establishes Edith Wharton's deliberate intention to focus readers on themes she emphatically regarded as central.

"Architecture" was a major concern in the creation of *The House of Mirth,* for there appears to be greater concentration on structural allusions here than in any other Wharton novel. Their importance seems confirmed by the letter from Edith Wharton to William Crary Brownell, 5 August 1905, in which she writes jubilantly, "Your seeing a certain amount of architecture in [*The House of Mirth*] rejoices me above everything—my theory of what the novel ought to be is so exorbitant."[4] The first structural allusion is the title taken from Ecclesiastes 7:4, supported by thematic allusions to Edward FitzGerald and Euripides. The second structural allusion refers to a sermon by Jonathan Edwards. A contrast to the Edwards allusion is created by thematic allusions to La Bruyère and John Selden. Third, plot allusions to George Gissing's novel *The Whirlpool* are structural in function, intensified by a thematic allusion to *The Merchant of Venice* as well as a topical thematic allusion to a contemporary Wall Street

Sir Joshua Reynolds, *Joanna Leigh, Mrs. R. B. Lloyd* (1776). Private Collection, London. Tableau Vivant: *The House of Mirth*.

scandal. Two other allusions complete the girders, one a structural allusion to Wordsworth's "She Was a Phantom of Delight" and the other an allusion to Sir Joshua Reynolds's *Joanna Leigh, Mrs. R. B. Lloyd*. Together the structural and thematic allusions offer a clearer understanding of the novel.

Religious and philosophical ideas of deism, Puritanism, and naturalism contrast to ideas of chance, free will, and artistic imagination. These themes pose questions rather than answer them, and the primary philosophical query is, "How does chance fit into a world apparently run by law?"

The novel demonstrates the unanswerability of the problem by raising opposing philosophical systems: Mrs. Peniston represents Law; Selden represents Chance. On the one hand, when Lily breaks the randomly applied laws of Mrs. Peniston's world, she is condemned and expelled. On the other hand, by sheer whim, Selden, the lawyer, destabilizes Lily's artistically designed laws of social response by introducing chance and doubt. Put another way, gambling and "being talked about" are not permitted in Mrs. Peniston's world, while in Lily's world they are permitted under certain conditions. Selden, who knows the laws of both worlds, interferes at random, like the practical-joker God of a Hardy tale, and causes Lily's death by upsetting the delicate environmental balance she created for her personal blossoming in the Trenor-Dorset world.

Meanwhile, the novel never closes the question of Lily's free will, for though Lily *believes* she is naturalistically predetermined by her education and environment, she does in fact make free choices, for instance not to succumb to Trenor and not to blackmail Bertha Dorset. Her ultimate free act is to use her artistic imagination to design self-portraits that create identity through internal and external images.

The Darwinian creature determined upon survival presumably would not have a choice as Gertie did not: "Reason, judgment, renunciation, all the sane daylight forces, were beaten back in the sharp struggle for self-preservation" (*HM* 262). If a Darwinian creature has a choice, it does not choose to destroy itself, except by mistake, in which case the element of chance overrides law, not possible in pure naturalism.

While naturalism and coincidence (fate) have been discussed often in the critical literature and have been irrefutably established as present in *The House of Mirth*, the systems are usually considered ends in themselves rather than part of a larger architecture. To show the larger philosophical architecture, however, several premises of the argument require evidence: the ideas of Puritanism, and deism, the ideas that Mrs. Peniston represents law, that Lily represents deism (as well as naturalism), and that Selden represents chance. The novel pits the philosophical systems against one another, and the problem of interpreting the conclusion is the problem of deciding which system has prevailed, if any. The thematic allusions help pull evidence out of the novel. Consider first the function of Ecclesiastes, to which the novel's title alludes (a "titular allusion").

Ecclesiastes' thematic refrain "all is vanity" structures the plot. "A good name is better than precious ointment: and the day of death than the day of one's birth" (Eccles. 7:1). Lily loses her good name after Rosedale sees her emerging from the Benedick. "Surely oppression maketh a wise man mad; and a gift destroyeth the heart" (Eccles. 7:7). Lily's response to the potential rape by Trenor can be considered "madness" caused by the oppression and obligation of his financial "gift," a context that modifies the melodramatic nature of Lily's reaction, and Lily is not "hasty" to be angry and blackmail Bertha. "Be not hasty in thy spirit to be angry: for anger resteth in the bosom of fools (Eccles. 7:9).

Using Lily's vanity and fear of aging, the novel builds on other parts of Ecclesiastes: "Vanity of vanities; all is vanity" (Eccles. 1:2). "Labor is vanity and avails nothing" (Eccles. 2:18) suggests those many "dull and ugly people," including Gerty Ferish, who Selden feels sacrificed to produce Lily (*HM* 7). "He that loveth silver shall not be satisfied with silver" (Eccles. 5:10) addresses Lily's extravagance, and Selden's observant detachment fits "better is the sight of the eyes than the wandering of the desire" (Eccles. 6:9).

When Ecclesiastes is considered thematically, Wharton's biblical allusion cannot be interpreted as affirming Christian values; or at least if she affirms them in this novel, it is not on the basis of Ecclesiastes, for the theme of Ecclesiastes is existentialist in quality, if not precisely in name, as the introduction to the Anchor Bible's translation explains: "Theologically, Ecclesiastes is the strangest book in the Bible because of its philosophical nihilism. Everything that happens to man appears to be predetermined, and fitted to its uniquely appropriated time, and what it all means (if anything) is an impenetrable mystery." The God of Ecclesiastes is "the mysterious, inscrutable Being whose existence must be presupposed as that which determines the life and fate of man, in a world man cannot change, and where all his effort and values are rendered meaningless."[5]

In the letter to Brownell quoted above, Wharton explained that she did not want the title to moralize by repeating its text on the title page: "In this case, where it inculcates a moral, I might surely be suspected of plagiarizing from Mrs. Margaret Sangster's beautiful volume 'Five Days with God' " (Wharton, *Letters* 94).[6] Edith Wharton did not necessarily want readers to interpret the title allusion in Christian terms. This "existential" version of God is more like a combination of the deist and Puritan versions, both of which depend on determinism.

As the representative of Puritanism, Mrs. Peniston rules strictly over "the house of mourning" that the author of Ecclesiastes recommends for the "heart of the wise." The "house of mourning" of verse 4 is not likely to be Gertie

Ferish's charity home for girls, for dingy as it may be, it is a place of hope. Rather, the "house of mourning" is Mrs. Peniston's dark mansion. With its "stifling odour of fresh mourning" (*HM* 357), dominated by the Dying Gladiator (*HM* 161), "shrouded" (*HM* 199) and "dreary as a tomb" (*HM* 160), where the prevalent wood is black walnut (*HM* 159), where Mrs. Peniston always wears "black brocade, with the cut jet fringe" (*HM* 201), where Grace Stepney "read out the deaths from the Times, and sincerely admired the purple satin drawing-room" curtains (*HM* 161). At Julia Peniston's funeral the dark drawing room "resembled a well-kept family vault, in which the last corpse had just been decently deposited" (*HM* 360).

The motif of death in this grimly proper house is naturally unattractive to Lily, who enjoys life's beauties and is drawn by Selden's amorphous "republic of the spirit." As a representative American, Lily has no vote at Mrs. Peniston's house even about redecorating her ugly bedroom. Even so, her heritage is Aunt Peniston's Puritanism, which creates a tension between naturalism and freedom because Puritanism paradoxically preaches both determinism and free will. Though the omniscient God knows what is destined to happen, man chooses to cause it, and since man's will is free, God cannot change the future.

The law of Mrs. Peniston's house is Puritanism, while Lily desires freedom. The first five letters of Mrs. Peniston's name suggest masculinity as well as penitence and parsimony. She herself represents the vengeful Puritan God whose laws result in the constant cleansing of conscience for reassurance of status among the Elect: "The first two weeks after return [to town] represented to Mrs. Peniston the domestic equivalent of a religious retreat. She 'went through' the linen and blankets in the precise spirit of the penitent exploring the inner folds of conscience; she sought for moths as the stricken soul seeks for lurking infirmities. The topmost shelf of every closet was made to yield up its secret, cellar and coal-bin were probed to their darkest depths, and as a final stage in the lustral rites, the entire house was swathed in penitential white and deluged with expiatory soap suds" (*HM* 157–58). Furthermore, Mrs. Peniston "was clearly destined by Providence to assume the charge of Lily" (*HM* 56). Her random financial support, her immovability, her remorseless pursuit of insects (including Lily whose intuitions are "thread-like feelers" [*HM* 190] whereas Grace Stepney has a mind like "moral fly-paper" [*HM* 196]), and Julia Peniston's passive observation of the world through her Dutch windows, dramatizes a retributive God's detachment from its fate. Mrs. Peniston "was apt to display a remarkable retrospective insight into [peoples'] ultimate fate, so that, when they had fulfilled their destiny, she was almost always able to say to Grace Stepney—the recipient of her prophecies—that she had known exactly what would happen" (*HM* 193). And when anyone violates a rule she is "as much aghast as if she had been accused of . . . violating any of the . . . cardinal laws of house-keeping" (*HM* 199). Mrs. Peniston dispenses the laws of Providence from a sitting-room decorated with the "fittings of the court-room" (*HM* 274).

The theme of Puritanism is further emphasized by an unmarked, unattrib-uted allusion—actually a combined thematic and structural allusion—to Jona-than Edwards's famous sermon "Sinners in the Hands of an Angry God." For the text of that sermon Edwards chose "Their foot shall slide in due time" (Deut. 32:35), a theme that Wharton carries out structurally and at which she hints in Grace Stepney's name. When Lily first comes to live with Mrs. Penis-ton, "She [finds] herself actually struggling for a foothold on the broad space which had once seemed her own for the asking" (*HM* 60). Lily's precarious footing on the soapy staircase, first at the Benedick and again at Mrs. Penis-ton's house, is analogous both to her social position and to her state of grace or moral position:

> There had been nothing in her training to develop any continuity of moral strength: what she craved, and really felt herself entitled to, was a situation in which the noblest attitude should also be the easiest. Hitherto, her inter-mittent impulses of resistance had sufficed to maintain her self-respect. If she slipped she recovered her footing, and it was only afterward that she was aware of having recovered it each time on a slightly lower level. [*HM* 422]

Before Lily's major fall (foreshadowed by Mr. Peniston's "seven-by-five paint-ing of Niagara" Falls [*HM* 162]), Selden "seemed to see her poised on the brink of a chasm, with one graceful foot advanced to assert her unconsciousness that the ground was failing her" (*HM* 309).

In his sermon Edwards portrays a vengeful Providence dangling His victim "over the pit of hell, much as one holds a spider, or some loathsome insect over the fire, abhors [him], and is dreadfully provoked."[7] Connecting Ecclesiastes' theme of vanity with an allusion to Edwards's sermon, the narrator comments of Lily, "No insect hangs its nest on threads as frail as those which will sustain the weight of human vanity" (*HM* 181).

Only the Hand of God can keep the sinner from hell. Mrs. Peniston's uncompassionate decision to "cut Lily off" when Lily confesses to gambling debts is equivalent to snipping the thread that drops her into hell, and as a thematic allusion, Edwards's words foreshadow the novel's conclusion: "It is to be ascribed to nothing else, that you did not go to hell the last night; that you was suffered to awake again in this world, after you closed your eyes to sleep" (Edwards 102).

An allusion that supports the Puritan theme by contrasting Lily's attitude is Edward FitzGerald's "The Rubaiyat of Omar Khayyam," a poem she carries in her luggage. Lily's attitude toward the Puritan brand of determinism and punishment is Ecclesiastes' admonition to "eat, drink and be merry," a theme repeated by FitzGerald. Furthermore, "The Rubaiyat" contains the famous lines, "The Moving Finger writes; and, having writ, / Moves on" (LI, l. 201) a line echoed in Reynolds's painting of Mrs. Lloyd, who is writing on a tree. The poem advises living for the moment: "Here with a Loaf of Bread beneath the Bough, / A Flask of Wine, a Book of Verse—and Thou" (XI, ll. 41–42). But the allusions to the Furies strongly suggest that Lily can never escape the heritage of a Puritan conscience. In addition, "Reni's" painting of Beatrice Cenci, the girl who murdered her father, decorates a small box in Mrs. Peniston's house (*HM* 274).[8] This combination of allusions suggests the possibility that because of her extravagant spending, Lily subconsciously feels responsible for the death of her father and that Lily's "social whirl" is a means of preventing the Furies of her guilt from rising to consciousness.

Lily's lavish "social whirl" is also a whirlpool. A structural allusion to George Gissing's *The Whirlpool* (1897) focuses on the themes of financial excess and the stock market. The similarity was originally spotted by C. S. Collinson. He summarizes the common features of the plots:

> Both heroines, Gissing's Alma Frothingham and Mrs. Wharton's Lily Bart, are shown as leading lives of unsatisfied ambition. . . . Both women belong to a society in which money and fashion predominate; both are deprived of an adequate personal income owing to their fathers' failure in business; both are "climbers" meeting with constant frustration; and finally both are victims of somewhat melodramatic coincidences. Their end is identical: an overdose of a narcotic, not apparently suicidal but taken at a moment of physical fatigue following mental stress.[9]

Gissing's novel begins with the protagonist gambling in the stock market. Like a Hardy novel it gives the impression that life is ruled by malevolent determinism.[10] And in her well-known article, Elaine Showalter notes what appears to be yet another structural allusion, this one to a contemporary popular novel, *Lily and Bertha*.[11]

Edith Wharton's structural allusions to Ecclesiastes, and Gissing's *The Whirlpool*, support an important topical thematic allusion first noticed by Wayne W. Westbrook, who finds *The House of Mirth* a "consciously constructed allegory of Wall Street."

According to Westbrook's research, hints of a Wall Street financial scandal began circulating in the spring and summer of 1905. A battle for the control of the Equitable Life Assurance Society resulted in complex stock exchange corruption involving a number of members of Congress and millions of dollars. Much of the corruption was thought to originate in the Albany, New York, home of legislative lobbyist Andrew C. Fields. The press dubbed it "the House of Mirth."[12]

In this context, of course, the Trenor, Rosedale, and Bry millions gained through gambling on stock market "tips" look even shadier, and by juxtaposition, Lily's participation in the stock market by accepting Trenor's offer to "invest her money" develops even darker shades of gray. So does her gambling at Bellomont. Bellomont is an additional thematic allusion to architecture and money, the Trenors' crude spelling of Portia's golden estate, "Belmont," in Shakespeare's *The Merchant of Venice*.[13] The stock market scandal emphasizes the novel's themes of gambling, chance, game playing, and risk taking and creates starker contrasts between Mrs. Peniston as representative of Puritan law, Lily as representative of deism, and Selden as representative of chance.

When Selden notes, with perfect lack of self-knowledge, that "In judging Miss Bart, he had always made use of the 'argument from design' " (*HM* 6), he makes a thematic allusion that supplies another clue to the overall structure of the novel. The "argument from design" is the philosophical basis for deism, the idea that one can infer the existence of God from order and laws in the universe. Lily and Selden each think in philosophical metaphors. Lily's thoughts combine deism and naturalism, which are deterministically consistent, but Selden's thoughts consist of a philosophically conflicting cross between deism and an indifferent and randomly judgmental Force that, as already noted, takes the form of risk and chance in the world of gambling.

The frequently used analogy for deist thought is the great clockmaker God who created the universe, wound it up, and threw it into space to run by its own laws. Imagery of whirling social "worlds" and "universes" recurs throughout the novel, in which, to Lily, "society is a revolving body which is apt to be judged according to its place in each man's heaven" (*HM* 79). She has a strong sense of being "just a screw or a cog in the great machine" (*HM* 498) but cannot understand the "laws of a universe which was so ready to leave her out of its calculations" (*HM* 42). The laws of Lily's universe are based on Darwinian evolutionary principles underlying the literary naturalism that produces characters whose fate seems predetermined. Environment, heredity, and chance render individuals unimportant specks without control over their futures or responsibility for their actions. But in *The House of Mirth* any naturalism must be ascribed to Lily, not to the author, for nearly all of the naturalistic descriptions in the novel are reported through Lily's thoughts, and naturalism is deterministically consistent with Puritanism.

Lily thinks of herself as "highly specialized" (*HM* 6), "a rare flower grown for exhibition" (*HM* 512) or (in an image that brings deism and naturalism together) a "mere spin-drift of the whirling surface of existence" (*HM* 515). Lily's habit of thinking this way has at least two consequences. One is that she projects her own worldview onto others, especially Selden. The other consequence is that by considering herself a victim of whichever system she finds most convenient for avoiding the Furies, she dodges the need to take conscious responsibility for her real or imagined guilt.

Ironically, Selden's impulsive nonsense, his satirical social aphorisms, dislodge Lily's convenient thinking. Selden's name is most likely an allusion to *Table Talk* by John Selden (1584–1654), a book Edith Wharton owned[14] that is similar in theme and attitude to *Les caractères ou les moeurs de ce siècle* by La Bruyère (1645–1696) that Lily finds in Selden's apartment on the visits that begin and conclude the action (*HM* 16, 492). Like the novel's Selden, John Selden and La Bruyère were lawyers. Both Selden's books and those of La Bruyère are collections of satirical observations on contemporary life and people ("table talk"), and Wharton's references to them constitute thematic allusions to the two authors' satirical attitude toward social law. The scene at the Brys' dinner on the Riviera during which Selden silently colloquizes on the "showy dulness of the talk" (*HM* 347), compared with the wealth of vocabulary the newspaper reporter would need to describe "the literary style" of Mrs. Dorset's gown (*HM* 348), illustrates the allusion.

A person who is satirical toward law and order must believe either that it does not exist or that it is an indifferent force, so the allusions tell us that Selden's statements and thoughts must be read ironically and compared with what he does. Like Mrs. Peniston, he is an observer who assumes he has a God-like right to judge Lily. An indifferent Force, he acts arbitrarily, always remaining emotionally detached. Since he talks social nonsense and never thinks of the possible consequences his frivolity might have for someone else, he shares responsibility with Lily for her fall.

In the first third of the novel Selden is neither reliable nor moral. While he often thinks of himself as conducting "experiments" and judging their results, laboratory experiments on people are unethical. Just by arbitrarily manipulating Lily's life, he is playing God. With "an impulse of curiosity" he decides it would be amusing to put Lily's social "skill to the test" (*HM* 4). As a result of this random impulse, and fully aware of the social implications for a woman alone with a man in his apartment, he invites her there for tea, beginning the chain of events that leads to Lily's death. The man Lily feels is neither "a prig nor a bounder" (*HM* 12) is actually both, simultaneously dangling Lily and a married woman, Bertha Dorset. Worse, by the prevailing social code, he behaves unlike a gentleman by failing to destroy Bertha's letters. Such a man can think nothing of the bantering that Lily finally stops without fully disbelieving the innuendo: "It's stupid of you to make love to me" (*HM* 12).

Selden's next impulse is to drop in at Bellomont, where he sits at dinner, talking to Bertha Dorset with the "joyous irresponsibility of a free man" (*HM* 85). Selden's impulse becomes a chance occurrence for Lily. Though he tells himself he has "renounced sentimental experiments" (*HM* 110), his behavior with Bertha indicates otherwise. Selden again meddles with Lily's feelings when he lies about having come to Bellomont to see *her.* During the ultimately disastrous Sunday walk Lily comments, "It is my business to get to church before the service is over," but Selden replies, "Exactly; and it is my business to prevent your doing so." Lily calls this "nonsense," but it is just another of her ironic misjudgments of Selden (*HM* 98). Morally he has no business interfering in her life for his own amusement, but he rationalizes selfishly that being the "unforeseen element in a career so accurately planned was stimulating" (*HM* 109). Because of Selden's whimsical interference, Lily not only misses a chance to marry Percy Gryce but makes a fatally permanent enemy of Bertha Dorset.

In the "republic of the spirit" scene, Selden weakens Lily's already wavering determination by introducing doubt about the validity of her aspirations. While readers tend to agree with him about the materialism of Lily's goals, worse evil than a loveless marriage based on business principles results from his game playing. He speaks nonsense about a "republic of the spirit," a place of personal freedom from money, poverty, ease, anxiety, and from all "material accidents" (*HM* 108), but on the one hand, the motives of the man who is still toying with Bertha Dorset's sexually free spirits can only be suspect. On the other, there can be no place free of "material accidents." The idea is similar to that in *The Age of Innocence* when Newland Archer tells Ellen Olenska that they can escape to another country where "categories like [mistress] won't exist" (*AI* 290), and she replies that there is no such country. Lily asks Selden perceptively, "why do you call your republic a republic? It is a close corporation and you create arbitrary objections in order to keep people out." He returns, "It is not *my* republic; if it were, I should have a *coup d'état* and seat you on the throne" (*HM* 113). This is more flirtatious nonsense, of course, because a republic with a monarchy is not a republic. As Lily says, Selden is acting arbitrarily, like a practical-joker God, and though she does not make the connection, she is aware that the "crude forms in which her friends took their pleasure included a loud enjoyment of . . . complications: the zest of surprising destiny in the act of playing a practical joke" (*HM* 158). But because of her pride in her attractions, and because of Selden's pretense of joking about not asking her to marry him because *she* doesn't want to marry *him,* implying that he wants to marry her when he doesn't want to marry at all, Lily believes that Selden is as God-like as he acts: "Ah, my dear Miss Bart, I am not divine Providence, to guarantee your enjoying the things you are trying to get!" (*HM* 113–14). Lily compares herself to Ned Silverton, who seemed to pass "under the spell of the terrible god of chance" (*HM* 41). And her sense of a "sudden glimpse into the laboratory where his faiths were formed" (*HM* 113) is a psychological projection of one of her own scientific rationalizations onto Selden.

Again by accident, Lily's social balance is upset when she encounters Selden at the Van Osburgh wedding: "The sight of Selden's dark head, in a pew almost facing her, disturbed for a moment the balance of her complacency. The rise of her blood as their eyes met was succeeded by a contrary motion, a wave of resistance and withdrawal. She did not wish to see him again, not because she feared his influence, but because his presence always had the effect of cheapening her aspirations, of throwing her whole world out of focus" (*HM* 141). Uncaring, Selden ignores Lily's request and approaches her anyway, further disappointing her in that after the intimacy of their walk, he had "gone back without an effort to the footing on which they had stood before their last talk together. Her vanity was stung" (*HM* 152). The theme of vanity in Ecclesiastes is thereby connected to the uncertain footing of Edwards's sermon. The manner of Selden's approach destroys Lily's ability to charm Rosedale, causing her to snub him and by doing so to anger Gus Trenor, a slip that leads to the attempted rape. Meanwhile, Selden enjoys the sight, leaning "against the window, a detached observer of the scene," so that "under the spell of his observation Lily felt herself powerless to exert her usual arts" (*HM* 153–54). Ironically, Lily later recalls these failures as "some malice of fortune" (*HM* 407).

When Selden finally decides to take responsible action to help her it is always after a hesitation that makes the move minimal and tardy. After making Lily believe he loves her in the tableaux vivants scene, he assumes the worst when he watches her emerge from the Trenor house; he runs away, once from New York, again from Italy. Then he blames *her*. For instance, he waits until just as they walk into the restaurant for the Brys' dinner to advise Lily to leave the yacht. Then on the way out after the Brys' dinner when Lily is thrown off the yacht, he cries, "Good God—if you'd listened to me!" (*HM* 353). Ultimately, then, Selden's irresponsible actions at the beginning of the novel, his decision to disappear in the middle of it, and his remiss hesitations later directly contribute to Lily's death. At her deathbed, however, he blames her for his arbitrary, judgmental aloofness, convincing himself that his "very detachment from the external influences which swayed her had increased his spiritual fastidiousness, and made it more difficult for him to live and love uncritically" (*HM* 532).

Two thematic allusions support another structural topic, the journey from life to death. Many floating and ship metaphors are illuminated in this context. One reference is to Thomas Cole's set of four paintings, *The Journey of Life,* engravings of which hang on the walls of cousins' "dingy" drawing rooms (*HM* 47). Cole's paintings are sentimental depictions of dreamlike scenery in which people set out on allegorical sea journeys of childhood, youth, manhood, and old age as angels guide their way.

The second thematic allusion to Tennyson's poem "Ulysses" features the voice of the aged hero about to embark on a last voyage because he has the urge always to be "roaming with a hungry heart." He claims, "I will drink life to the lees." Selden has not sought life but has escaped from it and by so doing has contributed to Lily's death. There is unmistakable irony, then, in Selden's kneeling by Lily's deathbed, "draining their last moment to its lees" (*HM* 533),[15] especially since Lily had been aware that because of his "strange assumption of authority" (*HM* 451), "his attitude of sober impartiality, the absence of all response to her appeal, turned her hurt pride to blind resentment of his interference. . . . he would never voluntarily have come to her aid" (*HM* 454).

Though Lily Bart and Lawrence Selden think in metaphors of scientific rationalism, their actions are based on other principles. While Selden bases his actions on principles of chance, as he seems to preach free will, Lily bases hers on principles of free will that she contradicts by gambling and making only passive use of her creativity.

The theme of Lily's artistic imagination is supported by two of the novel's major skeletal structural allusions, one to Wordsworth and one to Reynolds. The original title of *The House of Mirth* was to have been *A Moment's Ornament*.[16] Lily had been "brought up to be ornamental" (*HM* 480). The source for the phrase was Wordsworth's "She Was a Phantom of Delight"; the poem's voice is that of an observer like Lawrence Selden:

She was a phantom of delight
When first she gleamed upon my sight;
A lovely Apparition, sent
To be a moment's ornament

   [ll. 1–4]

The novel opens with Selden "refreshed by the sight of Miss Lily Bart" (*HM* 6), whose capacity to be ornamental, an art object, is demonstrated in the tableaux vivants scene. The context of his preaching to Lily about spiritual freedom in the "church" of Nature appears to derive from the romantic Wordsworthian ideal:

I saw her upon nearer view,
A Spirit, yet a Woman too!
Her household motions light and free,
And steps of virgin-liberty

   [ll. 11–14]

The "household motions" of Wordsworth's poem possibly suggested both Lily's intense desire to have a drawing room to do over, and her problematic attraction to Nettie Struther's baby, although that scene may be another allusion to a popular novel. "Steps of virgin-liberty" recalls the "republic of the spirit" scene. In addition, the word "steps" connects to the two scenes in which Lily meets the scrub woman on the steps of the Benedick and on the stairs of Mrs. Peniston's house, as well as the theme of her step-by-step fall.

The following stanza also supports the theme of the journey from life to death, and Lily's deistic description of herself as a cog in a machine (*HM* 498):

And now I see with eye serene
The very pulse of the machine;
A Being breathing thoughtful breath,
A Traveller between life and death

    [ll. 21–24]

The "Traveller between life and death" echoes Cole and Tennyson. The woman in Wordsworth's poem regains angelic status, just as Lily does for Selden, for to him the room in which he last sees her becomes a kind of heaven: "Irresistible sunlight poured a tempered golden flood into the room" (*HM* 526). The contrast between Selden's "heaven" and Jonathan Edwards's "hell" produces a final ironic punch.

Thematically related to Wordsworth's poem, the simple but ornamental deathbed "Sleeping Beauty portrait" over which Selden rhapsodizes is the last in a series of portraits that constitute the thematic structural allusion to Sir Joshua Reynolds, the eighteenth-century portraitist. The direct allusion occurs in the tableaux vivants scene when Lily recreates Reynolds's portrait of Mrs. Lloyd.[17]

Critics often describe the novel's sructure by the descending steps of Lily's fatal social decline, which, we have seen, derives from Edwards's sermon.[18] The "steps" also serve as gallerylike still portraits designed by Wharton to show Lily attempting to define her uniqueness, and thus to survive as an individual, against a social background over which she has tenuous control, especially when Selden interferes.

Lily is practiced in using "a happy shifting of lights," "well-poised lines and happy tints," as a "justifiable" means to an end (*HM* 187), and her appreciation of landscapes underscores her talent: "Purpling waters drew a sharp white line of foam at the base of the shore; against its irregular eminences, hotels and villas flashed from the greyish verdure of olive and eucalyptus; and the background of bare and finely-pencilled mountains quivered in a pale intensity of light. How beautiful it was—and how she loved beauty!" (*HM* 313).

The first portrait in the train station is followed immediately by a second in Selden's apartment where Lily's "profile [is] outlined against the warm background" (*HM* 16). She pauses before the mirror in an attitude revealing the "long slope of her slender sides, which [gives] a kind of wild-wood grace to her outline—as though she were a captured dryad" with a streak of "sylvan freedom" to her "artificiality" (*HM* 19).

This second portrait foreshadows the third and most important, that of the centrally placed Reynolds portrait, in which the "background of foliage against which she stood, served only to relieve the long dryad-like curves" (*HM* 217). This is Lily's masterpiece, the natural background of which repeats that of the "republic of the spirit" scene. As Mrs. Lloyd she is in complete control of the laws of her world, if only as the Wordsworthian "moment's ornament": "—you did love me for a moment. . . . But the moment is gone—" (*HM* 500).

The portrait of Joanna Leigh, Mrs. R. B. Lloyd, painted by Reynolds in 1776, the year of the American Revolution, depicts Mrs. Lloyd inscribing her husband's initials on a tree, a "fancy taken from *As You Like It*." The date of its creation again suggests the possibility that for a moment in her role as "Mrs. Lloyd" Lily achieved her version of the "republic of the spirit." In this light, the irony of Selden's response to Lily's death is intensified by the possible source of her emblem "beyond," if that is the "word that made all clear," in a poem by Robert Green Ingersoll, an agnostic and proponent of suicide (see Chapter 7 on *Twilight Sleep*).

> Is there beyond the silent night
>> An endless day?
> Is death a door that leads to light
>> We cannot say.
>
> ["Declaration of the Free," stanza 16][19]

A true "republic of the spirit," freedom from materialism, exists only in the republic of the grave.

As Lily's social status slips toward the coffin, the background of each successive, imitative world contains less context and meaning as when Rosedale views Lily's fourth dramatic portrait against the background of the tearoom: "The dark pencilling of fatigue under her eyes, the morbid blue-veined pallour of the temples, brought out the brightness of her hair and lips, as though all her ebbing vitality were centred there. Against the dull chocolate-coloured background of the restaurant, the purity of her head stood out as it had never done in the most brightly-lit ball-room" (*HM* 467–68). Lily's life becomes a series of substitutions of one background for another. As long as the background of the portrait is natural—like parks and gardens—Lily is secure, but she is a creature requiring personal aesthetic "roots," her own drawing room, to survive. Instead, her fifth and final portrait is her representation of Sleeping Beauty in a dingy boardinghouse bedroom.

So after Lily's succession of unsuitable backgrounds, we watch the "real Lily's" face vanishing in the "blank surface of the toilet-mirror" (*HM* 528) and conceivably also in the Emersonian "transparent eyeball." Though a supreme model, as an artist Lily never attains "the real thing" (*HM* 302) (an allusion to Henry James's story of the same name and on the same subject); she simply spends her life "posed" as herself. Not accidentally, in the background of Lily's room at her death, Selden finds "no token . . . of her personality" (*HM* 528).

Through the architecture of five primary structural allusions to Ecclesiastes, Edwards, Gissing, Wordsworth, and Reynolds (and probably others), supported by thematic allusions, Edith Wharton interconnected motifs of deism, Puritanism, chance, free will, and Darwinian naturalism that permit the novel to be read as an intensely ironic question about the contradiction between deterministic law, chance, and free will. Lily and Selden think in scientific rationalist modes, but their actions betray their thoughts, and Selden's Godlike "experiments" with Lily's moral and social life become the major factors that disrupt the predictability of her plans.

Since the assumption of social science is that the social order is rational, and therefore Lily's plans within it are rational, Selden's interference is perniciously irrational. While *The House of Mirth* demonstrates that law, chance, and free will paradoxically exist together, the structure of literary allusions balances Emerson's "journeying [social] atoms," and "animate poles" so nearly equally that the novel does not insist on chance as the solution to the dilemma it posits. Dilemmas and paradoxes, rape, and sleep/suicide themes are the first clues to Wharton's code even as they elaborate on nature, and the opposing, animate poles of the fifth stanza of Emerson's "The Sphinx."

The rootless socialites who whirl in groups (to appear again in *The Custom of the Country*) are also like "atoms whirling away from each other in some wild centrifugal dance" (*HM* 516), a metaphor also found in Emerson's poem:

> The journeying atoms,
>     Primordial wholes,
> Firmly draw, firmly drive,
>     By their animate poles.
>
> [Emerson, "The Sphinx," stanza 5, ll. 21–24]

Similar to the paradox of Selden's deliberate random interference, a chance incident in *The Reef* creates an unanswerable dilemma for Anna Leath who, driven by Furies of love and curiosity, but in search of truth, asks unceasing questions of the Sphinx, introducing that myth directly for the first time.

# 2 | The Reef
## Clustered Thematic Allusions

Aᴌᴛʜᴏᴜɢʜ *The House of Mirth* elaborates on structural allusions supported by thematic allusions, *The Reef* experiments by arranging the thematic allusions in clearer groups, or "clusters."[1] *The Reef* has been a particularly baffling novel for many readers. An anonymous reviewer for the *Nation*, representative of many who feel thwarted, argues that "the story is a paltry one," from a sense of frustration with what, to judge from its literary allusions, is the central issue and the very beauty of the novel: that "all possible solutions are equally unsatisfactory and undesirable," that "the theme is impossible of dramatic solution," and that it is equally impossible that Anna Leath and George Darrow "should ever be happy together—or apart."[2]

This reviewer's perception of paralyzing oxymoronic forces of love and hate, and other paradoxes, is exactly the subject of the novel and of its new experiments with thematic allusions that range from clusters of allusions to neoimpressionist painters Theodore Rousseau and Theo van Rijsselberghe. (Wharton knew the latter well enough to invite him to contribute to *The Book of the Homeless*.) These contrast with clusters of allusions to Greek art, Greek drama, and Homer's *Odyssey*. The process of tracing these allusions leads to the probable source of the puzzling title and another clue to Edith Wharton's riddle.

Relative to most of Wharton's other novels (*Ethan Frome* and *Summer* are exceptions), allusions in *The Reef* are spare. Wharton's experimentation focuses entirely on the psychological complexities of perception, especially of character and situation. Here for the first time allusions "cluster" into two broad general categories, the deliberately hazy perceptions of the neoimpressionists and the crystal sharp outlines of Greek art and literature.

The plot is also spare. George Darrow is engaged to Anna Leath, a widow to whom he had been betrothed in his youth. Crossing the channel to Paris to see his fiancée, he is arrested by a telegram from Anna citing an "unexpected obstacle" (*RF* 3) requiring delay of his visit. Angry at what he perceives to be a resurgence of her youthful coldness, Darrow meets a slight acquaintance, Sophy Viner, who says she has lost her trunk. Darrow "rescues" her and takes her to Paris, where they have an affair. On one occasion at the theater he meets

Owen Leath, Anna's stepson, who glimpses Sophy's pink opera cloak. When a letter of explanation finally arrives, Darrow throws it unread into the fire. Several months later, reconciled with Anna, he arrives at her château, Givré, only to find Sophy Viner installed as governess to Anna's daughter and engaged to marry Owen.

Here the novel shifts from Darrow's point of view to Anna's, following her psychological and moral anguish as she gradually discovers the truth, then attempts to decide whether to marry Darrow in spite of it. The story ends with Anna's effort to find Sophy so as to relinquish Darrow to her, but Sophy is abroad, so Anna is left unable to make an explicit decision. A conclusion without a resolution contributes to reader frustration, but Wharton's reasons for the stalemate have their foundation in the apparently irreconcilable contrast between the clear lines of Greek art and the purposely indistinct blur of impressionism.

When in her classical reserve and formality, Anna is described as a "fine portrait kept down to a few tones" (*RF* 127), she is being compared to part of a second cluster, Greek art, which was based on four subtle tones: black, white, brown, and red. She is a "kind of warrior . . . with . . . strong chin and close-bound hair, like that of an amazon in a frieze" (*RF* 193). Anna exemplifies the qualities for which Greek art is generally well known—cool marble placidity, poses that range from mannered or stiffly frigid to peacefully relaxed, and a muted, timeless appeal based on presumed moral superiority.

At the same time she is contrasted to the fluid, impermanent watercolor tints that represent Sophy. Anna's rival is described as "lightly washed in with water-colour" (*RF* 13). The conflict created by Anna's mixed feelings blurs the hard lines of her ordered classical thought patterns but also intensifies the passion aroused by an unconscious connection of sexuality to water, hence to watercolor. Anna discovers that Sophy's sexual experience with Darrow both disgusts and tantalizes her. Thus she finds herself trying to make the impossible reconciliation between classical reason and romantic emotion. Like Greek art, she has the "capacity of energy and passion which are paradoxically overwhelming precisely because they are so intelligently controlled."[3]

Whereas Sophy is associated with impermanence, fluidity, and the stormy seas of sexual passion, Anna is permanent but static, a condition that is emphasized by two direct allusions to poems by Keats with a Greek setting: "Ode on a Grecian Urn" and "Ode to Psyche." Implied as well is the château Givré as symbolic of Keats's "chamber of maiden thought." Although a widow, Anna had not been sexually awakened before the second advent of Darrow, and until their love is consummated, she can be considered the "still unravished bride of quietness" of Keats's "Ode on a Grecian Urn": "She suggested . . . a Greek vase on which the play of light is the only pattern" (*RF* 127). Darrow remembers the two of them fourteen years earlier: "They seemed, he and she, like the ghostly lovers of the Grecian Urn, forever pursuing without ever clasping each other. To this day he did not quite know what had parted them" (*RF* 30). What had parted them was Anna's discovery of his involvement with Kitty Mayne, a woman who had a reputation as "not a lady." (Wharton uses cat imagery for such women, as she does again, for instance, in *Twilight Sleep*.) Seeing the issue in the either/or terms of youth and old New York, she had broken her engagement. Later, when she is a mature woman with awakened passions, the decision does not seem as clear, so Anna struggles to perceive swimming colors in what had previously always appeared black and white.

Darrow, however, never attempts to reconcile contradictions: "George Darrow had had a fairly varied experience of feminine types, but the women he had frequented had either been pronouncedly 'ladies' or they had not. Grateful to both for ministering to the more complex masculine nature, and disposed to assume that they had been evolved, if not designed, to that end, he had instinctively kept the two groups apart in his mind, avoiding that intermediate society which attempts to conciliate both theories of life" (*RF* 26). Darrow's unquestioning acceptance of the contraries of the double standard gives him an innocent, charming quality, but as Elizabeth Ammons points out with little exaggeration, "Prince Charming turns out to be a liar, a hypocrite, a coward, and a libertine."[4]

Most of Keats's poems deal with the human and changeable opposed to the immortal and immutable. Anna is caught in a Keatsian dilemma by trying to marry Darrow's human, mutable personality to her own "immortal," essential one. Though she can empathize with Sophy and Darrow, that capacity does not go so far as to relieve her of fretfully seeking fact and reason (*RF* 341) and experiencing extreme emotional pain: "With a torturing precision she pictured them alone," but immediately she becomes remorseful, arrested by "a wave of contrary feeling" (*RF* 341). As she begins to discover Darrow's true character, Anna's many vacillations lead to an indecisiveness that creates empathetic frustration for the reader. Yet it is easy to see to what extent this difficulty originates in the very theme of the novel.

In her growing understanding of Darrow's character, Anna is compared to Psyche who, in the Greek myth, has never seen her lover until she lights a lamp against his wishes. Questioning Darrow about why he had not responded to her letter of explanation of the "obstacle," she feels the "tremor in her of Psyche holding up the lamp" (*RF* 112). She continually finds herself in moments of Keatsian intensity poised on the brink of experience like the lovers in the "Ode to Psyche," whose "lips touch'd not, but had not bade adieu" (*Psyche*, l. 17) and like the lovers on the Grecian Urn, who are neither apart nor together. Nevertheless, over the course of the novel, Anna develops psychologically from her struggle with indecision, her "branched thoughts, new grown with pleasant pain" (*Psyche*, l. 52), which emphasizes the oxymoronic theme of the novel.

Anna's capacity for development results from maturity and her residence in Europe among old traditions symbolized by Givré, the mansion of human life that Keats describes in his famous letter:

> I compare human life to a large Mansion of Many Apartments, two of which I can only describe. . . . The first we step into we call the infant or thought-less chamber. . . . We remain there a long while, and notwithstanding the doors of the second chamber remain wide open, showing a bright appearance, we care not to hasten to it; but are at length imperceptibly impelled by the awakening of the thinking principle—within us—we no sooner get into the second Chamber, which I shall call the Chamber of Maiden-Thought, than we become intoxicated with the light and atmosphere, we see nothing but pleasant wonders, and think of delaying forever there in delight.[5]

The "thinking principle" contrasted to intoxicating "light and atmosphere" describes both the contrast between Greek art and artistic impressionism and the conflict in Anna's mind.

The internal debate over Darrow awakens Anna's "thinking principle" and sharpens her vision of the "heart and nature of Man." Suddenly she finds herself "endowed with the fatal gift of reading the secret sense of every seemingly spontaneous look and movement" (*RF* 248). An atmosphere at Givré "full of a latent life" permits Anna the "deep inward stillness" necessary to what Keats called "soul making" (*RF* 85). In contrast, growing up in old New York, "Anna had wondered why everybody about her seemed to ignore all the passions and sensations which formed the stuff of great poetry and memorable action" (*RF* 86).

The Grecian quality of Anna's soul is first viewed through Darrow's eyes. His anger over the "unexpected obstacle" makes him scornful: "Even in his first moment of exasperation it struck him as characteristic that she should not have padded her postponement with a fib. Certainly her moral angles were not draped!" (*RF* 10). She never wishes "a 'best' " that is "made of someone else's worst" (*RF* 313). But Anna's solid soul is ensconced in Givré, her psychological mansion.

> The serene face of the old house seated in its park among the poplar-bordered meadows of middle France, had seemed, on her first sight of it, to hold out to her a fate as noble and dignified as its own mien. . . . the house had for a time become to her the very symbol of narrowness and monotony. Then, with the passing of years, it had gradually acquired a less inimical character, had become, not again a castle of dreams, evoker of fair images and romantic legend, but the shell of a life slowly adjusted to its dwelling.

Givré is the place one returns to, where one has duties, habits, and books, "the place one would naturally live in till one died: a dull house, an inconvenient house, of which one knew all the defects, the shabbinesses, the discomforts, but to which one was so used that one could hardly, after so long a time, think one's self away from it without suffering a certain loss of identity" (*RF* 84–85).

To Keats, "people are not souls 'til they acquire identities, till each one is personally itself."[6] While Anna has an identity associated with the house, it is as if the house were an allegory of a body without a soul. As Owen remarks to Anna: "Poor empty Givré! With so many rooms full and yet not a soul in it—except of course my grandmother, who *is* its soul!" (*RF* 105). Anna fears becoming like the first Mrs. Leath, a cold portrait with "stone-dead eyes" (*RF* 99) or like her mother-in-law, Madame de Chantelle, whose name is so much like a fungus, the chanterelle mushroom.

Still, the château has paradoxical sides, the romantic and the dull. The extinguished romance associated with the house is rekindled by the arrival of Darrow, and when Anna tries to perceive it as he will, her psychological awareness begins: "She seemed to be opening her own eyes upon it after a long interval of blindness" (*RF* 85). But Anna does not anticipate that the process of soul making, of creating an identity that includes passion, must involve a decision between living a calm but lonely life and living with Darrow tormented by doubts about his truthfulness and fidelity. For when he finally admits his affair with Sophy, Anna "seemed to look into the very ruins of his soul. . . . It was as though he and she had been looking at two sides of the same thing, and the side she had seen had been all light and life, and his a place of graves . . . " (*RF* 274, final ellipses Wharton's). Whichever life identity Anna chooses, that of lonely widow or that of troubled wife, she is Psyche "with awaken'd eyes" (*Psyche*, l. 6).

Unafraid of a life of sensation, Anna is ready, even eager, to experience it, facing the prospect with the deep inward stillness based on the classical qualities of her personality. Because her reason refuses to allow her to reconcile both sides of the dilemma of morality, soul making, and identity, she responds with Keatsian intensity: "Anna was intensely aware that as soon as they began to talk more intimately [she and Darrow] would feel that they knew each other less well" (*RF* 109). Paradoxes persist.

Sophy, on the other hand, is a mutable person who reacts to the feeling of the moment without thinking. She is "a shifting and uncrystallized mixture" of "any one of a dozen definable types" (*RF* 61). Darrow notes that the "freshness of the face at his side, reflecting the freshness of the season, suggested dapplings of sunlight through new leaves, the sound of a brook in the grass, the ripple of tree-shadows over breezy meadows . . . " (*RF* 58, Wharton's ellipses). To Darrow's suggestion that perhaps acting, a profession of changing roles (and a profession at the time considered nearly equal to prostitution) would not be the most proper vocation for a young lady, Sophy replies, "What—exactly—*do* you seem to see me permanently given up to?" (*RF* 170). There is no permanence about Sophy, so he can have no answer.

Sophy has been interpreted as a heroine by most contemporary critics, who admire her because she lives so fully. True enough, her exuberance, frankness, and sensitivity endow her with a nearly irresistible appeal as a modern "liberated" woman, and for readers unacquainted with the moral climate of Wharton's time, Sophy dominates the novel. James Tuttleton's observations are apt, however: "Sophy lives by no discernible principle except that of self-advancement, and the positiveness we may feel about her is largely the consequence of Anna's magnanimity in conferring on Sophy virtues that Anna herself wishes that she had."[7]

Recall that in Anna Leath's world, Sophy is not "a lady," in the moral sense that euphemism used to imply, though for the protection of her daughter and for the protection of her perception of Darrow, Anna desperately needs her to be one.

Rather, Sophy is a Siren. In *The Odyssey*, the goddess Circe tells Odysseus what obstacles to expect. If he succeeds in passing the singing Sirens (having tied himself to a mast to avoid their attractions), there will be reefs: "One course will bring you to a pair of precipitous rocks, washed by the boisterous breakers of dark-eyed Amphitrite; the gods call them the Moving Rocks. . . . The other course leads between two cliffs."[8] Circe recommends that Odysseus take his ship close to the lower of the two cliffs, and cautions him that to pass it with the least amount of damage, he must recognize a point where he "could shoot an arrow across." He never finds that point. Darrow's name now accrues meaning, especially written as if it were French: "d'arrow"; and his short channel crossing thereby becomes a moral Odyssey.

George observes the "prettiness" that is Sophy's siren quality: "She seemed simply to be aware of it as a note in the general harmony, and to enjoy sounding the note as a singer enjoys singing" (*RF* 61). To him she is an "unusually original and attractive creature" (*RF* 260), "one of the elemental creatures whose emotion is all in their pulses" (*RF* 262). His responsiveness to Sirens is further reflected in his attention to the "splash and ripple" (*RF* 226) of Owen's music in Madame de Chantelle's drawing room ("chantelle" is an anagram for "she sings" in French): "He sat motionless, as if spell-bound by the play of Madame de Chantelle's [knitting] needles and the pulsations of Owen's fitful music" (*RF* 156). Furthermore, Sophy comes from a family of Sirens. When Anna visits Sophy's sister, she felt she was "pulling back the veil from dingy distances of family history" (*RF* 365). On the last page of the novel, as Anna leaves, Laura calls out, "Do come again! I'd love to sing to you" (*RF* 367).

The Greek motifs of the allusions to Keats are underscored by the allusions to Greek drama. Much of Henry James's praise of the "Racinian unity" of *The Reef* is based on its classical organization in five acts, possibly a structural allusion to Racine. The controlled dramatic unities of Aristotle inspired Racine's drama and in turn Edith Wharton's novel in its carefully controlled settings, characters, and chronology. There are four main characters (Anna, Darrow, Sophy, and Owen), four minor characters (Adelaide Painter, Effie, Mme de Chantelle, and Mrs. McTarvie-Birch) and four "offstage" characters (Mr. Leath, Mrs. Murrett, "the Farlows," and Jimmy Brance). Time, too, is carefully controlled—the ten-day affair between Sophy and Darrow in spring (Sophy's youth) contrasts with a similar length of time at Givré in autumn (Anna's maturity). The novel's connection to Greek drama is also implied in Wharton's own comment that "one should know that there is a play in 'The Reef' all ready to be pulled out!—"[9]

In fact, Darrow takes Sophy to see a production of Racine's *Oedipe*, a play famous for its coincidences, and there Owen Leath gains the coincidental glimpse of pink that eventually results in Darrow's exposure. *Oedipe* is an allusion to the novel's theme of fate, destiny, and the gods. Mme de Chantelle's constant knitting brings to mind the three Fates traditionally symbolized by knitting women. The theme of Fate, carried forward from *The House of Mirth*, also serves to explain the coincidences so troubling to some critics.

*The Reef* opens with an allusion to Euripides' *Hippolytus*, later adapted to *Phaedra* by Seneca and—the source of Henry James's reference—*Phèdre* by Racine. When Darrow receives the "unexpected obstacle" telegram, the words "drip slowly and coldly" into a "brain . . . shaking, tossing, transposing them like the dice in some game of the gods of malice" (*RF* 3). Part of Wharton's careful plan alludes to *Hippolytus,* which opens with a game of chance between Aphrodite, representing promiscuity, and Artemis representing its opposite, chastity. In *The Reef* also, the characters' fates depend upon the arbitrariness of these gods.

As Darrow and Sophy converse during the intermission of the Greek play, Sophy rapturously exclaims that spirits are present, even during the intermission, "as if the gods were there all the while . . . pulling the strings" (*RF* 59), and Anna's daughter, Effie, an open, trusting child, admits Darrow into "full equality with the other gods of her Olympus" (*RF* 223). The novel suggests that random impulses of masculinity are, like Selden's in *The House of Mirth*, and like those of the gods, the sources of disturbing calamities. The events that occur are caused by the apparent arbitrariness of Darrow's and Owen's both making love to Sophy, who "happens" to Darrow like a storm or some other natural cataclysm. Sophie had "no literary or historic associations to which to attach her impressions: her education had evidently not comprised a course in Greek literature. But she felt . . . the ineluctable fatality of the tale, the dread sway in it of the same mysterious 'luck' which pulled the threads of her own small destiny. It was not literature to her, it was fact" (*RF* 60). Through Sophy, Darrow learns to understand fate as fact, as readers should be led to do in the world of this novel.

The classical unities derived from Aristotle's *Poetics*. Unity of action, time, and place were concepts that had a particular impact on Racine. The relationship of the five-book novel to the five-act classical play makes the allusions to *Phèdre* and *Oedipe* structural. *Phèdre* is a "reverberating allusion" (an allusion that echoes previous literature) in that Racine's seventeenth-century play derives from Greek and Roman sources (Euripides' *Hippolytus* and Seneca's *Phaedra and Hippolytus*). They are thematic as well, because their common themes, like the themes of *The Reef*, are fate, incest, and that of Keats's "Ode on a Grecian Urn," human passion constantly pursuing its object but destined to be forever frustrated. In praising *The Reef* for its "psychological Racinian unity, intensity and gracility,"[10] Henry James had obviously perceived its Grecian theme of fate and had noted the allusion to *Phèdre*. *Phèdre* and *Oedipe* both contain the themes of fate and incest, Phèdre having been predestined by the gods to succumb to her incestuous passion for her stepson (according to the play) and Oedipus having been doomed to marry his mother. The suggestion of incest in *The Reef* is that Darrow has been intimate with a woman who could become his step*daughter*-in-law and that Owen may be in love with his stepmother. Since the relatives concerned are not blood relations, these associations will seem tentative to modern readers until they consult the prohibitions of Leviticus that are so important to *The Mother's Recompense*.

Phèdre's stepson, Hippolytus, reminds her of her husband. She says to Hippolytus, "He breathes in you. I seem to see my husband still before me."[11] At the end she admits to her husband, Theseus, "I am the one, incestuous, infamous, / Who dared cast eyes on your chaste, gentle son" (*Phèdre*, l. 1623–24). In the same way, Anna's stepson, Owen, reminds her of her husband, Fraser Leath, and under some circumstances even Darrow reminds her of Leath: It was "almost as to Owen's father that she now appealed to Darrow" (*RF* 189–90). Furthermore, there is a brother-sister relationship between Anna and Owen: "Owen and I have always been on odd kind of brother-sister terms" (*RF* 114). Parallels emerge: Hippolytus is the son of Theseus, by Hippolyta, queen of the Amazons, and Anna is described as an "amazon in a frieze" (*RF* 193). That analogy makes Anna like a mother to Owen. In addition, Darrow thinks of Anna's daughter as the "mystical offspring of the early tenderness" between them (*RF* 138).

Owen is a problematic character who often steps out of the shadows— "He had a passion for prowling about the park at night-fall . . . " (*RF* 132, Wharton's ellipses). His personality is comprised of highs and lows, symptoms of manic depression, Teddy Wharton's disorder, the polarities of which are another way of expressing the novel's paradoxes and antitheses of perception. "I've been mad these last days, simply mad," Owen says, ironically stating the truth as he refers to the madness of love (*RF* 276). He has "the look of a young faun strayed in from the forest" (*RF* 155), phallic "gun in hand" (*RF* 154). A faun, of course, is a mythological creature who is half man, half goat—a satyr, but younger—a creature often represented as Pan playing the pipes, a detail that illuminates Owen's musicianship. The incest of *The Reef*, however, is primarily a matter of psychological perception indicative of an emotional closeness that means every action performed by one character affects the other three in spite of the aptly named Miss Painter, the friend with rocklike dependability.

The plot is not without a Greek deus ex machina, the "god from the machine," who often dropped from the sky with the aid of a mechanical device in the last act of Greek plays to untangle the plot's threads: "All their destinies were in Miss Painter's grasp" (*RF* 219). But Miss Painter is a dea ex machina without curiosity about the fates in which she intervenes and without omnipotence. When summoned by Madame de Chantelle, she descends upon the group as if she were goddess of a reef. Darrow perceives her acceptingly as a "granite image on the edge of a cliff" (*RF* 211), as "some wonderful automatic machine" (*RF* 212), and he sinks in the "lee of Miss Painter's granite bulk" (*RF* 226). Always hatted and booted for action, she can be called down from her lofty cliff to help at a moment's notice. Unfortunately, her mindless theocratic interventions accomplish little. This character alone fails to fit neatly into the Aristotelian structure of this so-called Jamesian novel.

*The Reef*'s reputation for being the most "Jamesian" of Wharton's novels is in part due to James's praise of it as "quite the finest thing" she had done and "both more done than even the best of [her] other doing and more worth it, through intrinsic value, interest and beauty" (Lewis 327). His only reservations had to do with Anna's "oscillations" and the nature of the American characters unreferred to the French milieu. Remarkably absent from his criticism is any mention of dissatisfaction with the enigmatic conclusion. Even so, it is hard to guess whether he fully comprehended the function of the literary allusions or the oxymoronic paralysis that Wharton was trying to illustrate—the "caught between a rock [reef] and a hard place" dilemma universal to human experience. James's apparent unfamiliarity with Wharton's intentions, if it was that, supports critics' growing sense of Wharton's literary independence of "the Master." The Jamesian quality that readers feel in *The Reef* is due not to instruction, influence, or imitation but rather to Edith Wharton's allusions to works by Henry James, particularly *The Ambassadors* (1903) and *The American Scene* (1906). In both cases the allusions center on issues of perception.

James's novels explore ways of knowing through observation by a "reflector." Wharton's use of two reflectors changes the technical problems, especially as she includes these reflectors' opposing points of view as one of many contrasts intended to join the oppositions, paradoxes, polarities, and oxymorons she creates by her thematic allusions. Nevertheless, Wharton finds the technique useful for both Darrow and Anna. Darrow fears not Anna's questions but "what might cry aloud in the intervals between them" (*RF* 193), while Anna finds herself fatally endowed with the ability to read the "secret sense" of every action (*RF* 248). Like the scene between Madame Merle and Osmond observed by Isabel Archer in *Portrait of a Lady*, and like that between Darrow and Sophy watched by Owen, moments in which people are seen comfortably sharing lengthy silences reveal the existence of intimate secrets.

Among the unseen social forces experienced as a series of impressions for James was the position of American men whom he viewed in *The American Scene* as supplying all the canvas of life and "the women all the embroidery."[12] Wharton alludes to this image to provide yet another paradox for Anna, who "learned to regard the substance of life as a mere canvas for the embroideries of poet and painter" (*RF* 87). For James, paradox of viewpoint was a desirable achievement, as when Lambert Strether in *The Ambassadors* comprehends the "slow rush." Such a viewpoint is not indecisive or oscillating, but the discernment that opposing views might have such equal merit that they admit of no logical choice. Anna achieves this capacity. She learns the equal value of cool Greek reason represented by Hellenic art and passionate impulse represented by French impressionism and neoimpressionism, a late outgrowth of which was pointillism.

One of the functions of both allusions to James was to emphasize the manner in which George Darrow views the world. He looks out upon it with a kind of moral pointillism when he observes Sophy after he "picks her up": "She seemed hardly conscious of sensations of form and colour, or of any imaginative suggestion, and the spectacle before them . . . broke up, under her scrutiny, into a thousand minor points" (*RF* 38). Darrow allows himself to "receive his own sensations through the medium of hers" (*RF* 60). Most of Darrow's perceptions, however, are described as "blurred," "shimmering," or "impressionistic." Both he and Sophy are described by a mode of impressionism that Wharton beautifully arranged to contrast with the novel's Greek classicism.

The title of the novel has forever puzzled readers who from time to time attempt to relate a reef in some way to Wharton's life or resort to clever acrostics.[13] But just as Edith Wharton used a painting by Sir Joshua Reynolds as a structural allusion in *The House of Mirth*—only the beginning of many art allusions in her novels—here she supplies a titular art allusion to *The Reef* as part of the thematic cluster of allusions to perception. *The Reef*, a painting by the Belgian neoimpressionist Theo van Rijsselberghe (1862–1926), depicts a rock outcropping on the coast of Brittany. The painting is executed in blue and violet pointillist dots.

Theo van Rijsselberghe, *The Reef* (1889). The Kröller-Müller Foundation, Amsterdam. Titular Allusion: *The Reef.*

Theodore Rousseau, *Le Givré* (1845). Walters Art Gallery, Baltimore. Thematic Allusion: *The Reef.*

Another neoimpressionist, Theodore Rousseau, painted *Le Givré* (1845), an impelling landscape of a frost-coated meadow after which Wharton named Anna Leath's eighteenth-century French château. One meaning of *givré* is "frost," and the manion *is* cold without a soul, but a second meaning is "time," which, by suggesting sea foam, ties it to the theme of the reef and the Siren's watercolor world.[14] In addition, one of the meanings of "reef," when it is used as a verb, is "to draw up or gather in" (as in "to reef a sail"). A psychological gathering in of information, perceptions, and impressions is the common thread that holds one cluster of literary allusions together, and a subcategory under perception is the theme of contradicting perceptions.

The theory behind impressionism rests on contradiction. Contrasting colors are dabbed next to one another on the canvas. Yellow and blue, for instance, stimulate the eye to try to blend them into green. The inability of the optic nerve to merge the colors causes an illusion of shimmering and vibrating.[15] This sense of wavering is the visual reflection of Anna Leath's new psychological state and Darrow's old one. Since her marriage Anna has adjusted her reserved but passionate personality to a stasis now disturbed by her attraction to Darrow. But Darrow, upset by the "unexpected obstacle" caused by Anna's family responsibilities, responds with rage reflected by the "angry sea beyond" [which] "as if from the crest of the waves, stung and blinded him with a fresh fury of derision" (*RF* 3). As a result, when Anna discovers that he has petulantly indulged in an affair with a Siren, the ship of their plan flounders on the Odyssean reef, "an obstacle."

In an attempt to extricate herself from her reef, Anna sleeps with Darrow, an episode so subtly handled that it eludes most readers. On Anna's last evening with him before taking the train to Paris, her "eye fell on the notecase she had given him. It was worn at the corners with the friction of his pocket and distended with thickly packed papers. . . . she put her hand out and touched it." After that Darrow catches her in his arms (*RF* 342–43). Seeing the sexual imagery of the passage depends on recognizing the note case as a means of intercourse; the distension, the pocket, and the urge to touch then become clear. The point of the scene is that Anna had expected intimacy with Darrow to clarify her decision, but it changes nothing. Finally, at the end of the novel she decides to give up Darrow to Sophy, but Sophy has left for India with her former employer, leaving Anna still to decide whether or not she can marry Darrow. The novel ends as it begins, with lovers "pulled together and apart like marionettes on the wires of the wind" (*RF* 13).

The themes revealed by the two clusters of allusions to Grecian and impressionist themes include the dilemma already found in *The House of Mirth* and paradoxically add "pleasant pain" to the major thematic clue of Lily's "suicide." *The Reef* dramatizes in Anna the question of Emerson's narrator to the Sphinx: "Have I a lover / Who is noble and free?" (stanza 12, l. 94).

Darrow's careless affairs with Lady Ulrica, Kitty Mayne, Sophy, and undoubt-edly many others, selfishly create pain for both Anna and Sophy, each in her own way the "old playfellow" of Emerson's "The Sphinx." Anna has moved beyond "questioning the Sphinx" to "trying to find an answer to it" (*RF* 94). Here Darrow's secrets make a Sphinx of him, for ironically, the situation de-veloped not unlike Anna's first marriage, in which "there were so many things between them that were never spoken of, or even indirectly alluded to" (*RF* 100). But caught by a Fury of his own making, Darrow gets pain he deserves when he is (again paradoxically) fated to be hemmed in by Anna's logic (*RF* 195). Either Anna will refuse him, or she will accept him but she will never trust him.

Owen, whose mental health is tenuous, conceivably suffers enough from Darrow's actions to unbalance him further. Most frightening, then, is that while Anna and Sophy are emotionally distracted, little Effie runs as wild as a dog, "flying down one of the long alleys at the head of her pack" (*RF* 168), vulnerable to the faun who plays Pan's pipes, the stepbrother who prowls in the dark and then brags, "Nobody knows where I go, or what I see [or whom]" (*RF* 155).

The allusions to the neoimpressionists and Keats, Greek drama, Homer, and Henry James support themes of oxymoronic contraries, of impressionistic perceptions, of fate and incest. They elucidate reasons that the novel bothers so many critics, who object to its lack of solution and its apparent dependence on coincidence, and they explain its "Jamesianism." *Phaedra* appears to con-stitute Wharton's first use of a "reverberating allusion" (though there is the kernel of one in *The House of Mirth*), while the art allusions serve to demon-strate how each of the main characters views the world: Darrow impressionis-tically, Sophy in the impermanent tints of watercolor, Anna with the clearness of Greek light, but Owen, whose mentally disturbed perceptions swing into polarities, lives in the shadows of chiaroscuro. Here also, for the first time, we find the beauty of two sets of contrary "clusters" of thematic allusions, those to perception—neoimpressionists and James—and those to ancient Greece—Greek art, *The Odyssey, Oedipe,* Racine's *Phèdre,* and Keats's "Ode to Psyche" and "Ode on a Grecian Urn." They are neatly arranged, as Gloria Erlich so astutely points out, under symbols of umbrellas: Darrow's protects him from rain and consequences; Anna's parasol shades her from the sun of happiness. As Wharton's novels develop, however, the umbrella becomes a symbol for a more encompassing type of allusion.

The themes revealed by the clusters of allusions include the dilemma al-ready found in *The House of Mirth* and add the paradoxical "pleasant pain" and incest to the list of clues to the code. But there is much more to the riddle than the dilemma—Anna Leath is "still questioning the Sphinx" (*RF* 94), dramatizing the question of Emerson's narrator to the Sphinx, "Have I a lover / Who is noble and free?" Darrow's breezily careless affairs create complications when Anna, his "old playfellow" meets the sexually free Sophy:

> The waves unashamed
>> In difference sweet,
> Play glad with the breezes,
>> Old playfellows meet;
>>> ["The Sphinx," stanza 4, ll. 25-28]

Darrow's unashamed Siren is a protégée of a Fury: He "remembered [Sophy] as one of the shadowy sidling presences in the background of that awful house in Chelsea, one of the dumb appendages of the shrieking unescapable Mrs. Murrett, into whose talons he had fallen in the course of his headlong pursuit of Lady Ulrica Crispin. . . . how it clung!" (*RF* 15–16). The novel hints of incest, a subject that becomes the focus again in *The Mother's Recompense*. The shocking quality of incest, however, should not be allowed to overshadow the interesting discoveries that emerge from the unique "mythic allusions" of *The Custom of the Country,* in which Wharton develops her water symbol when poisonous mythical reptiles invade old New York.

# 3 | *The Custom of the Country*
Mythic Allusions

The broad range of *The Custom of the Country* is often contrasted to the spare unity of *The Reef,* published by Scribner's in October 1913 with great success.[1] Edith Wharton's technical development in this novel is the coalescence of clusters of thematic allusions, mostly allusions to creation myths or literature with mythological content. The effort forms a supporting myth for a body of American literature that (compared to European literature) has little but derivative myth. Wharton points out that American ideals, as represented by the population of the Midwest, had been "based on the myth of 'old families' ruling New York from a throne of Revolutionary tradition" (CC 193), a theme she continues in a different way in *The Age of Innocence.* Except for Washington Irving's adaptations of German mythology in stories like "Rip Van Winkle," rags-to-riches morality tales like the *Autobiography of Benjamin Franklin,* and a few poems like "The Midnight Ride of Paul Revere," American culture was thin broth for a lover of the world's literary stew. So far it had provided almost nothing of its own to which to allude, a problem for an author who aspired to write important American literature and a problem Edith Wharton apparently set out to help alleviate. Her reference to *The Custom of the Country* as her "great American novel" is most interesting, since much of it is set in Europe.[2]

Nearly picaresque, the novel contrasts the unmarried Lily Bart's one-year social descent to the much-married Undine Spragg's twelve-year social ascent. It begins with her marriage to Ralph Marvell of old New York aristocracy, her affair with the nouveau riche Peter Van Degen, her marriage to French nobleman Raymond de Chelles, and the final union with her male counterpart, the rustic billionaire Elmer Moffatt. Undine, like America, accrues wealth without any culture except that purchased from Europe.

Undine's parents moved to New York from Apex City for Undine's social advancement. The only surviving child of three, two of whom died in a typhoid epidemic in Apex, Undine manipulates her guilt-ridden parents. Irregular construction shortcuts during development of Apex's real estate and water systems were the source of Mr. Spragg's financial gain and human loss. Moving to New York at the Spragg's financial, physical, and psychological expense is a parental attempt to assuage guilt, win Undine's love by bribery, show off her beauty, and remove her from the threatening influence of Elmer Moffatt. The three languish at the Hotel Stentorian until Undine meets Ralph Marvell and launches a victorious campaign to marry him.

The book follows Undine and Ralph through the conflict of their European honeymoon and the birth and neglect of their son to her flight with Peter Van Degen. When Van Degen learns that Undine refused to visit her critically ill husband, he realizes she could treat him the same way, so he abandons her.

Next, Undine embarks on a plan to marry Raymond de Chelles, a difficult goal to achieve because of his Roman Catholicism. She is divorced, and Catholics then were not permitted to marry divorcées. To extort enough money from Ralph to try to bribe Vatican officials for an annulment, Undine threatens to take custody of their son. Despairing of raising enough money to ransom his son, Ralph commits suicide. Undine prevails, but she is quickly disillusioned when she is forced to live quietly rather than reign over a glittering social elite. When she revolts, de Chelles punishes her by refusing to conceive the son who would ensure her acceptance by old French families. In retaliation she sells his Boucher heirloom tapestries to the now mightily prosperous Elmer Moffatt. Undine immediately divorces de Chelles for Moffatt. As the novel ends, however, having learned that divorce will prevent her from becoming an ambassador's wife, Undine remains dissatisfied.

Since myths are a channel for various energies, Cynthia Griffin Wolff's reading of the themes of Undine's energy versus the passivity of old New York offers a useful approach to the novel's mythical subtext, which is constructed of a set of literary allusions that combine to become a creation myth. Following Wharton's method, which appears to be unique in American literature, the following story emerges from the allusions as the novel's foundational American creation myth: Once, when the brave new world (America) began, its Adam and Eve (the Spraggs) disobeyed God by poisoning the fertile Water of Creativity on the western edge of Eden. When their children were poisoned, the four elements from which they had been created became unbalanced, causing their metamorphosis into a plague of gold-devouring reptiles raging with energy that emerged from the West to invade Eastern Eden. The Titan gods of old New York were blindly passive, and because they averted their eyes, they fell into the dragon's pit, their gold and daughters overtaken by reptilian fiends. The race dies, but the genetic energy of their half-reptile, half-Titan sons and daughters makes possible a cultural redemption. The traditional culture of the East can be combined with the wealth and vitality of the West.

The novel's allusions unveil themes of great floods, of diseases of poisoned water—typhoid and pneumonia—and of "poisoned" creatures who develop the capacity of metamorphosis: undines, lamias, basilisks, toads, and satans. They become human but soulless monsters who seek the healing element of gold. With ruthlessness that passes for magic, they marry for gold, divorce and remarry for money, then cheat for it in politics, real estate, and the stock market. In the stormy wake and imbalance of the elements caused by passion, they leave devastation and shipwreck. Yet, however complete their devastation may seem, there is a chance that culture can be reborn by drowning (or being baptized) into new life.

No joy permeates this vision; still, it is neither deterministic nor, necessarily, a version of the "fortunate fall" of Puritan typology. "Increasing enlightenment produced a revolt of Apex Puritanism" (CC 353). Undine feels that she has "cast in [her] lot with a fallen cause" when she learns that she had "given herself to the exclusive and dowdy when the future belonged to the showy and the promiscuous" (CC 193). Any hope that exists requires the new generation to mend the broken thread of its historical continuity to culture and the arts, not to retrogress or remain static but to create a culturally enriched future for both East and West.

The title is a convenient way to enter the novel's world of literary allusions.[3] Apparently Charles Scribner wrote Edith Wharton questioning her choice. On November 27, 1911, she replied:

> Thank you for enquiring about the title of "The Custom of the Country."—It is unfortunate, indeed; but, as Mrs. Fraser's book came out at least ten years ago, & was of so entirely different a character, I am wondering if there would be any confusion or any harm done to the sale if I keep the title? Of course I have a perfect right to, as it is "in the public domain," & Beaumont & Fletcher (weren't they the originators?—No. I think it was a later dramatist) can't be disturbed by our pilferings!—In any event, thank you for announcing "The Wake," on the chance that I may have to use that title as a substitute.[4]

The letter seems a masterpiece of indirection about the matter of allusion which she disparages as "pilferings."

Edith Wharton had good reason for wishing to keep her allusive title. The custom of this bawdy play's title is that whenever a virgin is married, the duke of the country has a right either to break the bride's maidenhead or to accept a ransom:

> . . . O the wicked Custom of this Country,
> The barbarous, most inhumane, damned Custom.
> . . . That when a Maid is contracted
> And ready to the tye o' th' Church, the Governour,
> He that commands in chief, must have her Maiden-
>     head,

Or Ransom it for money at his pleasure.
. . . . . . . . . . . . . . . . . . . . . . . . . . . . .
                 . . . all
Your sad misfortunes had original
From the barbarous Custom practis'd in my Country

The lascivious duke prefers the first option. The heroine is too pure to accept such behavior, so she and her bridegroom escape by ship after the ceremony, whereupon they are shipwrecked in a strange country whose customs are unfamiliar. The "custom of the country" amounts to prostitution of the bride. The allusion to the play connects the themes of marriage and the marketplace as Wolff, who first noticed the source of the title, remarks: "This is a world whose moral center has been lost—a world where everything is for sale" and "marriage and divorce are no more than a means of bartering."[5] In Wharton's novel that "custom," that prostitution, is divorce and remarriage for money, but of course Undine does the prostituting, going so far as to use her son as collateral. She considers him "an acquisition," a "bale of goods," whom "she'd be ashamed to sell . . . cheap" (CC 478, 440, 447).

Wharton was right that the title derived from a later author in that Massinger succeeded Fletcher as coauthor of Beaumont's plays. The allusion to the play sets up yet another parallel, the radical economic changes of the Jacobean era with those of the novel's era. The Jacobean age witnessed the shaping of a capitalist system that destroyed a tradition of individualism and social morality when the economy suddenly changed from a stable, rural agricultural society to an unstable, urban environment in which individuals competed.[6] Invasion of the formerly aristocratic society by the middle classes is a theme that the play and the novel have in common. The same kinds of characters occur, especially the merchant ambitious to become a gentleman—in this case Elmer Moffatt, who embodies forces of appetite and materialism dominant in both Jacobean and American society. And as in the Jacobean comedy, the merchant who becomes rich while remaining rustic creates superb material for satire.

Mr. Dagonet, Ralph Marvell's grandfather, is a man from old New York whose sarcasms had "as little bearing on life as the humours of a Restoration comedy" (CC 311) and whose notion of Undine's and Ralph's divorce was "almost as remote from reality [as Ralph's]. All he asked was that his grandson should 'thrash' somebody, and he could not be made to understand that the modern drama of divorce is sometimes cast without a Lovelace" (CC 337).

Lovelace is probably the villain rapist of Richardson's eighteenth-century novel *Clarissa* (an allusion that Wharton uses later in *The Glimpses of the Moon*) but may doubly allude to the empty-headed fop of the Restoration comedy *Three Weeks After Marriage* by Arthur Murray, which, like Reynolds's portrait of Mrs. Lloyd, is dated 1776.

Three Weeks After Marriage (in which indigent fops marry daughters of rich merchants for their money), like *Clarissa,* and like *The Custom of the Country,* reinforces Wharton's themes of the western "invaders" concerned with the procurement of wealth at the expense of family life, tradition, honor, and morality. And her allusions to creation myths tell a story about the genesis of these invaders. "You might as well tell me there was nobody but Adam in the garden when Eve picked the apple," Mr. Dagonet says to Ralph during their discussion of the impending divorce (CC 337). Undine was among those who have "cast in their lot with a fallen cause" (CC 193). She inherited this condition from her father who, when Ralph sent his name down to the "subterranean restaurant" of the hotel where Mr. Spragg lived, "appeared between the limp portières of the 'Adam' writing-room" (CC 439). Together Ralph and Undine pretend to be a new Adam and Eve: "One of the *humours* of their first weeks together had consisted in picturing themselves as a primeval couple setting forth across a virgin continent and subsisting on the adjectives which Ralph was to trap for his epic" (CC 146, italics mine). But Ralph's old New York passivity—he should have been trapping active verbs—is no match for Undine's energy, and he is eventually replaced as Adam by the midwesterner Elmer Moffatt.[7]

Moffatt appears in Apex as if suddenly created from the rib of Eve: "No one in Apex knew where young Moffatt had come from" (CC 549). He married his Eve without God's "Voice that Breathed o'er Eden" (CC 467). Having no ancestral background, no history, and like the nomadic medieval conquerors, no home, Moffatt arrives in Apex not only as an Adam but as Satan having suddenly appeared to tempt the Sons of Jonadad to drink wine. In the scene in which Moffatt and his cronies get drunk at a church function, Wharton summons a verse from Jeremiah: "And we have obeyed the command of Jonadab ben Rechab, our ancestor, in every particular, drinking no wine as long as we live . . . and building no houses to dwell in" (Jer. 35:8,9).

Members of the de Chelles family remark on wandering Americans. It seems "natural that the Americans, who had no homes, who were born and died in hotels, should have contracted nomadic habits" (CC 512). Adam and Eve, cast out of Paradise, were also wanderers, and biblical myth is based on the search of their descendants for a homeland, which, when established, required fierce wars to retain. Furthermore, the historical tales told of vanquished civilizations frequently involve advanced but complacent societies overrun by nomads like Visigoths. Ralph thinks of the invasion ironically: "The daughters of his own race sold themselves to the Invaders; the daughters of the Invaders bought their husbands as they bought an opera-box. It ought all to have been transacted on the Stock Exchange" (CC 78).

Secure European culture is contrasted with old New York by reducing "Invaders" like Undine and Moffatt to "intruders" when they arrive on the continent (CC 78, 499). So much rootlessness emphasizes a lack of the kind of permanence in America that makes possible great artistic civilizations. Wharton alludes to great French art, like that of the French painters Gauguin and Boucher, in *The Custom of the Country* to emphasize further the contrast between the complexity of great civilizations and the apparent simplicity of the primitive.

Richard Lawson pointed out the source of Undine's name in the old German tale recorded by La Mott Fouqué.[8] The story is about a water nymph who can acquire a soul only by marrying a mortal and bearing his child but ends tragically with the return of the undine to her subterranean world and the subsequent suicide of Huldbrand, her husband. Parallels between this myth and the plot of *The Custom of the Country* suggest that the story is a structural allusion.

An allusion to Gauguin can be deduced by combining Undine's name with the Edenic allusions. Gauguin's paintings include one entitled *Undine* (1889), upon which he based a woodcut entitled *Be Mysterious* (1890). "Mysterious" is a one-word clue used again and again in *The Custom of the Country.* To Gauguin the undine symbolized the perilous feminine character of treacherous waters. The nude figure's sensuality recalls the fall associating it with Undine's cold sexuality—her prostitution of herself in marriages contracted only for social and financial gain.

Gauguin, the great primitive painter, left France for his Tahitian "paradise," then poisoned it with syphilis, thereby producing his own fallen paradise. Gauguin was obsessed with the Edenic theme: "Milton's version of the forfeit of Eden was a direct inspiration to Gauguin in the evolution of his own Eve saga."[9] The precise nature of Wharton's Edenic myth is not meant to parallel Gauguin's; rather, the Edenic theme and its subtle link to Milton are important because among other things these creation myths "layer" the allusions ("layered allusions" are discussed in Chapter 5).

One source describes the undine as "rich in the spoils of pearls and coral from the deep bed of ocean,"[10] language that explains Undine's attachment to Van Degen's pearls, the grasping gesture of "her hand absently occupied with the twist of pearls he had given her," and her insistence on a portrait by Popple when a wealthy patron announces that Popple is the only artist who can "do pearls" (CC 231, 187).

Structural allusions are reinforced by significant themes, one of which is the nymph's absence of soul. Undine has no feelings except as expressed by performances, rationalizations, or acquisitions, and a soul is not among the things Undine is interested in acquiring. Lack of soul is a quality of the fall; Undine's lack of soul suggests that she embodies traits of both Eve and Satan as tempters. Satan's traditional reptilian form makes it normal for him to seek water like the undines that are also mythologically wicked creatures and like the sea nymph that Ralph imagines Undine to be: "Undine's figure wavered nereid-like" (*CC* 144).

Boucher, on the other hand, is considered a competent example of highly sophisticated eighteenth-century rococo decorative art. In the world of Boucher, mythological themes are excuses for exhibiting frankly sensuous female figures; the paintings seldom include men. Boucher's backgrounds were fanciful, energyless renditions of natural settings, devoid of firm architectural structure. They never attempted to relate background to foreground figures. But as a decorator he was unsurpassed, having a "rich and varied talent, brilliance of execution, and light hearted voluptuousness."[11] He designed magnificent tapestries that were then manufactured by Gobelins' weavers. Their sophistication is recognized by Elmer Moffatt, who helps Undine trick de Chelles into selling them. The theme of interweaving varied strands of society to create cultural depth is carried out by allusions yet to be discussed: the motion of the waves of water and of Undine's hair, the "wavering limbs" of Shelley's *Prometheus Unbound,* and Keats's Lamia, who "Dissolv'd, or brighter shone, or interwreathed / [her] lusters with the gloomier tapestries—" (ll. 46–53). Wharton's literary allusions to Keats and Shelley weave the strands together "like the Gobelins' weavers, on the wrong side of the tapestry" (*BG* 197).

Uncultured Undine had not previously heard of Boucher or of the "famous Berlin comedians who were performing Shakespeare at the German Theatre" (*CC* 37). Nevertheless, Ralph is moved to find her "Ariel-like, suggesting, from the first, not so much of the recoil of ignorance as the coolness of the element from which she took her name" (*CC* 152). Part of his great error is mistaking her dominant humor for air rather than water: "She might have been some fabled creature whose home was in a beam of light" (*CC* 21). But Undine is primarily a creature of water, the "poisoned" survivor of typhoid's waterborne filth.

Water and air allusions to Shakespeare and Ariel point to *The Tempest,* and one of the themes informing *The Tempest* is the medieval concept of the four elements representing the bodily humors that rule health. The waves of the stormy sea shipwreck Prospero and Miranda, who find themselves, like Adam and Eve, in a "brave new world." And like Wharton's Adamic conquerors, Prospero, whose own kingdom was seized, immediately invades, usurping the position of the earth monster Caliban and indenturing him and Ariel, the air spirit. Fire is in the lightning, the stars, and Prospero's white magic, which is taken for granted by Miranda, just as Mr. Spragg's moneymaking magic is taken for granted by Undine. As for Mr. Spragg, the question of preserving his daughter's virginity is just as prominent as it is in Prospero's mind. There must be no fall, no original sin, in the brave new world.

Still Prospero must pay for his own original sin, that of neglecting his dukedom in favor of magic, metaphorically drowning into life in the shipwreck of the tempest. He eventually restores social balance by forgiving those who trespassed against him, breaking his magic staff, releasing his slaves, and returning to his responsibilities.

Like Prospero, Ralph is seen "drowning into life" as he recovers from pneumonia, the illness caused by water in the lungs—too much "Undine" in the air. He is literally dying in the *"noyade* [drowning] of marriage" (*CC* 224-25). In his sickbed, he "became a leaf on the air, a feather on a current, a straw on the tide, the spray of the wave spinning itself to sunshine as the wave toppled over into gulfs of blue . . . " (*CC* 327 Wharton's ellipses). As "time and life stole back on him" (*CC* 328) in an unmarked, unattributed allusion, he finds that he is like the shipwrecked Gulliver pinned to the beach in a new world of Lilliputians: "He woke on a stony beach, his legs and arms still lashed to his sides and the thongs cutting into him; but the fierce sky was hidden, and hidden by his own languid lids. He felt the ecstasy of decreasing pain, and courage came to him to open his eyes and look about him . . . " (*CC* 327, Wharton's ellipses).

Never realizing the potential strength of his heritage against the invaders, Ralph continues his quest for a magic method of supplying Undine with ransom for Paul. He never reaches a state of forgiveness, and he never assumes his inherited responsibilities royally, as Prospero does. His death is inevitable because he is fallen and unredeemed.

Wharton cleverly weaves the medieval "elements"—water, air, fire, and earth—into the Boucher tapestry scene. Undine argues with Raymond de Chelles about rescuing his brother from financial ruin because she wants the money spent on her. She broods over the wealth represented by the tapestries. " 'It's so cold here—and the tapestries smell so of rain'. . . . 'I suppose they ought to be taken down and aired,' " de Chelles said. "She thought: 'In *this* air—'. . . . " The couple then walks into the library, "alone over the fire." Undine resumes the fight. "Why on earth do *we* have to pull him out?" (*CC* 498- 99). Her disagreement with Madame de Chelles over the parlor fires (*CC* 517) shows, oddly, that Undine needs fire to maintain those illusions. As a nomad, she has no earth either, no piece of real estate to call home and no "earth mother" nurturance to give her son. Even at the close of the novel when she and Moffatt own a palatial house—in Paris—the mansion is merely a stage for entertaining between travels. Undine's elements are out of balance.

Undine's humors are also out of balance. By medieval philosophy, the four bodily humors must be equalized to maintain health. A predominance of cold and dry earth produced melancholy; cold, moist water produced phlegm; too much hot, moist air produced blood; and hot, dry fire produced choler. The typhoid caused by evil in the western environment has poisoned Undine's water element, causing an overabundance of pneumonialike phlegm, so that she is intellectually dull, cool (cold and damp like the tapestries) morally imperturbable, and sexually cold. In this context it is easy to see why Undine needs blazing fires and spotlights to survive.

It is relevant to note that the patient whose humors are out of balance will seek gold: "Gold was the king of metal, the sum of all metallic virtues, and alchemically it was a mixture of the elements in perfect proportion. The same perfect proportion in the human body caused health. . . . Alchemy was the link between the perfect metal and perfect health in the patient."[12] Undine seeks gold for survival and pleasure, while Ralph seeks gold to ransom his son. The entire diseased society seeks gold: "All these [planetary social] systems joyously revolved about their central sun of gold" (CC 193). Wharton shows ailing non-culture vainly attempting to cure its ills through economic success, and in the process she makes the first part of her own myth: a new world is created, with its elements thrown out of balance by poisoned water, so that gold-seeking monsters come out of the west.

Wharton alludes to yet another creation myth when Ralph Marvell dreams of becoming a writer: "I saw the vision of a book I mean to do. It came to me suddenly, magnificently, swooped down on me as that big white moon swooped down on the black landscape, tore at me like a great white eagle—like the bird of Jove! After all, imagination *was* the eagle that devoured Prometheus!" (CC 152). In Aeschylus's *Prometheus Bound*, the gods chain the Titan Prometheus to a rock. He is tortured by an eagle that preys on his perpetually renewing liver, punishment for sharing the element fire with man. Since he also taught man the arts and sciences, he represents intellectuality both in this version and in Shelley's *Prometheus Unbound*, which Wharton knew from childhood.

Wharton's allusions to nereids, reptiles, and poison undoubtedly originate in Shelley:

Behold the Nereids under the green sea,
Their wavering limbs borne on the wind-like stream,
Their white arms lifted o'er their streaming hair

    [*Prometheus*, act 3, scene 2, ll. 45–47]

In this poem people are foul, and women like Undine, who should be "From custom's evil taint exempt and pure," are "ugliest of all things evil" (*Prometheus*, act 3, scene 3, l. 156). The invading conquerers take the forms of reptiles and even the American eagle.

Thou knowest that toads, and snakes, and loathly worms
And venomous and malicious beasts, and boughs
That bore ill berries in the woods, were ever
An hindrance to my walks o'er the green world:

    [*Prometheus*, act 3, scene 3, ll. 36–38]

Exempt from old customs of the country, which included a similar moral code for business and private life, the reptilian invaders overwhelm the blind, sleeping New York Titans, whose limited energy is morally undirected.

The eagles—birds of prey—are more specifically Elmer Moffatt and Undine's father, whom Ralph meets "descending from his eyrie" in Moffatt's office building (*CC* 262). Discussing Elmer Moffatt with Undine, Ralph hears her describe the "Titanic scale" of Moffatt's schemes and comments, "Jove, I wish I could put him in a book! There's something epic about him—a kind of epic effrontery" (*CC* 254). But Ralph, whose eyes ache with light in the presence of Undine, is blind to the effrontery of this epic attack by liver-devouring eagles and gold-seeking reptiles.

A cluster of allusions to reptilian beasts capable of metamorphoses supplies this part of Wharton's myth. The myths of the nereids, naiads, and undines directly connect them to the myths of the reptiles. The nereids live in the salty sea, while the naiads live in freshwater streams and rivers, although Wharton seems to use the terms interchangeably, a departure from her usual precision. The Greek myth about naiads concerns the love of the river god Achelous for Dejanira: "When the fable says that Achelous loved Dejanira, and sought a union with her, the meaning is that the river in its windings flowed through part of Dejanira's kingdom. It was said to take the form of a snake because of its winding."[13] Undine is described as a snake, "always doubling and twisting on herself" (*CC* 6). She is "what the gods had made her—a creature of skin-deep reactions" (*CC* 224). Elmer Moffatt is also reptilian. "His redness, his glossiness, his baldness, and the carefully brushed ring of hair" describe a "monster released from a magician's bottle," making Moffatt and Undine counterparts, each concerned, as Mr. Spragg puts it, "to take care of their own skins" (*CC* 468, 261). The naturalist Bowen perceptively describes Undine as a "monstrously perfect result of the system" (*CC* 208).

Like Undine, who is always acting a different part, Moffatt has qualities of metamorphoses. He "seemed to promise the capacity to develop into any character he might care to assume" (*CC* 108). He hypnotizes Ralph with the crystal toy that he holds in his hand (*CC* 468), and the "jovial cunning" of his "prematurely astute black eyes" (*CC* 108), whose unwavering gaze under Undine's scrutiny connects him not only with Undine's inclement gazes (*CC* 46) but also with the basilisk. Pliny describes the basilisk as advancing upright, unlike other serpents, and as having the power to split rocks and destroy shrubs merely by breathing on them. The monster could kill with a look.

Undine, too, is not simply a snake. She is Lamia, the reptile metamorphosed into a woman who attempts to marry a mortal but dies when she is recognized by the philosopher Apollonius.[14] In a striking similarity to the original tale, Lycius, the unfortunate human victim of the undine, dies. The description of Undine posing for her portrait by Popple is hardly less colorful than that of Keats's "palpitating snake, / Bright and cirque-couchant in a dusky brake" (*Lamia* I, ll. 46–47): "She was dressed for the sitting in something faint and shining, above which the long curves of her neck looked dead white in the cold light of the studio; and her hair, all a shadowless rosy gold, was starred with a hard glitter of diamonds" (CC 189). And "every movement she made seemed to start at the nape of her neck, just below the lifted roll of reddish-gold hair, and flow without a break through her whole slim length" (CC 6). With Ralph on their honeymoon, she sits under a tree Eve-like, her movements suggesting a need to twist and curve around it: "Her beautiful back could not adapt itself to the irregularities of the tree-trunk, and she moved a little now and then in the effort to find an easier position" (CC 141). Later Ralph realizes that "she would go on eluding and doubling, watching him" (CC 222).

Keats was inspired by, and obliquely alludes to, Milton's Satan, so that *Lamia* becomes a "layered allusion," an allusion that alludes to literature containing yet another allusion:

> With burnisht Neck of verdant Gold, erect
> Amidst his circling Spires, that on the grass
> Floated redundant: pleasing was his shape,
> And lovely, never since of Serpent kind
>
> [*Lamia* IX, ll. 497–503]

Keats's version emphasizes dazzling color and rolling curves and perhaps reveals the source of the tapestry episode:

> She was a gordian shape of dazzling hue,
> Vermillian-spotted, golden, green, and blue;
> Striped like a zebra, freckled like a pard,
> Eyed like a peacock, and all crimson barr'd;
> And full of silver moons, that, as she breathed,
> Dissolv'd, or brighter shone, or interwreathed
> Their lusters with the gloomier tapestries—
>
> [*Lamia* I, ll. 46–53]

Discovered by Hermes as he seeks the nymph he loves, "fast by the springs where she to bathe was wont" (*Lamia* I, l. 17), the lamia befriends the nereid:

> I took compassion on her, bade her steep
> Her hair in weird syrops, that would keep
> Her loveliness invisible, yet free
>
> [*Lamia* I, ll. 106–108]

Because she, too, longs to be free to go "Down through the tress-lifting waves [with] the Nereids fair" (*Lamia* I, l. 207), Lamia promises Hermes he will find his lover if he will transform her back into a woman. Therefore, she becomes a beautiful woman with a "neck regal white" (*Lamia* I, l. 243) whose only desire, like Undine's, is to spend her days "with feast and rioting to blend" (*Lamia* I, l. 214) and lead "days as happy as the gold coin could invent" (*Lamia* I, l. 313), even if she must sell some gloomy tapestries to do it.

The lamia and the nereids are thus connected by Undine's "waving and floating" hair (CC 154) as well as by Mrs. Spragg's explanation of the genesis of Undine's name: "We called her after a hair-waver father put on the market the week she was born— . . . It's from *un*doolay, you know, the French for crimping" (CC 80).

Like Keats's serpent-woman, Undine must be seen but never recognized in order to survive. Wharton constantly refers to Undine's attraction to glitter, blaze, and dazzle, both in her person and in her surroundings: "The white and gold room, with its blazing wall-brackets, formed a sufficiently brilliant background to carry out the illusion" (CC 21). She makes Ralph's eyes ache "with excess of light" (CC 141). She is not recognized by Ralph, who sees only romance, though ironically he knows "what strange specimens from the depths slip through the wide meshes of the watering-place world" (CC 159). And in France, Undine gravitates to the watering places a lamia or an undine might be expected to frequent. As if consciously aware of the devastation of being unseen, Undine controls Ralph by turning her eyes away from him, but de Chelles is her Apollonius, the only one who *recognizes* her, and when he does he kills her by refusing to see her. When Undine asks him to sell his ancestral home, "the suggestion seemed to strike him as something monstrously, almost fiendishly significant. . . . His glance followed hers to the tapestries" (CC 526–27). "He looked at her as though the place where she stood were empty" (CC 527). Only Moffatt, the basilisk, can look directly at Undine (CC 109).

Undine has no soul and no self beyond the evil acquisitiveness symbolized by her inelastic fingers (CC 142), for her "pliancy and variety were imitative rather than spontaneous" (CC 148). Ralph thinks of her, however, as "*divers and ondoyant*" (CC 79)—divers and wavering like a flame—but the phrase could possibly be translated "various and pliant." An ironic allusion to Ralph's misinterpretation of Undine, the phrase is taken from an essay entitled "By Various Means We Arrive at the Same End" in the first volume of Montaigne's *Essays*. The essay's subject is the courage by which certain historical figures achieved the mercy of their conquerers, as opposed to others who achieved mercy by demeaning and humiliating themselves. The complete statement is: "Certes, c'est un sujet merveilleusement vain, divers et ondoyant que l'homme. Il est malaise d'y fonder jugement constant et uniforme."[15] But the correct translation provides more irony: "Truly man is a marvellously vain, fickle, and unstable creature, on whom it is difficult to found a certain and uniform judgment."[16] Unstable, Ralph never achieves mercy from the conquering Lamia.

As a woman the Lamia operates with a Satanic magic to ensnare Lycius in a sensuous tapestry of evil. Undine is also associated with magic. Her trance-like happiness in assuming that her father can mysteriously acquire unlimited money is dependence on magic. "Money still seemed to her like some mysterious and uncertain stream which occasionally vanished underground but was sure to bubble up again at one's feet" (CC 495). This particular kind of magic hints at Coleridge's "Kubla Kahn," with its suggestions of demonism. Undine moves with "supernatural ease" (CC 167) but a sinister metamorphosis occurs when her will is crossed: "She seemed to grow inaccessible, implacable—her eyes were like the eyes of an enemy" (CC 165). Undine is viewed by Ralph as "embodying [a] spirit of shifting magic" (CC 139)—her hand "held the magic wand of expression" (CC 142), and she designs to travel on Peter Van Degen's yacht, the *Sorceress* (CC 169).

Another "invader," the nouveau riche Peter Van Degen, is also of the reptilian family. His "batrachian countenance" and "grotesque saurian head" place him among frogs and toads (CC 66, 49). Another of the myths of the naiads involves the goddess Latona who, exhausted by the pursuit of Juno, stops to drink at a pond of clear water. Inexplicably and evilly, local rustics refuse to allow her to slake her thirst, threatening her with violence. Further insulting her, they wade into the pond to stir up the mud, making the water unfit to drink. In revenge, Latona weaves a spell: " 'May they never quit that pool, but pass their lives there!' And it came to pass accordingly. They now live in the water, sometimes totally submerged . . . [and] are not ashamed to croak in the midst of it. . . . Their backs are green, their disproportioned bellies white, and in short they are now frogs, and dwell in the slimy pool."[17] The water in Apex, having been poisoned by speculators wading in the mud of graft, carried typhoid and caused the deaths of two Spragg children and several townspeople. Mr. Spragg, himself poisoned by the incident, begins the Apex pure water campaign but in the course of it deals unethically with his father-in-law's real estate holdings. Though he becomes rich from civic utilities and real estate, Puritan-like, he is able to view his dishonest wealth as a reward from God. Something elemental about the West, its abundance of riches, and its ignorance of culture causes its inhabitants a bestial illness of soul.

Eventually Spragg's dishonesty results in the "Ararat investigation." Noah's ark is said to have rested on Mount Ararat after the flood (Gen. 8:4). One of God's reasons for the flood was that "when men began to multiply on earth and daughters were born to them, the sons of heaven saw how beautiful the daughters of man were, and so they took for their wives as many of them as they chose" (Gen. 6:2). The allusion returns us to the "custom of the country," divorce.

The reptiles—basilisk, lamia, and frog—constitute "invaders." The American eagle that descends upon the sleepy Titans at the firesides of old New York represents them all. The myth is completed when the Westerners metamorphose into beasts that invade and ravish old New York.

The two major clusters of allusions to creation myths and to beasts are mythological. The first cluster, the creation myths of Genesis, *The Tempest* (and the medieval four elements) are joined by the myth of Prometheus, which also contains a connecting allusion to a supernatural eagle. The second cluster of allusions is to mythical reptiles, Keats's "Lamia," and the myths of the basilisk and of Latona's frogs. "Lamia" and Gauguin's *Undine* are both underscored by a secondary layer of allusions to Milton's Satan in *Paradise Lost*. Another subcategorical cluster consists of the shipwreck themes in Beaumont and Massinger's *The Custom of the Country,* Shakespeare's *The Tempest,* and Swift's *Gulliver's Travels.* The brilliant result of the combined allusions is a literary structural foundation that forms an American Genesis myth of a plague of reptiles that conquers and transforms New York. Neglected children like Paul Marvell, son of a marriage between conqueror and conquered, who has intellectual curiosity, have every chance of combining the best of both "races" and of reviving American culture. This is the hope of the novel. But they must be nurtured.[18]

An almost unnoticed character like Effie Leath, Paul is the first sign of another clue to the riddle of the Sphinx. Like *The House of Mirth* and *The Reef, The Custom of the Country* concludes with the protagonist on the horns of a dilemma. In the first novel readers sympathize with Lily Bart, in the second they are frustrated by Anna Leath, and in this they feel that Undine and other lamias, dragons, and entrancing basilisks in search of gold deserve their plight.

> The fiend that man harries
> > Is love of the Best;
> Yawns the pit of the Dragon,
> > Lit by rays from the Blest.
> [Emerson, "The Sphinx," stanza 10, ll. 73-76]

Added to the questionable death of Lily Bart, Ralph Marvell's suicide begins an evolving pattern, and another important matter resurfaces, the neglect of children. That topic melds with the topic of the dilemma for Newland Archer in *The Age of Innocence;* Archer faces equally unsatisfactory choices. As he sees it, choosing between May and Ellen means choosing between living death and revolution.

# 4 | *The Age of Innocence*
## Branching Thematic Allusions

Lᴵᴷᴱ *The House of Mirth, The Age of Innocence* is a favorite novel.[1] Winner of the 1921 Pulitzer Prize, it has been much read by critics, and judging from what is revealed by the literary allusions, for the most part it has been well read. Nonetheless, some surprises emerge from echoes of the outside world, and from the wildness and dark places of the novel, churning under the surface of its literary allusions. Three primary types of allusions are represented: structural, clustered, and "branching" thematic allusions.

The function of two "structural allusions," Gounod's *Faust* and Dion Boucicault's *The Shaughraun,* have been described by Wagner, Gargano, and Moseley.[2] Most of the remaining allusions are thematic allusions that cluster into four major groups: themes of innocence, themes of living death, themes of revolt, and themes of inaccessible love. While thematic and structural allusions are not new developments, the title may be the first instance of a "reverberating art allusion," an allusion to a painting that appears to allude to an earlier painting of the same name. Sir Joshua Reynolds's title *The Age of Innocence* echoes Louis Gabriel Blanchet's satirical painting of mischievous children (1731). Wharton further developed reverberating art and literary allusions in *The Glimpses of the Moon.* The primary beauty of *The Age of Innocence* is its four related clusters of branching thematic allusions that reveal more themes symbolized by the Sphinx and the Furies.

Newland Archer precipitously announces his engagement to May Welland in order to protect her "innocence" from the influence of her sophisticated cousin, Ellen Olenska, who, having escaped an abusive husband, expected her old New York family to help her obtain a divorce. Instead, the family, through Archer, advises her to remain married. Reluctantly, she follows their advice, but the two fall in love. Nevertheless, Archer marries May. After several clandestine meetings, Newland and Ellen realize that they must either elope or separate forever. Before they can decide, May announces her pregnancy to Ellen, then throws an elaborate farewell banquet in Ellen's honor, effectively expelling her from old New York society. A generation later, when both are widowed, Newland finds himself in Paris on a bench beneath Ellen's window, unable to meet her though he has dreamed of her for twenty years. He decides

Sir Joshua Reynolds, *The Age of Innocence* (1788). The Tate Gallery, London. Reverberating Titular Allusion: *The Age of Innocence.*

that he has missed "the flower of life" and that she is more real to him in his mind.

There are several literary allusions to innocence, the most obvious occurring in the novel's title. In addition, allusions to "The Babes in the Wood" (*AI* 47), Drake's "The Culprit Fay" (*AI* 102), Washington Irving's *The Alhambra*

(*AI* 146), Balzac's *Contes drôlatiques* (*AI* 85), and Gounod's *Faust* (*AI* 3) all support the theme of innocence. The questions are to what extent is the theme satirical, and who is innocent of what?

Most readers interpret the word "innocence" sexually, but there are two types of innocence in the novel, sexual and social. May is described by Newland Archer as the innocent child he wishes would not possess the "innocence that seals the mind against imagination and the heart against experience!" (*AI* 146). He recognizes that "all this frankness and innocence [is] only an artificial product" (*AI* 46). As if describing the children in the Blanchet painting, he muses: "Untrained human nature was not frank and innocent; it was full of the twists and defenses of an instinctive guile" (*AI* 46). May is socially, if not sexually, experienced. Her polished social skills attract Newland: "She was always going to understand; she was always going to say the right thing" (*AI* 14). "Nothing about his betrothed pleased him more than her resolute determination to carry to its utmost limit that ritual of ignoring the 'unpleasant' in which they both had been brought up" (*AI* 26). Even so, she is sexually more aware than Newland supposes: "You mustn't think that a girl knows as little as her parents imagine. One hears and one notices—one has one's feelings and ideas" (*AI* 149). A detail often raised about May's innocence is that she saves her marriage by behaving deceitfully, lying to Ellen Olenska about her pregnancy. This is not sexual deceit but social deceit about a sexual subject supported by the social code of old New York.

Ellen's sexual innocence is in question not only because of her separation from the count, and "a shadow of a shade" on her reputation (*AI* 26), but because she is willing to face the hard realities of an affair with Newland and offer to "once come to you" (*AI* 312) then return to Europe. Nevertheless, at first she is innocent of the social codes of New York. And while May is rather less sexually innocent than Newland imagines, Ellen is probably somewhat more innocent. The "shadows and shades," the hints of an affair with M. Rivière, who helped her escape from her husband, can be neutralized by examining the allusion to Fitz-Greene Halleck and Joseph Rodman Drake, apparently a gay couple, who wrote a number of poems together. A member of the Knickerbocker Group, Drake was the author of "The Culprit Fay," a poem about a fairy the size of an insect who must perform heroic deeds to expiate the crime of allowing an innocent human maiden to see him. The hint of homosexuality in the situation of a male fairy who must avoid women creates irony in the following passage: "Mrs. Archer and her group felt a certain timidity concerning these [literary] persons. They were *odd*, they were uncertain, they had things one didn't know about in the background of their lives and minds. . . . and Mrs. Archer was always at pains to tell her children how much more agreeable and cultivated society had been when it included such figures

as Washington Irving, Fitz-Greene Halleck and the poet of 'The Culprit Fay' "
(*AI* 102, emphasis mine).

Old New York viewed "such unhappy persons as Joseph Drake, author
of 'The Culprit Fay,' balanced between 'fame and infamy' as not quite of the
best society, and writing not quite the best poetry."[3] Like the "long-haired men
and short-haired women" who filled the house of the Blenkers (*AI* 220),
M. Rivière had ventured unsuccessfully into authorship (*AI* 199). If his words
are read doubly, he seems to be one of the "unhappy" persons who are nonetheless full citizens elsewhere: "Things that are accepted in certain other societies," he says to Newland, "or at least put up with as part of a general convenient give-and-take—become unthinkable, simply unthinkable" in America (*AI*
253). If he had had an affair with Ellen Olenska, her husband would hardly
have made Rivière his emissary. All told, especially since she is married, Ellen
seems sexually experienced but socially innocent, at least in old New York.

But the most innocent character is Newland Archer, who does not understand M. Rivière. Strictly, Archer is not sexually innocent, having sown his
wild oats with Mrs. Thorley Rushworth, but neither that "mild agitation" nor
his "sincere but placid" love for May prepares him for the passion he feels for
Ellen. His initial ambivalence between his sympathy toward her and his assumption that she is guilty of those "shadows and shades" may be similar to
the ambivalence expressed by Fitz-Greene Halleck in his poem "To Ellen,"
which furnishes the possible source for Ellen's name: "Are there two Ellens of
the mind? / Or have I lived at last to find / The Ellen of my heart?"[4]

The allusions to Halleck and Drake are underscored by the allusion to
Washington Irving's *The Alhambra* (*AI* 146), which includes a tale of three
innocent princesses imprisoned in a tower to protect them from men. The imprisonment has the opposite effect, and they escape.[5]

That Edith Wharton had a humorous attitude toward two sexually innocent marriage partners can be inferred from a comment in her notebook concerning an earlier version of the plot: "At last he and Ellen fly together (contrast between bridal night with May & *this one*)."[6] The thinking behind the
note seems borne out by the content of the allusion to Balzac's *Contes drôlatiques* ("humorous tales"), which features two stories, "Innocence" and "The
Danger of Being Too Innocent." The latter is a ribald story about the marriage
of a boy and girl who had been kept so perfectly pure that their bumbling
attempts to discover what is supposed to happen in the bedroom provide
amusement.[7]

That context turns Newland's minimal sexual experience toward irony:
"He could not deplore . . . that he had not a blank page to offer his bride in
exchange for the unblemished one she was to give to him. He could not get
away from the fact that if he had been brought up as she had they would have

been no more fit to find their way about than the Babes in the Wood" (*AI* 46–47).

"The Babes in the Wood" is a rather gruesome tale, *The Children in the Wood,* an old ballad from the Percy collection in which a wicked uncle abandons two infants to die in the woods.[8] The issue of the survival of the innocent applies not only to Ellen but to Newland Archer because he has the child's inability to distinguish between "vision" (or fantasy) and reality. He is innocent of understanding social reality, so that May can manipulate the system dexterously while Newland is blind to her maneuvering.

Both socially and sexually naive as the novel opens, Newland Archer is daydreaming over an operatic performance of Gounod's *Faust,* based on Goethe's play. The scene features innocent fourteen-year-old Marguerite just before she is sexually victimized by the fifty-year-old Faust, whom the devil has provided with the body of a noble youth. Without distinguishing fiction from reality, Archer then shifts his gaze from one stage to another, the opera box opposite, in which he admires May, imagining that she can be a "miracle of fire and ice," then notes the entrance of Ellen Olenska (*AI* 7), which results in a dramatic impulse. He rushes to the box to "protect" May by announcing their engagement early. This very impulse sets in motion a pattern of events that prevents his ever linking with Ellen, and the same medieval sense of honor motivating that impulse will prevent him from deserting his pregnant wife.

At their wedding, a stage show itself, Newland muses that "real people were living somewhere, and real things happening to them . . . " (*AI* 182, Wharton's ellipses). Though May at first represents the fiction of chivalric romance, she soon represents the real. When he first sees May at St. Augustine, Florida, Newland thinks: "Here was truth, here was reality, here was the life that belonged to him" (*AI* 141).[9] But it's a reality in which beautiful fictional things do not happen: The advancement of their wedding date was a dream to May. "It was like hearing him read aloud out of his poetry books the beautiful things that could not possibly happen in real life" (*AI* 147). After Newland sees Ellen at the pier in Newport, he makes a dramatic exit patterned after the Boucicault play, realizing, "Reality was what awaited him in the house on the bank"—May (*AI* 215). It's a safe and familiar reality: "The whole chain of tyrannical trifles binding one hour to the next, and each member of the household to all the others, made any less systematized and affluent existence seem unreal and precarious" (*AI* 217). But he cannot give up hope for beauty and passion, so gradually he replaces the reality of May with a fictional dream life with Ellen: "He had built up within himself a kind of sanctuary in which she throned among his secret thoughts and longings. Little by little it became the scene of his real life, of his only rational activities. . . . Outside it, in the scene of his actual life, he moved with a growing sense of unreality . . . so absent from everything most densely real" (*AI* 262). Ellen tries to show him the practical ramifications of his desires: "We'll look, not at visions, but at realities." But he replies, "I don't know what you mean by realities. The only reality to me is this" (*AI* 289). May, an expert at interpreting the reality represented by "arbitrary signs," recognizes the meaning of Archer's absentness when, "absorbed in other visions, [he] had forgotten his promise" to drive home with May after meeting Ellen with May's carriage (*AI* 293). "Could it be possible that the sense of unreality in which he felt himself imprisoned had communicated itself to his wife?" (*AI* 324). It had, and she acted out of her social experience to protect herself from any resulting "unpleasantness."

What Newland Archer loses by remaining in his innocent dream world is indeed "the flower of life," and to him Ellen had "become the composite vision of all that he had missed" (*AI* 347). Twenty years later, Newland thinks that Ellen is the flower of life he missed—and inexplicably chooses to continue to miss (even after inspiration by an "effulgent Titian") when he decides, "It's more real to me here than if I went up" (*AI* 361). Evidence suggests, however, that the "flower of life" that Newland missed is something altogether different, the clue to which can be found in the stories by Balzac.

"Innocence" is an anecdotal joke about children clamoring to see a nude Adam and Eve by Titian. When one child asks how to tell Adam apart from Eve, the other replies, "You silly! . . . to know that, they would have to be dressed!"[10] But the anecdote contains a passage about children that Wharton seems to have felt apt: "Watch them playing, prettily and *innocently* . . . , and you will agree with me that they are in every way lovable; besides which they are flower and fruit—the fruit of love, the *flower of life*. . . . Do not expect a man to be innocent after the manner of children, because there is an, I know not what, ingredient of reason in the naïveté of a man, while the naïveté of children is candid, immaculate"[11] (emphasis mine).

By living in dreams, chivalric fictions, and books, Newland Archer missed—if indeed he did miss it—the ability to live awake and fully "the real things of this life" that he learned about, ironically, in his library. His memories of May's pregnancy announcement, christenings, the babies' first steps, the engagement and marriage of his daughter, the future of his children, even his friendship with President Roosevelt, are all set in his library (*AI* 344). It is not in Ellen that he has missed the "flower of life" but in his children. Somehow even sadder is the thought that Newland has not missed the "flower of life" but thinks he has.

The failure of Newland Archer and other innocent Americans to live fully awake—a theme that Wharton took up again in *Twilight Sleep*—is emphasized through allusions to *La sonnambula* (*AI* 58), and a cluster of allusions to Tennyson (*AI* 46), Labiche (*AI* 128), and Poe (*AI* 137) that have two themes in common, death-in-life and voyages of exploration: "Incredible dream: . . . struck from all three allusions to Edgar Poe and Jules Verne" (*Around the World in Eighty Days*) (*AI* 137, 337). The themes take several forms, from passive resistance, frozen motion, sleep, and sleepwalking to live burial (a theme that occurs in Wharton's work disturbingly often), but together they represent a new kind of cluster—thematic allusions containing more than one theme, or "branching thematic allusions."

In *La sonnambula* (1831), a comic opera by Vincenzo Bellini, complications arise when the heroine sleepwalks into the wrong bedroom the night before her wedding. Wharton's allusion to it underscores the many instances of the sleepy passivity of persons from old New York such as May, who prefers not to travel, such as Mrs. Archer and Archer himself at the conclusion of the novel, who, like Melville's Bartleby, "prefer not to" try to meet new people (*AI* 103), and like the van der Luydens, who escape to their country home when problems surface. In fact, much of the "action" of the novel involves forms of passivity.

Newland, for instance, had attempted to interest May in Tennyson's "Ulysses" and "The Lotus Eaters" without success: "When he had gone the brief round of her he returned discouraged" (*AI* 46). The allusion to "Ulysses" is ironic. Late in life Ulysses "cannot rest from travel"; he must "drink life to the lees" (*Ulysses*, ll. 6–7) and begin a new journey, which late in *his* life Newland refuses to do. He has become used to living in half dreams of Ellen like "The Lotus Eaters," who found how "sweet it was to dream of Fatherland, / Of child, and wife, and slave" (*Lotus Eaters*, ll. 39–40), and "How sweet it were, hearing the downward stream / With half-shut eyes ever to seem / Falling asleep in a half-dream! (*Lotus Eaters*, ll. 99–101) like Archer, "stopped at the sight [of Ellen at the pier] as if he had waked from sleep. That vision of the past was a dream" (*AI* 215). When May greets Archer in the library after his last meeting with Ellen, he is sitting "without conscious thoughts, without sense of the lapse of time, in a deep and grave amazement that seemed to suspend life rather than quicken it. . . . What he had dreamed of had been so different that there was a mortal chill in his rapture." May enters and remarks, "I believe you've been asleep!" (*AI* 314).

At May's farewell banquet for Ellen, in passive acceptance that never changes later in life, Archer thinks: " 'It's to show me . . . what would happen to me—' and a deathly sense of the superiority of implication and analogy over direct action, and of silence over rash words, closed in on him like the doors of the family vault" (*AI* 335–36).

Figuring even more prominently in the novel is the cluster of allusions to voyages of exploration that bring together "Ulysses' " theme of exploration and the theme of wakeful dreaming or living death of "The Lotus Eaters."

Wharton directly mentions *Le voyage de Monsieur Perrichon* (1860) by Eugène Labiche. The play is a comic farce, the climax of which involves a fall into a glacial crevasse. The author casts old New York in January as that glacial crevasse: "Archer had seen, on has last visit to Paris, the delicious play of Labiche, *Le Voyage de M. Perrichon,* and he remembered M. Perrichon's dogged and undiscouraged attachment to the young man whom he had pulled out of the glacier." Ironically, he thinks, "The van der Luydens had rescued Madame Olenska from a doom almost as icy" (*AI* 128–29). But Ellen, who actually makes van der Luyden dinners "a little less funereal" (*AI* 87), risks being pulled into the crevasse, for Mrs. van der Luyden has been "rather gruesomely preserved in the airless atmosphere of a perfectly irreproachable existence, as bodies caught in glaciers keep for years a rosy life-in-death" (*AI* 53).

May is constantly described as cool, frosty, or chill. She blows out lights, she is associated with dying fires, and Newland seems doomed to catch the paralyzing cold. After his separation from Ellen, he leans out the window of his library for some air, but May admonishes him that he will freeze to death. " 'Catch my death!' he echoed; and he felt like adding: 'But I've caught it already. I *am* dead—I've been dead for months and months' " (*AI* 295). Images of precipices, abysses, and vortices connect the Labiche themes to Poe's "The Maelstrom" (*AI* 116).

In Poe's *The Narrative of Arthur Gorden Pym,*[12] an "intraauthorial allusion" (a reference to another work by the same author), Pym stows away on a ship hiding in a coffinlike box in the hold, a symbolic live burial. After reaching an island, he is buried in a landslide and a number of adventures later sails "uncharted waters toward the South Pole," passing glaciers and icebergs but discovering a warm land with a black landscape at the edge of a chasm that features strange hieroglyphics:

> A range of singular looking indentures in the surface of the marl . . . might have been taken for the intentional . . . representation of a human figure. . . . the rest of them bore also some little resemblance to alphabetical characters. . . . We now found ourselves [in a wild place where] the surface of the ground in every other direction was strewn with huge tumuli, apparently the wreck of some gigantic structures of art. . . . Scoriae were abundant, and large shapeless blocks of the black granite, intermingled with others of marl. (Poe's note: The marl was also black; indeed, we noticed no light-colored substances of any kind upon the island.) [186]

Newland feels that marriage is a "voyage on uncharted seas" when in fact it's a journey preplanned by society. The image of warm black vegetation occurs during Archer's talk with May when she asks him frankly if there is someone else. "He lower[s] his head, staring at the black leaf-pattern on the sunny path at their feet" (*AI* 148), and lies. "They lived in a kind of hieroglyphic world, where the real thing was never said or done or even thought, but only represented by a set of arbitrary signs" (*AI* 45), and "there were moments when [Newland Archer] felt as if he were being buried alive under his future" (*AI* 140). His entire life is spent "in a deep and grave amazement that seemed to suspend life rather than quicken it. 'This was what had to be, then . . . this was what had to be,' he kept repeating to himself, as if he hung in the clutch of doom. What he had dreamed of had been so different that there was a mortal chill in his rapture" (*AI* 314, Wharton's ellipses). The death-in-life theme is supported by another intraauthorial allusion. In this case the allusion to Washington Irving's *The Alhambra* crosses over to "Rip Van Winkle," the legendary resident of the Catskills who slept twenty years. Behind that story lies the motif of the American Revolution symbolized by the hieroglyph of the tavern sign renamed for George Washington by crossing out "George III." It seemed to have occurred while old New York, Washington Irving's "Knickerbocker" country, was asleep, as does the invasion of old New York by the Titans in *The Custom of the Country.*

The plethora of literary and art allusions in *The Age of Innocence* splits into two major categories with branching thematic clusters to the French and Italian revolutions. In a "branching thematic cluster" the members of a cluster fork to form two subtopics. In this case an encompassing "umbrella" allusion to revolutions alludes either to the French Revolution or to the Italian Revolution.

Allusions to the French Revolution begin with general references to Thackeray (*AI* 34, 46, 103), whose *Vanity Fair* takes place during the French Revolution. Allusions point, like May's arrows, to Dickens's *A Tale of Two Cities* (*AI* 34), again about the French Revolution, to David's *The Coronation of Napoleon* (*AI* 98) and Meissonier, another painter of Napoleon (*AI* 209), and to Michelet, historian of the French Revolution (*AI* 294), among others. These allusions support three ideas: Newland Archer's inclination toward a social and intellectual revolt that is reflected in his reading, the futility of Ellen's being "wholly in revolt" against her past (*AI* 139), and such scarcity of revolt in old New York that it becomes worth commenting about Mrs. Welland in "one of her rare revolts against fate" (*AI* 280). A line from *The Custom of the Country* sums up the theme's irony, citing the "myth of 'old families' ruling New York from a throne of Revolutionary tradition" (*CC* 193). The several allusions to revolt range from the comparison of Grandmother Mingott to Catherine the Great, who ran European revolutions from the Russian throne, to the Frenchman M. Rivière, who helped Ellen revolt against her husband. A sly allusion to Ralph Waldo Emerson in Professor Emerson Sillerton's name adds to the list of those who do "revolutionary things" (*AI* 220). These revolutionaries are contrasted to Archer when the poet-journalist Ned Winsett, who is "starving to death" for ideas, is associated with a statement by M. Rivière. "You see, Monsieur, it's worth everything, isn't it, to keep one's intellectual liberty, not to enslave one's powers of appreciation, one's critical independence? It was because of that that I abandoned journalism, and took to so much duller work: tutoring and private secretaryship. There is a good deal of drudgery, of course; but one preserves one's moral freedom" (*AI* 200).

The second twig of the branching thematic allusions to revolt generally concerns Italy—the novels with an "Italian atmosphere" like those of Ouida, George Eliot's *Middlemarch,* which features the Casaubons' Italian honeymoon (*AI* 139), the Italian travel memoirs of Baroness Bunsen (*AI* 192), and Hawthorne's *The Marble Faun* (*AI* 34). Ellen returns to New York with Italian possessions.

The allusions branch again. The first subcategory is the political aesthetic revolutions of the Italian Renaissance: Dante and Petrarch (*AI* 70), the background for *Romeo and Juliet* (*AI* 307), Renaissance painters Botticelli and Fra Angelico (*AI* 71), art critics, historians, and novelists of the Italian Renaissance like the Goncourts (*AI* 104, 199, 201), Walter Pater (*AI* 71), Paul Bourget (*AI 104),* Vernon Lee and John Addington Symonds *(AI* 71), and, of course, Columbus, the Italian Renaissance discoverer of America (*AI* 154).

The second subcategory of references to "Italian revolt" is a set of allusions to the Victorian Pre-Raphaelite Brotherhood, Rossetti (*AI* 139), Swinburne (*AI* 85), and Morris (*AI* 103). The Pre-Raphaelites looked to Raphael and the Italian Renaissance for inspiration to revolt against the prevailing Victorian aesthetic.

Then the allusions to revolution branch as well. One branch supports a theme of inaccessible, unsatisfied, or forbidden love. A diagram would resemble branches, or roots, of a tree. The "branching allusions" seem furthermore meant to reflect the branches and roots of literary and social families.

Naturally, Newland Archer's desire to revolt against his family and old New York is a result of his longing for Ellen Olenska's love. While to Ellen New York is a chilly heaven and her old life hell—"I'm sure I'm dead and buried, and this dear old place is heaven" (*AI* 18)—Archer's version of heaven is a romantic European country where ideas like "mistress" don't exist. He wants to elope with Ellen:

> "I want—I want somehow to get away with you into a world where words like that—categories like that—won't exist. Where we shall be simply two human beings who love each other, who are the whole of life to each other; and nothing else on earth will matter. . . . "
>
> "Oh, my dear—where is that country? Have you ever been there. . . . I know so many who've tried to find it; and, believe me, they all got out by mistake at wayside stations: at places like Boulogne, or Pisa, or Monte Carlo" [*AI* 290].

For Newland Archer, Italy at first seems to be that magic world, since he connects it with Ellen. The theme is reflected in the rooms in which he fantasizes bedroom scenes from plays—the revolutionary Catherine Mingot's "ceilings on which an Italian house-painter had lavished all the divinities of Olympus" (*AI* 212). When he is dreaming about May, Newland thinks, "We'll read *Faust* together . . . by the Italian lakes . . . " (*AI* 7, Wharton's ellipses). But the Italian escape would probably have been as disappointing as Dorothea Brooke's Italian honeymoon if it had occurred. But it doesn't occur because of May's capacity to stand her ground against change: "They had not gone to the Italian Lakes: on reflection, Archer had not been able to picture his wife in that particular setting. . . . Once or twice, in the mountains, Archer had pointed southward and said: 'There's Italy'; and May, her feet in a gentian-bed, had smiled cheerfully, and replied: 'It would be lovely to go there next winter, if only you didn't have to be in New York' " (*AI* 194).

Ellen's warnings about "wayside stations" are scarcely necessary, for the impetus against elopement, against "revolution" of any kind, is built into Archer's chill, sleepy old New York roots. His feet, like May's, are firmly planted. In response to Winsett's desire to emigrate, he reacts with all his "old inherited ideas": "Emigrate! As if a gentleman could abandon his own country! One could no more do that than one could roll up one's sleeves and go down into the muck. A gentleman simply stayed at home and abstained" (*AI* 126). Later in life, he and May take the "old-fashioned tour" of Europe, but he declines to join his children in Italy (*AI* 351). The novel's implied hope is that the new generation is more open to change than the old.

That Newland prefers living in a dream state much like Platonic love rather than the real "heaven" of an actively happy life is supported by literary allusions to Shakespeare (*AI* 307), Irving (*AI* 102, 146), Dante (*AI* 70), Petrarch (*AI* 70), Mérimée (*AI* 103, 200), Rossetti (*AI* 139), Morris (*AI* 103), and Vernon Lee's *Euphorion* (*AI* 71). Each item alludes to lovers separated by circumstances beyond their control. Romeo and Juliet are separated by a family feud, Irving's princesses are imprisoned in a tower, Dante and Petrarch are separated from Beatrice and Laura by death, and curmudgeonly Mérimée is kept from his *Inconnue* by geography.

Two other allusions, one to Flaubert (probably *Madame Bovary* is meant) and one to Rossetti's *The House of Life* are more specifically about extramarital love. Rossetti's *The House of Life* is a sequence of love sonnets thought to be addressed to the wife of the artist William Morris. Madame Bovary, of course, was, like Newland Archer, a dreamer trying to escape her mundane existence through reading and extramarital romance. Finally, Vernon Lee's *Euphorion,* a collection of "studies of the antique and the mediaeval in the Renaissance," features a long essay on "Mediaeval Love," according to which the ideal Platonic love of Dante's *Divine Comedy* was made possible by a foundation in courtly love poetry that actually reflected the love of the knight for a *married,* rather than an eligible, lady.[13]

Since Rossetti was influenced by poetry of courtly love, and Wharton knew that, it is not surprising to find that the sonnets of *The House of Life,* like "Love's Lovers," reflect the frustrated longings of unsatisfied love and do so using the images of Cupid and blindness upon which Wharton elaborates in *The Age of Innocence:*

> Love's Lovers
>
> Some ladies love the jewels in Love's zone
> And gold-tipped darts he hath for painless play
> In idle scornful hours he flings away;
> And some that listen to his lute's soft tone
> Do love to vaunt the silver praise their own;
> Some prize his blindfold sight; and there be they
> Who kissed his wings which brought him yesterday
> And thank his wings to-day that he is flown.
>
> My lady only loves the heart of Love:
> Therefore Love's heart, my lady, hath for thee
> His bower of unimagined flower and tree:
> There kneels he now, and all-unhungered of
> Thine eyes gray-lit in shadowing hair above,
> Seals with thy mouth his immortality.

In his search for Ellen in the Blenker's garden, Archer finds a "wooden Cupid who had lost his bow and arrow but continued to take ineffectual aim" (*AI* 224). More successful with the bow and arrow is May, who, though like Mrs. Beaufort she pretends to be blind to her husband's "private weaknesses," is sharp-eyed enough to win the jeweled arrow at the Beaufort's garden party: "That's the only kind of target she'll ever hit," Beaufort says ironically, for May, several times described as the goddess Diana, aims at Ellen Olenska, whose last name means "deer," and hits the bullseye (*AI* 211).[14]

The thematic allusions cluster into four major groups supporting themes of innocence, living death, revolt, and inaccessible love, several of the allusions sharing double themes. Naturally, the themes are interdependent. A state of innocence can be monotonous, a living death, but that is also a description of the state of sin according to Medora Manson: "To me the only death is monotony. I always say to Ellen: Beware of monotony; it's the mother of all the deadly sins" (*AI* 208). A revolt leading to adulterous love is sin, but the novel forces the reader to question sexual or social innocence if, by definition, it must be blind to "unpleasantness" and exclude intellectual stimulation, experience, and appropriate change.

Even though Archer claims to want change (he has a "haunting horror of doing the same thing every day at the same hour" [*AI* 84]), in the museum, a place of intellectual stimulation, he and Ellen are already buried in a necropolis with the sarcophagi and mummies (*AI* 311). To justify his desire to revolt, Archer psychologically projects his own feelings onto May, wondering whether the "deadly monotony of their lives had laid its weight on her also" (*AI* 293). But because of the influence, culture, and training of old New York, an ideal love with someone like Ellen is inaccessible to a man whose every revolutionary idea dissolves at its first contact with habit. When, on his honeymoon, he sees some of the women who "ought to be free," he finds them "queer cosmopolitan women deep in complicated love affairs" (*AI* 196). And "if one had habitually breathed the New York air there were times when anything less crystalline"—like the Italian "way-stations" of Pisa and Bolougne—"seemed stifling" (*AI* 95).

In this way, thematic allusions to literary topics of innocence, death-in-life, revolution, and inaccessible love reinforce these major motifs of the novel. Ironically, in *The Age of Innocence,* Newland Archer *needs* enough Furies to stir him out of his daydreams "un-hungered." And as Emerson Sillerton keeps track of the branches of a firmly rooted family, his name recalls Emerson's "The Sphinx":

> Out of sleep a waking
>   Out of waking a sleep
> Life death overtaking;
>   Deep underneath deep?
>     ["The Sphinx," stanza 2, ll. 13–16]

The theme of innocent childhood as the "flower of life," and the "fate of the manchild" ("The Sphinx," stanza 2) contrast to the danger (real or not) implied by the allusions to homosexuality. All the while "historic allusions" and "allusion[s] to democratic principles" (*AI* 3), allusions to allusions, and allusions to a code at the beginning of the novel (*AI* 38, 39) lead to hints of a message at the end in a cross-novel repetition of the phrase, "I've got a message for you" (*AI* 354).

Trapped in a variation of the dilemma, Newland Archer fails to recognize that neglect of cultural education results in living death and that neglect of sexual education endangers children by leaving them prey to Faustian pederasts, and that it ruins the lives of adults who base marriages on mistaken assumptions. Representing Americans, Newland Archer, "Whose soul sees the perfect / Which his eyes seek in vain" (*Sphinx,* stanza 10, ll. 79–80), is blind to the knowledge that while his children are one "flower of life," there are many others in maturity, like the cultural riches of Europe and the potential love of Ellen Olenska. *The Glimpses of the Moon* elaborates on the marriage based on mistaken assumptions, as it introduces the next clue to the code, adds pieces to the neglected child puzzle, and unexpectedly reintroduces the rape theme.

# 5 | *The Glimpses of the Moon*
### Reverberating Art Allusions

MOST CRITICS HAVE ignored *The Glimpses of the Moon*[1] (the title of which alludes to *Hamlet*), tacitly agreeing that it is "sentimental and conventional."[2] Some express more severe disappointment, declaring that "Wharton has begun—probably entirely without realizing it—to borrow from her own earlier work."[3] But the feathery light quality of the novel is actually humor heavily structured through literary allusion, and the "borrowing" is a form of "self-allusion." Wharton narrowed this known technique of an author's alluding to biographical events to allude only to her work. This modification is here called "autoallusion."

Susan Branch and Nick Lansing descend from formerly wealthy old New York families. Though he "writes" and she "manages," each is dependent on the hospitality of well-to-do friends. They meet and fall in love but are too poor to marry without a pact to "manage" for a year on cash wedding gifts, then divorce, marry for money, and part friends.

But after their marriage Nick disapproves of the way Susy "manages." When Susy packs their trunks to leave Strefford's Italian villa at Como, lent them for their honeymoon, she includes four boxes of Strefford's cigars because Nick enjoys them. He considers that stealing; she considers the cigars a gift. A second incident occurs when the couple arrives at the Venetian palace loaned to them by Ellie Vanderlyn, where, Susan finds, the unspoken expectation is that in exchange for use of the house, she must deceive Nelson Vanderlyn about his wife's affairs. Susy knows that Nick will disapprove of such deception, but to remain with him in the beauty of that palace, she accedes.

When Nick discovers the lie, he stalks off to join the Hickses, wealthy Americans, on their cruise. Susy visits wealthy friends, thinking Nick is accepting the terms of their bargain by taking the opportunity to marry Coral Hicks. She becomes "engaged" to Lord Strefford. Realizing she still loves Nick, Susy leaves for Paris to care for Grace and Nat Fulmer's five children so that the parents can pursue careers in music and art. The responsibilities of child care teach Susy courage to face Nick, so she writes asking him to finalize divorce details. After the visit the reunited couple takes the Fulmer children with them on a second honeymoon.

The source of the contradiction between Wharton's perception of her subject as "difficult"[4] and the critics' view of her novel as "trivial"[5] can be found in the complexly thematic, clustered, layered, reverberating (see Chapters 9 and 10), autoallusive, and metaphysical allusions. For the first time Wharton displays her humor in a novel that becomes fascinating in its continued allusion to Emerson's poem. *The Glimpses of the Moon* is comprised in part of several jokes. One of them is that Wharton uses her own popular novel, a novel that just happens to have "mirth" in the title, as a structural allusion. She then combines the titular structural allusion with thematic allusions, especially those from *Marius the Epicurean* and *Hamlet,* to create something altogether different, a bit of romantic lunacy, moon madness complete with ghosts and vampires.

The first point that must be addressed is complaints that "Wharton has begun—probably entirely without realizing it—to borrow from her own earlier work." Misunderstood as "borrowing," intentional autoallusion functions structurally as a joke on the novel's theme of borrowing houses. Wharton alludes to *The House of Mirth*. The scene at the beginning in which Susy visits Nick's bachelor apartment and leaves by running down three flights of stairs (*GM* 11, 12) recalls Lily's visit to Selden at the Benedick at the beginning of *The House of Mirth*. In the center, Nick's proposal on the hill with a view is remarkably like the "republic of the spirit" scene in the middle of *The House of Mirth,* when Susy deplores her "hateful useless love of beauty . . . , the curse it had always been to her, the blessing it might have been if only she had had the material means to gratify and to express it!" (*GM* 192, Wharton's ellipses). When she then goes on to characterize her "hideous" hotel (*GM* 192) as she had described the "dingy stairs" of Nick's (*GM* 8), she echoes Lily's words as well as the description of her "dingy" boardinghouse. A closing episode in which Susy watches the working women and thinks, "Why shouldn't I earn my living by trimming hats?" (*GM* 270) recalls Lily's similar statement and the scenes in which she tries it and fails. Susy sitting exhausted on a bench watching Paris just before being rescued by Grace Fulmer recalls Lily sitting on a bench watching New York just before being rescued by Nettie Struther. The regularity of allusions to *The House of Mirth* and their parallels to the plot show them to be, collectively, a structural allusion like those discussed in the first chapter. Moreover, there is a humorous quality to Wharton's use of the first of her novels to contain structural allusions *as* a structural allusion.

Like *The House of Mirth,* "Glimpses" uses the technique of thematic allusion; the first set of clustered thematic allusions concerns bargains. As the novel opens, Nick and Susy are ecstatically "glimpsing" the moon while Susy recalls their bargain: "When she made the bargain she meant it to be an honest one. . . . Why shouldn't they marry; belong to each other openly and honourably, if for ever so short a time, and with the definite understanding that whenever either of them got the chance to do better he or she should be immediately released? The law of their country facilitated such exchanges, and society was beginning to view them as indulgently as the law" (*GM* 21). The unmarked one-word clue, "bargain," an emphasis on the contractual exchange of marriage, is probably an explication of a Renaissance sonnet by Sir Philip Sidney:

> My true-love hath my heart, and I have his,
> By just exchange one for the other given:
> I hold his dear, and mine he cannot miss,
> There never was a better bargain given.
>
> [*The Bargain*, stanza 1, ll. 1–4]

The seeds of Nick and Susy's disaster are contained in the bargain itself, which is based, first, on ignoring human experience of the marriage bond, and second, on a misunderstanding by each of what the other is suggesting. Each suggests an agreement based on contrasting philosophical views of life attractive to, but unrecognized by, the other—Nick's "perpendicular" view and Susy's "Epicurean" view. Complications increase until they come together, as Emerson suggests, "to vision profounder," a vision clarified by the sun, not obscured by the moon.

The couple's breakup occurs when Nick suddenly realizes what he has never asked, just *how* Susy "manages": "If there were certain links in the chain that Lansing had never been able to put his hand on, certain arrangements and contrivances that still needed further elucidation, why, he was lazily resolved to clear them up with her some day" (*GM* 23). When he discovers that her management involves morally unacceptable compromises, they argue and he stalks off. Before he does, the fact of misperceptions between them begins to arise when Susy reminds him of their bargain "with the half-conscious sense of having been unfairly treated":

> When they had entered into their queer compact, Nick had known as well as she on what compromises and concessions the life they were to live together must be based. . . .
> "After all—you were right when you wanted me to be your mistress."
> He turned on her with an astonished stare. "You—my mistress? . . . But the compact—I'd almost forgotten it. . . . The thing was absurd, of course; a mere joke." [*GM* 109–11]

But Susy is "modern," a feeling person, while Nick is morally "old fashioned," a reasoner who certainly never asked Susy to be his mistress. When the original conversation is reread as it was recalled by Nick, the nature of the mixup becomes evident. Nick drops reason and reacts emotionally. Susy drops emotion and reacts reasonably. The result is that each has a completely different understanding about the nature of their agreement: "His next utterance was a boyish outburst against the tyranny of the existing order of things, abruptly followed by the passionate query why, since he and she couldn't alter it, and since they both had the habit of looking at facts as they were, they wouldn't be utter fools not to take their chance of being happy in the only way that was open to them?" (*GM* 20).

Nick is emotionally proposing "the only way that was open," marriage, but Susy, misled by the passionate outburst, responds in a reasoning mode to what she understands as a suggestion that she be Nick's mistress. She wants their relationship to be honest: "If such happiness ever came to her she did not want it shorn of half its brightness by the need of fibbing and plotting and dodging" (*GM* 21). In so saying, she "set forth her reasons" with what Nick thinks is her "usual lucid impartiality" (*GM* 20).

Susy is deeply hurt by Nick's quarrelsome accusations, and Nick is equally wounded by her apparent lack of reasonable appreciation of his moral values. This hurt, compounded by the failure of both to recognize the emotional bond that develops in marriage, is also featured in Sidney's sonnet: "For as from me, on him his hurt did light, / So still methought in me his hurt did smart." Susy "hid her face in her hands. It seemed to her, now, that nothing mattered except that their love for each other, their faith in each other, should be saved from some unhealable hurt" (*GM* 105). Meanwhile, Nick leaves without any word or attempt to mend the situation, and the author's disapproval of Nick's idea of household management is manifest in a related thematic allusion to "managing."

After Nick leaves, enveloped "in the Nessus-shirt of his memories" (*GM* 312), he joins the Hickses on their yacht, the *Ibis,* eventually replacing Mr. Buttles as social secretary. The Hickses are wealthy American "Primitives" who travel Europe "promoting art," sharing with Nick an especially keen interest in archeology. In one conversation, the "modern young secretaries, Mr. Beck and Mr. Buttles, showed a touching tendency to share [Eldorada's] view, and spoke of Mr. Hicks as 'promoting art,' in the spirit of Pandolfino celebrating the munificence of the Medicis" (*GM* 61).

Agnolo Pandolfini (1360–1446) was a Florentine public official and Renaissance humanist. The primary information about him is in the writings of Vespasiano, which describe Pandolfini's involvements in the affairs of the Medici and his devotion to letters. "Vespasiano records that on his wedding night Pandolfini told his bride what he expected of her in the management of the household, and advised her to take it to heart as he did not intend to repeat it."[6]

The allusions to Sir Philip Sidney and to Pandolfini reinforce the themes of the marriage bargain and the necessity of "management," while a cluster of allusions to Pope, Shakespeare, Richardson, the opera *Don Giovanni,* and a reverberating allusion to paintings by Correggio, Van Dyke, and Vanderlyn support themes of rape and abandonment.

Nick's abandonment of Susy is foreshadowed when he tells her before their engagement that he is "free as air" (*GM* 10) and in so saying seems to Susy to assume an attitude expressed by Alexander Pope in another poem of love and passion, "Eloisa to Abelard," that the moment you constrain love with law it disappears:

> Curse on all laws but those which love has made!
> Love, free as air, at sign of human ties,
> Spreads his light wings, and in a moment flies.
>
>     [*Eloisa to Abelard,* ll. 74–76]

Nick, however, does believe in imposing both legal and moral laws, and he assumes that Susy knows them. Pandolfini at least explained his expectations to his wife while the threat contained in Pandolfini's reported words cuts off communication and places husband and wife in an adversarial relationship.

In Susy's view, Nick in his "Nessus-shirt" (*GM* 312) has turned against her. The shirt of Nessus signals a layered allusion to abandonment as well as to poisonous eroticism in the context of Antony turning against Cleopatra. In a singularly sensual speech addressed to the departing Cleopatra, Antony feels he should have killed her:

> Thou fell'st into my fury, for one death
> Might have prevented many. Eros, ho!
> The shirt of Nessus is upon me; teach me,
> Alcides, thou mine ancestor, thy rage.
> Let me lodge Lichas on the horns o' th' moon,
> And with those hands that grasped the heaviest club
> Subdue my worthiest self. The witch shall die:
>
>     [*Antony and Cleopatra,* act 4, scene 12, ll. 41–47]

Antony claims to be the descendant of Hercules (Alcides), who killed the centaur Nessus with a poisoned arrow for trying to rape his wife, Deianira. In revenge, the dying Nessus soaked his shirt in poisoned blood and gave it to Deianira as a love charm. But she sent it to her husband, Hercules, who in dying agony threw Lichas, the messenger who brought it, high into the air toward the moon, a detail that reflects the novel's title theme.

Like Antony, who in a moment of passionate fury is capable of raping Cleopatra, erotic feelings increase Nick's anger: "It was as if a sickness long

Antonio Correggio, *Venus, Satyr and Cupid* (c. 1518). (Referred to in some sources as the "Antiope.") Musée du Louvre, Paris. Cliché des Musées Nationaux—Paris. Reverberating Allusion: *The Glimpses of the Moon.*

John Vanderlyn, *Ariadne Asleep on the Island of Naxos* (1809–14). Courtesy of the Pennsylvania Academy of the Fine Arts, Philadelphia. Gift of Mrs. Sarah Harrison (The Joseph Harrison, Jr. Collection). Reverberating Allusion: *The Glimpses of the Moon.*

smouldering in him had broken out and become acute, enveloping him in the Nessus-shirt of his memories" (*GM* 312). The allusion itself intensifies when clustered with allusions to Robert Browning, to the opera *Don Giovanni,* to Richardson's novel *Clarissa,* and to Nick's preference in art, all of which create a cluster of thematic allusions to rape. In turn, the cluster is supported by reverbating art allusions to rape, a rape, it should be emphasized, that, like incest in *The Mother's Recompense,* is more psychological and symbolic than actual.

While reading on the Hickses' yacht, Nick recalls taking Susy to the Louvre before the breakup: "His own momentary mood was for Correggio and Frago-nard, the laughter of the Music Lesson and the bold pagan joys of the Antiope. . . . Closing his book he stole a glance at Coral" (*GM* 184). Wharton ties Cor-reggio's *Venus, Satyr and Cupid* (sometimes called "Antiope") to Antony's fu-rious allusion to "Alcides." An allusion to "Vandyke" (Coral's pronunciation of Van Dyck) (*GM* 227), who painted a more threatening than "joyful" *Rape of Antiope,* the nude figure of which repeats those of the Correggio and the Vanderlyn, creates a layered art allusion (the allusion to the painter Vanderlyn is in the name of Susy's American friends). Vanderlyn's famous *Ariadne Asleep on the Island of Naxos* was adapted from his own copy of Correggio's "Antiope" made just previous to painting the "Ariadne."[7]

Such a cluster of thematic allusions seems heavy-handed, especially in a comedy. Nick's "rape" is actually a rape of Susy's identity that results from their first disagreement over the cigars, just as his abandonment of her results from their second disagreement over Ellie's letters.

Although Susy does envy Ellie Vanderlyn somewhat, because she can order couture clothing by the trunkful, her own trunks of clothing so represent her identity that she could not look at the cases of Ellie's laces, silks, and furs "without picturing herself in [the clothes], and wondering by what new miracle of management she could give herself the air of being dressed by the same consummate artists" (*GM* 78). But Nick has no sense of Susy as an individual, and not until he sees her as "not the bundle of qualities and defects into which his critical spirit had tried to sort her out, but the soft blur of identity, of personality," and one "mysteriously independent," do problems begin to be solved (*GM* 285).

Nick believes that the way Susy "coaxed reluctant things into a trunk was a symbol of the way she fitted discordant facts into her life," and "he had grown to shrink from even . . . harmless evidence of her always knowing how to 'manage' " (*GM* 29). When he discovers Streffy's cigars in their trunks, Nick demands that Susy hand them over: "Lansing had time for an exasperated sense of the disproportion between his anger and its cause. And this made him still angrier" (*GM* 30). Since three of the cigar boxes are packed in Nick's trunk, Nick demands the key, which Susy gives him. For half an hour he "battled with the lock" (*GM* 30) and "broken-nailed and perspiring, extracted the cigars and stalked with them into the deserted drawing room" to put them back (*GM* 31).

The battle with the lock is a visual pun on Pope's "The Rape of the Lock," an intraauthorial allusion that crosses from Pope's *Eloisa to Abelard.* In that context the Freudian symbolism of the key in the lock, and of the stolen cigars in a woman's trunk, becomes clear. Nick feels he is the "reluctant thing" coaxed into Susy's trunk. But with a twist, Wharton has had Susy put three boxes of the cigars in Nick's own trunk so that three quarters of his "rape" turns against himself. Or, to change the terminology of rape to its root meaning, *theft*—recall the stolen glance at Coral—the attempted theft of Susy's identity fails, especially since she has freely handed him the box of cigars from her own trunk. Nevertheless, the episode creates a sorrow for her that she later describes as "ravaging" (*GM* 344). While the allusions to Pope, Mozart, Richardson, and Shakespeare, and the reverberating allusion to paintings by Correggio, Van Dyck, and Vanderlyn, support the themes of rape and abandonment, a second set of art allusions to Tiepolo and Velasquez, Renaissance women, and probably Picasso indicate more of the novel's jokes.

After Nick leaves Susy, he randomly boards a train. Upon reaching Milan he gets off and orders coffee, which, "instead of clearing his thoughts, had merely accelerated their pace" (*GM* 123–24). Nick drinks a great deal of coffee from this point in the novel, without fully awakening, which recalls the "twilight sleep" theme of *The Age of Innocence*. In the coffee shop he is approached by Mr. Buttles, who has recently left the Hickses' employ because of a disagreement with Coral Hicks. Nick thinks the break is over Buttles's "conscientious objections to Tiepolo" (*GM* 125). He feels sorry for the spectacled Mr. Buttles, regarding him as a "limp image of unrequited passion," a hopeless suitor for Coral (*GM* 127). Coral and Mr. Buttles, juxtaposed as they are with Tiepolo's angels, are two of Wharton's "guardian angel" figures, each of whom views the world clearly but through different types of lenses.[8]

Earlier in the novel Nick runs across Coral with her field glasses in the Church of the Scalzi "under the whirl of rose-and-lemon angels in Tiepolo's great vault" (*GM* 91). In the course of their conversation she admits openly: "I am in love—Oh, there's Eldorada and Mr. Beck! . . . I told them that if they'd meet me here to-day I'd try to make them understand Tiepolo. Because, you see, at home we've [sic] never really *have* understood Tiepolo; and Mr. Beck and Eldorada are the only ones to realize it. Mr. Buttles simply won't". . . . "I *am* in love . . . and that's the reason why I find art such a *re*-source" (*GM* 95). (While "*re*-source" may simply reflect Coral's untutored grammar and pronunciation, it could also be Wharton's hint about her reverberating art allusions.) Nick misunderstands Coral's situation, too. Forgetting chronology, he presumptuously believes Coral is frankly admitting her love for *him* and that he caused Coral's rejection of Mr. Buttles. The disagreement between Mr. Buttles and Coral, however, was not a lover's quarrel, and not over Nick and the artistic value of Tiepolo but over Coral's "pagan" way of life, which Mr. Buttles connects with loose Renaissance morality: "If Miss Hicks chooses to surrender herself momentarily to the unwholesome spell of the Italian decadence it is not for me to protest or to criticize" (*GM* 125). Further confusion occurs because Nick (and the reader) are humorously teased by the author into believing that Tiepolo was a Renaissance artist, when in fact he painted in the eighteenth century. A similar joke occurs when Violet Melrose is about to take artist Nat Fulmer to Paris: "Such a marvellous experience, to be there when he and Velasquez meet!" (*GM* 175). She must mean the paintings. Velasquez had been dead since the Renaissance.

Pablo Picasso, *Gertrude Stein* (1906). The Metropolitan Museum of Art, New York. Art Allusion: *The Glimpses of the Moon.*

Coral, with her "queer apostles and parasites" (*GM* 61), is a lesbian woman in love with Eldorada.[9] For this reason Mr. Buttles connects her with decadence. Coral, however, does not consider herself decadent and even associates herself with Tiepolo's angels. She is consistently described in masculine terms —as handsome, strong, courageous, primitive, and massive with hard and material ideals (*GM* 291). The following passage is often misread: "Coral Hicks was *never* lovely: but she certainly looked unusually handsome. Perhaps it was the long dress of black velvet which, outlined against a shaded lamp, made her strong build seem slenderer. . . . " (*GM* 287, emphasis mine). The description of Coral (whose passions are art and archaeology) with its code words for the portrait, "shade" and "outline," and her description as "primitive," refusing to wear jewelry, and as an "inspiration" (*GM* 239), seem to allude to Picasso's *Portrait of Gertrude Stein* (1906).[10] That painting depicts an earth goddess in her "uniform" of brown velvet corduroy wearing no jewelry *except* a coral brooch. The portrait is famous for Picasso's decision to execute Stein's frank expression after an Iberian mask. (The mask is a symbol important in regard to Susy as well.) In addition, coral is a symbol of healing.[11]

Gertrude Stein, who was a great promoter and collector of art, particularly of Matisse and Picasso, also studied medicine at Radcliffe with William James. Compare Coral's education at Bryn Mawr, add the fact that the role played by Coral Hicks in the novel is that of healer and peacemaker, that her name alludes to Edouard Hicks, American primitive painter most famous for his many "Peaceable Kingdoms," and the allusions tell the story.

Having surreptitiously (and sympathetically) slipped lesbianism into this novel, Edith Wharton carries over her bold joke to stereotypical male homosexuality. Soon the Princess of Teutoburg and her son, the Prince Anastasius, who "adored his mother," join the Hickeses' entourage. Besides hovering over his mother and enduring "delicate health," the prince is described effeminately as "not a warrior" but "stooping, pacific and spectacled" (*GM* 231), words intended to cast doubts on his masculinity and to make the reader suspect that he and his aide-de-camp may be homosexuals. And when the "smiling aide-de-camp had caught Nick's eye," "Nick had flushed to the forehead. . . . He had contrived to let the aide-de-camp feel that he was too deficient in humour to be worth exchanging glances with; but even this had not restored his self-respect" (*GM* 238). But Nick's insight is limited to the Prince and his aide-de-camp. He does not recognize that Coral is a homosexual woman, though Strefford does: "*Queer* child, Coral," he tells Susy (*GM* 58, emphasis mine). Coral tells Nick she agreed to marry the prince and "wear a crown" because she wishes to become "prominent" and to "promote culture, like those Renaissance women" (*GM* 289–90).

The Renaissance women to whom Coral refers were probably the Sforzas. Two of them, Ippolita Maria Sforza (1445–1488), a student of classical literature and philosophy, and Isabella (1503–1561), a writer, were patrons of the arts. There was also a third, Caterina Sforza (1463–1509), who, though she married several times and gave birth to eight children, was a warrior. She eventually became known for "the man's heart that beat in her woman's breast."[12]

"Flushed and tear-stained" Eldorada is the person most visibly upset by the news that Coral will marry the Prince. As secretary and companion to Coral ("I am in love— Oh there's Eldorada"), she is an Alice B. Toklas figure who tells Nick: " 'You'll find her looking lovely—' and jerked away with a sob as he entered" (*GM* 287). Note that it is only Eldorada who finds Coral "lovely." Strong-minded as she is, Coral is understandably upset by pressure to marry the Prince and, believing Nick enlightened, openly seeks his opinion. Still misunderstanding the situation, he accidentally gives correct advice: "Ask yourself—ask your parents" (*GM* 289). The cluster of joking allusions to Tiepolo and Velasquez, Renaissance women, and Picasso reveals some of the novel's humor, but themes of madness and healing established through allusions to the Bible, Le Fanu, and *Hamlet* add depth to the joke.

When Nick finally understands about the Prince, "the scales [are lifted] from his eyes": "Innumerable dim corners of memory had been flooded with light by that one quick glance of the aide-de-camp's: things he had heard, hints he had let pass, smiles, insinuations, cordialities, rumours of the improbability of the Prince's founding a family" (*GM* 241). The scales' falling from his eyes alludes to Acts 9:18, in which Saul recovers his eyesight, is baptized to "vision profound," and begins to recover moral and physical strength.

After he had been with the Hickses a day or two, Nick "confessed [to Coral] that he had not been well" (*GM* 181) and spent "three weeks of drug taking" on the yacht. The drugs of scenery and study were "merely a form of anaesthetic: He swallowed them with the careless greed of the sufferer who seeks only to still pain and deaden memory" (*GM* 179).

Nick absorbs a great deal of the caffeine drug coffee before he finds himself on the Hickses' yacht. "As he drank his coffee his thoughts gradually cleared. It became obvious to him that he had behaved like a madman or a petulant child—he preferred to think it was like a madman" (*GM* 131).

Nick's caffeine madness most probably refers to Joseph Sheridan Le Fanu, to whom Wharton alludes directly later in the novel as well as in the preface to *Ghosts* (*GM* 227). In Le Fanu's famous ghost story "Green Tea," when the protagonist becomes addicted to strong green tea drunk while studying pagan religions, he hallucinates an evil monkey.[13] Literally, he has a "monkey on his back"—an addiction. "Carmilla," in the same volume, is a story about the moon madness of lesbian vampirism.

The novel does not support the idea of Coral as a vampire, however. And as Michael Begnal says in his book on Le Fanu: "Behind the window dressing of vampirism Le Fanu is presenting a study of aberrant sexuality" the lesson of which is that "it is the soul that must be cleansed."[14] Instead, the vampires are Susy's women friends who suck the financial blood from their husbands and adulterous lovers.

"She caught Susy's wrists in vehement fingers." "You don't know what horrors women will do—and even girls!" says Ellie Vanderlyn to Susy when Strefford becomes rich and interesting (*GM* 213). She then turns to the subject of her lover, Algie Bockheimer: "I'm in mortal terror of losing him. And I do assure you there's no other way of keeping them [than perpetually guarding them from other women] when they're as hideously rich as that!" (*GM* 214). Ellie shuddered.

"I think you're abominable," Susy exclaimed. And Wharton emphasizes this biblical code word for sexual perversions (from Leviticus) by repeating it: "A-bo-mi-nable? A-bo-mi-nable? Susy!" "Yes . . . with Nelson . . . and Clarissa . . . and your past together . . . and all the money you can possibly want . . . and that man! Abominable" (*GM* 215). Finally, another of Susy's adulterous friends, Violet Melrose, is described as a "vampire in pearls who sought only to feed on the notoriety [from affairs] which all her millions could not create for her" (*GM* 145–46).

There are a number of disabling wrist grabbings in the novel. Nick grabs Susy's wrists controllingly several times, but here Ellie has Susy by the wrists. In "Carmilla," Le Fanu points out: "One sign of the vampire is the power of the hand. The slender hand of Mircalla [Carmilla] closed like a vice of steel on the General's wrist when he raised the hatchet to strike. But its power is not confined to its grasp; it leaves a numbness in the limb it seizes, which is slowly, if ever, recovered from" ("Carmilla," 288).

And in *Hamlet,* Ophelia describes Hamlet's frightening entrance into her bedroom by the maddening light of the moon. Will he rape her? He came with his clothing disheveled: "with his doublet all unbraced. . . . As if he had been loosed out of hell / To speak of horrors—he comes before me."

| | |
|---|---|
| Polonius: | Mad for thy love? . . . What said he? |
| Ophelia: | He took me by the wrist and held me hard. |

[act 2, scene 1, ll. 78–88]

Ophelia's suicide is the ultimate loss of her identity.

So Wharton has deflected the topic of Coral's homosexuality to the idea of the moral illness of Nick and the couple's friends. For a long time Nick's "life seemed as flat as a convalescent's first days after the fever has dropped" (*GM* 283). His healing, of course, is a cure from his mad rapist mentality and caffeine addiction that led him to regard *The Rape of Antiope* as a "pagan joy." Eventually he becomes disgusted with pagan life aboard the yacht and resolves to leave. But before this change takes place, he first needs a "cure" from "symptoms" brought on by the bargain, the mad adventure (*GM* 14), and from his tendency to regard himself as a deity but his wife as a piece of property: "From the moment that she had become his property he had built up in himself a conception of her answering to some deep-seated need of veneration. She was his, he had chosen her, she had taken her place in the long line of Lansing women who had been loved, honoured, and probably deceived, by bygone Lansing men" (*GM* 64). Intuitively, Lansing's new friends call him "Old Nicks," slang for the devil (*GM* 237). He further needs a cure from the tendency to make sarcastic remarks like that he made to Susy on the choice of Como for their honeymoon: "—with all due respect to you—it wasn't much of a mental strain to decide on Como." Luckily Susy has a strong sense of self and, though disturbed, is not destroyed by Nick's cutting comment: "His wife instantly challenged this belittling of her capacity" (*GM* 2).

Nick's illnesses are, of course, moral and begin with "moral languor" (*GM* 179). But he is in good hands, for in Rome, the Hickses had "gaily defied fever" (*GM* 230), and Coral had sent Susy a note (misinterpreted by her) that said in part, "You may count on our taking the best care of him" (*GM* 138). But when the Hickses become "addicted" to imperious demands on his time, Nick learns how it feels to be a "paraded and petted piece of property," that it is "a good deal more distasteful than he could have imagined" (*GM* 283). Gradually, through Coral's example of "originality," he begins to realize that a woman can have an identity of her own, be separate, "prominent," influential, and courageous enough to explain to her parents why she refuses to marry a Prince. Ironically, when Nick feels his physical and moral health returning, he expresses himself in terms of possession once again: "But she's mine, Nick cried, in a fierce triumph of recovery. . . . " (*GM* 320, Wharton's ellipses). But she is his because she has volunteered to be, for no other reason.

Thus allusions to the Bible, and to Le Fanu's ghost stories "Green Tea" and "Carmilla" as well as to *Hamlet*, humorously introduce themes of the madness of Nick's "rapist mentality" and thematic allusions to healing that include Walter Pater's *Marius the Epicurean* and an intraauthorial allusion to *The Renaissance*, both thematic allusions to healing.

While Nick is with the Hickses, Susy stays with Fred and Ursula Gillow, a situation more ambiguous for her than Nick's is for him. There she can survive in sensuous luxury, but Ursula (whose surname means "a loose and wanton woman," according to the *Oxford English Dictionary*), is carrying on one of her several extramarital affairs, while Susy is exposed to the questionable courtship of Strefford. The very attributes to which Nick is attracted in Susy, her love of the sensuous and her ability to "manage," are the attributes that constantly place her in compromised positions.

Susy is a "feeling" person with regard to both physical touch and emotion. Her "succumbing to the familiar spell of . . . furs and laces and brocades" (*GM* 168), chinchilla, the deep blue sparkle of sapphires, her physical attraction to Nick, and her emotional response to people, laughter, and music stem from the same basis as her appreciation of the moon and roses, of art and poetry. To her it is an accident of life that most of these "whim[s] of the moment," including marriage, are expensive luxuries (*GM* 168). So though Susy is an Epicurean, she is neither materialistic nor a hedonistic lover of pure pleasure for its own sake.

The "Marius" to which Susy refers is Walter Pater's novel *Marius the Epicurean* (1885), a philosophical romance that takes place in pagan Rome.[15] The novel's subjects include "various crazes concerning health and disease" and they are related to Nick's experiences by themes of health and illness. An autobiographical apologia for Pater's aesthetic values, the book seemed, to the many who read both *Marius* and the last line of Pater's *The Renaissance,* to imply that people should live for the moment because that is the only certainty in an ever-changing universe: "To burn always with this hard gem-like flame, to maintain this ecstasy, is success in life."[16] Epicureans further believe that the senses are the source of all knowledge, so failure to try to live perfectly in the moment is failure to live life fully.

Though she knows and understands Epicurean principles intuitively because she lives by them, Susy is deluded by her love for Nick into thinking he understands and agrees: "The mere fact that he was engaged on a philosophic romance, and not a mere novel, seemed the proof of an intrinsic superiority" (*GM* 56). But Nick neither understands nor agrees: he "winced more than he triumphed when Susy produced her allusion to *Marius*. . . . He knew enough of his subject to know that he did not know enough to write about it; but he consoled himself by remembering that *Wilhelm Meister* has survived many weighty volumes on aesthetics" (*GM* 63). When he thinks "he could develop his theory of Oriental influences in Western art at the expense of less learning than if he had tried to put his ideas into an essay" (*GM* 63), Nick is committing the two sins of pride of inexperienced writers, writing on something he doesn't understand and taking educational shortcuts. Nevertheless, the episode demonstrates that, though he seems to be a positivist, Nick is attracted to Epicureanism and is therefore also attracted to Susy.

Without knowing it, as a man of the old-fashioned "perpendicular" ideas of Episcopalian New York, somewhat like Newland Archer, he is actually in opposition to Epicureanism as described by Pater: pitched to a really high and serious key, the precept "—*Be perfect in regard to what is here and now*: the precept of 'culture,' as it is called, or of a complete education—might at least save [Marius] from . . . vulgarity" (*Marius* 84). Nick is being neither perfect nor educated about writing his book and, like Archer, sleepwalks through most of his life in spite of caffeine.

Pater makes quite clear the difference between hedonism and Epicureanism. The emphasis of the Epicureanism of Cyrenaic, he says, is "not pleasure, but fullness of life,[17] and 'insight' as conducing to that fullness—energy, variety, and choice of experience, including noble pain and sorrow even, loves such as those of the moral life, such as Seneca and Epictetus—whatever form of human life, in short, might be heroic, impassioned, ideal: from these the 'new Cyrenaicism' of Marius took its criterion of values" (*Marius* 87).

Living in the moment, however, does not provide for the future, and literature and art alone are insufficient for "fullness of life." A harmonious future is necessary, a theme that is carried out by cross-generic thematic allusions to music in *Marius* and *Don Giovanni,* by the poetry of Browning and FitzGerald, and by the paintings of Fragonard and Matisse.

The novel does not endorse the myopia that made Nick and Susy's original bargain so impossible. There must be a future for mankind, for family, and for Susy, who is now "out of a job" (*GM* 199). The solution to Susy's future is in Pater, under a layered allusion to FitzGerald's "Rubaiyat of Omar Khayyam" (seen already as a structural allusion in *The House of Mirth*) that ends with an allusion to the Gospel of Luke 2:46: *"Let us eat and drink, for to-morrow we die!*—is a proposal, the real import of which differs immensely according to the natural taste . . . [and] may come to be identical with—'My meat is to do what is just and kind'; while the soul, which can make no sincere claim to have apprehended anything beyond the evil of immediate experience, yet never loses a sense of happiness in conforming to the highest moral ideal it can clearly define for itself; and actually, though but with so faint hope, does the 'Father's business' " (*Marius* 83). Pater argues that if the means of living in the moment justify the ends, as hedonists believe, then a teleology of imagination is implied, a "blessedness of vision," and so a future. One way to understand this is through the study of music: "The study of music, in that wider Platonic sense, according to which, music comprehends all those matters over which the Muses of Greek mythology preside, would conduct one to an exquisite appreciation of all the finer traits of nature and of man. . . . one's existence, from day to day, came to be like a well-executed piece of music; that 'perpetual motion' in things . . . according itself to a kind of cadence or harmony" (*Marius* 85–86).

Here the two plot lines begin to merge, for Nick learns to be less "Perpendicular" and leans toward Susy's brand of Epicureanism or New Cyrenaicism. His healing under Coral's care progresses, for he does have a positive side that Wharton presented with his negative one in the earlier allusion during a trip to the Louvre: "They had stood before the little Crucifixion of Mantegna. He had not been looking at the picture, or watching to see what impression it produced on Susy. His own momentary mood was for Correggio and Fragonard, the laughter of the Music Lesson and the bold pagan joys of the Antiope" (*GM* 184). Nick is attracted not only to the paintings of sex and rape but also to Fragonard's *Music Lesson.* He had later taken note that "the Princess

Jean Fragonard, *The Music Lesson* (1770). Musée du Louvre, Cliché des Musées Na-tionaux—Paris. Thematic Allusion: *The Glimpses of the Moon.*

Mother adored . . . Matisse" (*GM* 235). Matisse also painted a *Music Lesson,* so that this is a reverberating allusion. Now Susy has a chance of "reaching a responsive chord" in Nick, saving him from "some unhealable hurt" (*GM* 105) impossible before he came under Coral's healing "management"; Coral "always made him feel, in her presence, like a member of an orchestra under a masterful *bâton*" (*GM* 136).

Susy is also influenced by music. Coming from the window of the Vander-lyns' palace in Venice she hears "What of soul I wonder?" The song is a popu-larization of Browning's "A Toccata of Galuppi's." The toccata, a musical form developed by Bach, is literally a "touch piece" and thus connects with the sensuousness of Epicureanism. Browning reproduced the musical form in his poem, which addresses the eighteenth-century Venetian composer, a contem-porary of Tiepolo.

Like much of the novel, the poem takes place in Venice: "What, they lived once thus at Venice where the merchants were the kings." The poet describes "balls and masks begun at midnight" and the sexual attraction between a couple listening to Galuppi play: "—She, to bite her mask's black velvet, he, to finger on his sword / While you sat and played Toccatas, stately at the clavichord?" The poem goes on to contrast sex and death:

As for Venice and its people merely born to bloom
    and drop,
Here on earth they bore their fruitage, mirth and
    folly were the crop;
What of soul was left, I wonder, when the kissing
    had to stop?

The night Susy hears this poem put to music drifting from the Venetian palace window is the night Nick has left her and she has tried to forget by plunging into a party with her friends: "She began to hum the first bars of Donna Anna's entrance in *Don Giovanni*," Mozart's opera about rape and murder. "Pity I haven't got a black cloak and a mask. . . ." (*GM* 117–18, Wharton's ellipses). She had tried to cover her tears with makeup, and her face, her identity, is now a "painted image" in danger from Nick and from Strefford (*GM* 122). " 'Oh, your face will do,' said Strefford, laying his hand on her arm" (*GM* 118).

Nick has seen that Susy's "mask of paint and powder was carefully enough adjusted to hide any ravages [Wharton's code for rape] the scene between them might have left" (*GM* 129). Nick thinks: "After all, she had merely obeyed the instinct of self-preservation, the old hard habit of keeping up, going ahead and hiding her troubles; unless indeed the habit had already engendered indifference, and it had become as easy for her as for most of her friends to pass from drama to dancing, from sorrow to the cinema. What of soul was left, he wondered—?" (*GM* 128). Nick is correct in the first half of the sentence, but when he says "unless" he again begins, in effect, judgmentally to "rape" Susy's true identity, to degrade her courage in his own self-pity.

Susy refers to this upright judgmental quality of Nick's as "perpendicular": "Ah, Nick had become perpendicular! . . . After all, most people went through life making a given set of gestures, like dance-steps learned in advance. If your dancing manual told you at a given time to be perpendicular, you had to be, automatically—and that was Nick!" (*GM* 113, Wharton's ellipses).

In a letter about Jane Austen, Mary Russell Mitford wrote, "A friend of mine . . . says that she has stiffened into the most perpendicular, precise taciturn piece of single blessedness that ever existed," a quotation that may be a joking self-allusion to descriptions of Wharton herself such as those found in Lubbock's biography. Miss Mitford, however, is considered an unreliable source. The joke is that though Susy considers Nick morally "perpendicular," he is more likely to be physically horizontal, dreaming and dozing, than "perpendicular."[18] For though she is unlikely ever to stiffen perpendicularly, Susy is modifying in Nick's direction by learning "dignity" even as Nick learns his "music lesson": "Dignity! It was odd what weight that word had come to have for her. She had dimly felt its significance, felt the need of its presence in her inmost soul, even in the young thoughtless days when she had seemed to sacrifice so little to the austere divinities. And since she had been Nick Lansing's wife she had consciously acknowledged it, had suffered and agonized when she fell beneath its standard" (*GM* 165). Even so, since Nick has still not written, Susy sees a lawyer and divorce proceedings begin.

From the cluster of allusions to music in *Marius* and *Don Giovanni*, Browning's "Toccata," and FitzGerald's "Rubaiyat," and in "The Music Lessons" by Fragonard and probably Matisse (*GM* 235), Susy learns about cross-generic creative harmony. Echoing Kate Clephane, she feels like a ghost who needs to come back to life and resume her identity, a theme highlighted by a cluster of allusions to ghosts: the myth of Isis, *Hamlet* and "the glimpses of the moon," and Goethe's *Faust*.

Thus, by the time she joins the Fulmer children, Susy understands the need to plan for the future, having grown beyond the Epicurean idea of having "no sincere claim to have apprehended anything beyond the veil of immediate experience" (*Marius* 83). To live always in that moment was exactly Susy's hope as the novel opened with the lovers gazing at a "splash of moonlight on the water. Apples of silver in a net-work of gold. . . . " (*GM* 3, Wharton's ellipses).[19]

The inspiration for this beautifully poetic image is probably Marius's contemplation of the discovery of the sculptured head of Medusa "drawn up in a fisherman's net, with the fine golden laminae still clinging here and there to the bronze" (*Marius* 12), and his contemplation of a woman: "The golden fibre in the hair, the gold threadwork in the gown marked her as the mistress" (*Marius* 34) though Wharton humorously reduces the image to Ursula's "gold-meshed bag" (*GM* 201) entangled as the characters are in an expensive net of moon madness over love and money.

The moon is a complex symbol of love, lunacy, maternity, dreams, death, and ghosts, all of them used as "metaphysical allusions" so named because they function much like the conceits of metaphysical poetry. For example, in one of John Donne's poems, "A Valediction: Of Weeping," the poet bends and twists the image of a circle into various shapes. That plasticity is the particular quality of the metaphysical "conceit," or metaphor. Donne crafts the circle deftly into a coin, a piece of fruit, a tear, a ball, a globe, and finally the moon. Edith Wharton performs similar magic with her metaphysical allusions throughout *The Glimpses of the Moon*. She takes the magic image of the moon from *Hamlet,* changes its color from silver, to white, to gold, to orange, then transforms it into the peach Susy peels for Clarissa, bursts it into blooms of yellow roses, splatters it into a network of silver coins, then turns the coins into Ursula's gold-net purse, practicing the metamorphosis of the Sphinx:

> Uprose the merry Sphinx,
> > And crouched no more in stone;
> She melted into purple cloud,
> > She silvered in the moon;
> She spired into a yellow flame;
> > She flowered in blossoms red;
> She flowed into a foaming wave:
> > She stood Monadnoc's head.
>
> > [*Sphinx,* stanza 16, ll. 121–28]

All the while Wharton's images relate to an allusion to Henry Vaughn's metaphysical poem "The World" and refer back not only to *Hamlet* but also to the transformational lunacy of another Shakespearean play, *A Midsummer Night's Dream.* The author supports all of her images with literary and art allusion.

The yacht featured in *Marius* is the *Isis,* an allusion to an Egyptian bird worshiped as the symbol of the light and shade of the moon. When Nick first boards the Hickes' yacht, the *Ibis,* he thinks he is merely going for a "moonlight sail" (*GM* 181). But the significance of the incident is increased by the primary moon symbol contained in the titular allusion to the scene in which Hamlet encounters the ghost of his father:

> > What may this mean,
> That thou, dead corse, again in complete steel
> Revisit'st thus the glimpses of the moon,
> Making night hideous, and we fools of nature
> So horridly to shake our disposition
> With thoughts beyond the reaches of our souls?
>
> > [*Hamlet,* act 1, scene 4, ll. 51–56]

In part, the apparition is the ghost of Hamlet's past, and Susy, learning to plan for the future discovering "what of soul," must also deal with the past: "She had given [Nick] glimpses of her past," but she had not dealt with its ghost (*GM* 25).

Again, one of her rich friends gives her an opportunity to prostitute herself by taking charge of the Fulmer children while the friend has an affair with Nat

Fulmer: "The offer gave her a salutary glimpse of the way in which, as the years passed, and she lost her freshness and novelty, she would more and more be used as a convenience ... nursery governess or companion. She called to mind several elderly women ... who ... had long since been ruthlessly relegated to these slave-ant offices. Never in the world would she join their numbers" (*GM* 176). Ironically, she does become nursery governess and companion but in an honest bargain with Grace Fulmer. Nevertheless, emotionally she feels just as dead as she did earlier, when the "queer emptiness in which her thoughts rattled about as thoughts might, she supposed, in the first moments after death—before one got used to it. To get used to being dead: that seemed to be her immediate business. And she felt such a novice at it—felt so horribly alive! ... Nelson ... probably never would understand, or be able to communicate, the lesson when he had mastered it" (*GM* 281).

And before joining the Fulmer family, who can communicate to her the "music" lesson, the lesson of living a richly harmonious intellectual and moral life, she "seemed to be looking at [Paris] from the other side of the grave; and as she got up and wandered down the Champs Elysées, half empty in the evening lull between dusk and dinner, she felt as if the glittering avenue were really changed into the Field of Shadows from which it takes its name, and as if she were a ghost among ghosts" (*GM* 271). The symbols of ghosts proliferate when Susy finds the five Fulmer children an "apprenticeship of motherhood" whose "self-multiplication was equalled only by the manner in which they could dwindle, vanish." She finds the "changes from ubiquity to invisibility ... maddening" and considers hunting for them in the "subterranean closet where the trunks were kept." If "the rape of the lock" serves, as well as Wharton's favorite allusion to Faust's subterranean Mother goddesses (discussed in Chapter 11 on *The Gods Arrive*), she will indeed find them there (*GM* 295–96).

In her mind Nick has now become part of her past, but through the experience of child care she has developed identity and the courage to face him. She writes to Nick, asking him to visit her to settle final details concerning their divorce.

Nick, though he feels "the penetrating ghost of her" (*GM* 312), tries at first to "escape even a distant glimpse" of Susy. He feels himself "the only creature visible in a ghostly and besetting multitude" (*GM* 313). Finally, almost in spite of himself, he does get a glimpse of Susy, "transformed, transfigured": "For an instant she stood out from the blackness behind her, and through the veil of the winter night, a thing apart, an unconditioned vision, the eternal image of the woman and the child" (*GM* 319). The moonlight glimpse is instrumental in creating a change of heart in Nick and after a few more scenes he relents and through the influence of the children, he and Susy come back to life on a second honeymoon.

In this vastly underestimated novel, about which a great deal more needs elucidation, Edith Wharton successfully employs clusters of thematic allusions to rape, jokes and healing, music, and ghosts to support a lighthearted story that nevertheless contains an important moral point about conducting marriage honestly and responsibly.[20] That responsibility includes planning a future that allows for the possibility of a family.

For the first time in a novel Wharton uses reverberating art allusion, branching allusion, and structural autoallusion. Here too, for the first time, she produced a cluster of layered allusions all of which share a *secondary* allusion to one of her primary thematic allusions, *Antony and Cleopatra*.

Tiepolo painted an *Antony and Cleopatra*. In Le Fanu's "Carmilla," at the foot of Carmilla's bed a "somber piece of tapestry" represents "Cleopatra pressing the fangs of the asp to her breast," the viper's fangs of course alluding to the vampire's pointed teeth (*Carmilla* 235). Furthermore, *Antony and Cleopatra* is part of a cluster of allusions to passionate love: Sidney's "The Bargain," Pope's "Eloisa to Abelard," and Browning's "Toccata." Susy's surname, "Branch," entitles our branching allusions, twigs on a literary family tree, that are all too beautifully "managed" on their "sphinx-guarded threshold" (*GM* 142) to be coincidental.

In the novel so far, clues to the code have included the dilemma, the neglected child in danger (Clarissa in this novel, for what is Strefford doing, giving expensive jewelry to a little girl?) the bridges between America and Europe, men and women, past and present, and between the arts (a literary allusion to a painting of a music lesson, for instance) and the theme of pain. Also, three additions to the list of clues to Edith Wharton's code stress the need for self-discipline. It may be too easy to stay in a half-awake horizontal position, to practice forms of rape and homosexuality, and to use drugs. And the result, to Edith Wharton, is night veiling the couple's morning when Nick and Susy should be by "one music enchanted" as described by Emerson in "The Sphinx":

> By one music enchanted
>     One deity stirred,—
> Each the other adorning,
>     Accompany still;
> Night veileth the morning,
>     The vapor the hill.
>
>     [*Sphinx*, stanza 5, ll. 35–40]

For once a dilemma is solved. Even the Furies are relatively calm in *The Glimpses of the Moon*, perhaps because "the Sphinx guards the threshold."

But Kate Clephane of *The Mother's Recompense* is less fortunate. Her choices are followed by coincidences perfect for the relentless attention of the Furies. Themes of the neglected child and the specter of incest arise again, this time managed at the conclusion by a literary figure that seems molded like a metaphysical conceit from Lily Bart's gambling at cards, the bridge.

# 6 | *The Mother's Recompense*
### Umbrella Allusions

THE FIRST "umbrella allusions" were the large categories of thematic clusters symbolized by the parasol and the bumbershoot that divided the structure and imagery of *The Reef* into contrasting sides: sun/rain, Anna/Sophy, Greek art/ watercolor, and so forth. But *The Mother's Recompense* is entirely shaded by the one umbrella allusion to incest from Leviticus described at the end of the chapter. This "umbrella" covers every possible incestuous combination, but with her usual irony, Wharton makes the mother the perpetrator, not the father, and everyone, not just the child, is victimized by precipitous action followed by the fateful Furies.

The "neglected child" in *The Mother's Recompense* is Kate Clephane's daughter, Anne, whose mother reluctantly abandons her to her husband and mother-in-law.[1] Chronologically, events begin with Kate Clephane's stifling marriage to a man of old New York. When her daughter is three years old, Kate escapes with a lover, eventually divorcing her husband and settling on the Riviera. Citing "immorality," the Clephanes never again permit Kate to see her daughter.

One morning nearly twenty years later, Kate awakens depressed over the dissolution of a passionate love affair with Chris Fenno, a man a dozen years younger than she. The affair had ended two years earlier, when he abandoned Kate to enlist in the Great War. Kate's maid hands her a telegram that reads "Mrs. Clephane dead—" (*MR* 7). Kate takes it to be some horrible practical joke until she realizes that the Mrs. Clephane in question is not herself but her mother-in-law and that her daughter is requesting her to rejoin the family. Joyfully she reestablishes an affectionate relationship with her daughter and their old family friend, Fred Landers, who had always wanted to marry her.

Kate's life would be perfect except that she regrets that Anne doesn't yet feel close enough to confide in her about being in love. Her discovery of the odd coincidence that Anne is engaged to Chris Fenno produces not only feelings of jealousy but an inexplicable sense of horror. Her indecision about whether to tell her daughter about Fenno recalls Anna Leath's dilemma, but after coming near suicide, Kate decides not to tell Anne and not to marry Fred but to to resume her lonely life in Europe. Her unexplained decision to remain single has driven some critics to pronounce the novel a failure.

Structural allusions to mother-daughter relations supply a frame on which to hang a psychologically haunting story about the need for love, a story full of the shadows of midnight imaginings, of mysteries, specters, and terrors, all originating in the subconscious but lived out in the daylight setting of a novel of manners. Wharton continues to experiment here with literary allusion, both structurally and thematically, in a way that adds great depth to her work.

Begin with the ghost in the flyleaf: "My excuses are due to the decorous shade of Grace Aguilar, loved of our grandmothers, for deliberately appropriating, and applying to uses so different, the title of one of the most admired of her tales. E. W." (*MR* v). Aguilar's "tale" is a sentimental, melodramatic novel of manners mostly forgotten today.[2] Grace Aguilar is one of many (now) obscure Victorian novelists whose original *The Mother's Recompense,* written in 1836 at the age of nineteen, was a sequel to a novel called *Home Influence.* At the time of its publication in 1850 the author had died, and the preface was written by her mother, Sarah Aguilar. The theme of the novel is filial devotion and obedience, especially to the saintly Mrs. Hamilton, the heroine mother, who is the epitome of the "angel in the house" and the ironic antithesis to Kate Clephane, who eventually feels like a "ghost" in the house. Plot problems in the original novel are caused by the willful secretiveness of Caroline, who keeps her infatuations from her parents, and by the mistreatment of Lilla and Annie Grahame by their neglectful mother, stern father, and abusive governess. The reward of the happy ending, the mother's recompense, is entirely due to Mrs. Hamilton's devoted Christian maternity.

Caroline's lament demonstrates the novel's melodramatic tone: " 'Oh! were the counsels, the example, the appeal of her mother all forgotten? Was this a mother's recompense? Alas! Alas!' . . . I have brought down endless misery on myself—that matters not; but oh, I will not cause them further suffering. I will no longer wring the heart of my gentle mother, who has so often prayed for her erring child."[3]

Irony is at once evident in Wharton's own restrained tone and the novel's deliberate lack of Christian resolution. Wharton has *not* entirely put the plot to "uses so different" from Grace Aguilar's, for besides using the title (a "titular allusion") as a structural element, she borrowed given names for Anne Clephane and her best friend, the "disagreeable" Lilla Gates, from the original. Both Annes and Lillas had stern fathers and neglectful mothers. Both Annes are secretive about their love affairs and have intimate girlfriends who, their mothers fear, might negatively influence their morals.

While Kate worries that her daughter won't confide in her, Aguilar's novel insists on an openness between parent and child that is tyrannically inquisitive.

Caroline's sister, Emmeline, has written a private letter to a girlfriend expressing some secret sorrows: " 'With me, dearest,' [says Mrs. Hamilton to her
daughter] 'there must be no control, no reserve; if there be the least appearance
of either, you will inflict more pain on my heart than from your infancy you
have ever done, for I shall think my own counsels have alienated from me the
confidence of my child.' "[4] With the complete approval of the author, Mrs.
Hamilton demands to read all of her daughter's mail. But Wharton's Anne
Clephane is not about to have *her* privacy invaded, nor is her mother willing
to invade it, a circumstance that creates perilous psychological mysteries as
well as "pain on" Kate's heart. The black-and-white world of Grace Aguilar is
replaced by one in which there is extreme danger of "mother and daughter
[becoming] like two ghosts in a gray world of disenchantment" (*MR* 140), a
world of loneliness and desolation for both. The word "desolation" is key.

On 9 June 1925 Wharton wrote to Margaret Chanler, "No one else has
noticed 'desolation is a delicate thing,' or understood that the key is there."[5]
"Desolation is a delicate thing" is a structural allusion to the epigram by Percy
Bysshe Shelley on the title page, echoed in Wharton's comment that "as my
work reaches its close, I feel so sure that it is either nothing, or far more than
they know. . . . And I wonder, a little desolately, which." The epigram is from
Shelley's *Prometheus Unbound* (*Prometheus* I, l. 772). The Chorus of Spirits
asks "Hast thou beheld the form of Love?" (*Prometheus* I, l. 763). The Fifth
Spirit responds that she saw the "Shape" of love:

> His footsteps paved the world with light—but as I
>    past 'twas fading
> And hollow Ruin yawned behind. Great Sages bound
>    in madness
> And headless patriots and pale youths who perished
>    unupbraiding,
> Gleamed in the Night I wandered o'er—till thou, O
>    King of sadness,
> Turned by thy smile the worst I saw to recollected
>    gladness.
>    [*Prometheus* I, ll. 767-71]

To this the Sixth Spirit responds, "Ah, sister! Desolation is a delicate thing"
to those who are "soothed to false repose," to those who "Dream visions of
aerial joys, and call the monster, Love, / And wake, and find the shadow Pain"
(*Prometheus* I, ll. 778-79).

Here in Shelley's *Prometheus Unbound,* a second structural allusion, is the
summary of the *surface* of Wharton's psychological plot with repetition of the
theme of pain to be featured also in *Twilight Sleep.* Kate beholds the *shape* of

love in her affair with Chris Fenno, but whatever love he has for her fades, and as an excuse to leave her, he, *pale youth*, volunteers for war. Kate is abandoned to desperate loneliness with only *recollected gladness* to ease her pain. When she reunites with her daughter, she is *soothed to false repose*, which turns to *desolation* and *pain* when she meets Chris again only to discover his love for Anne. That revelation causes not only jealousies and fears of social *ruin* but also repetition of the abandonments of Kate by Fenno and of Anne by Kate.

If *Prometheus Unbound* can be said to have a companion piece, it is Percy Shelley's *The Cenci*, a psychological drama about father-daughter incest. This play, an intraauthorial allusion, descended from a Renaissance revenge tragedy in which Count Cenci's rape of his daughter and subsequent imprisonment of her in a torture chamber drives her to order him murdered. *The Cenci* is the first of a series of branching thematic allusions under the umbrella theme of incest, two branches to father-daughter incest (older and younger generations), and one each to mother-child incest, uncle-niece incest, and brother-sister incest.

The matter of psychological father-daughter incest alluded to in *The Cenci* arises through Kate's feeling that though Chris was not Anne's father, he should have been if passion were the criterion. Therefore, in Kate's mind, if Anne marries Chris, she would commit incest with her "father."

According to Stuart Curran (to simplify a lengthy discussion),[6] *Prometheus* and *The Cenci* pose parallel problems, but whereas Shelley's solution to the evils of *Prometheus Unbound* is forgiveness, his solution to the incestuous (and other) evils of *The Cenci* is murder (although Beatrice triumphs by forgiving everyone before her execution): "Canst thou forgive even the unforgiving, / When their full hearts break thus, thus!" (*Cenci*, act 5, scene 3, ll. 105–106). The dark undersurface of *The Mother's Recompense* contains the source of Kate's incestuous ghost and the "struggle" between alternative solutions identical to Shelley's: Kate can solve her dilemma either by "murdering" Anne—"To destroy Anne's happiness seemed an act of murderous cruelty" (*MR* 218)—or by forgiving her and taking responsibility for the past actions, *and* the coincidences that resulted from them, that placed her in the situation she finds so intolerable. Of Chris's illness, "she felt herself responsible, almost guilty" (*MR* 174); and she recognizes the need to forgive herself when she tells Fred Landers at the end of the novel, "I'd never really forgiven myself for leaving Anne" (*MR* 256). She forgives Anne's temper and accusations. The problem remains why, as her daughter asks, if everyone is forgiven, must Kate go away? (*MR* 227). Part of the reason is that Kate Clephane, like Beatrice, cannot bear to witness those things that raise a "formless horror" in her mind:

I who can feign no image in my mind
Of that which has transformed me. I, whose

thought
Is like a ghost shrouded and folded up
In its formless horror.

[*Cenci,* act 3, scene 1, l. 10]

The horror of incest is a psychological "ghost" in the sense that incest both does and does not exist. No physical incest has occurred, or will occur, since there are no blood relatives except mother and daughter. But incest seems no less real for its existence in Kate's subconscious: "Was she jealous of her daughter? Was she physically jealous? Was that the real secret of her repugnance, her instinctive revulsion? Was that why she had felt from the first as if some incestuous horror hung between them?" (*MR* 221).

An allusion to Mary Shelley's *Frankenstein* creates a monster in Kate's mind similar to reptilian monsters in *The Custom of the Country.* Each Shelley "calls the Monster Love." In an accidentally Frankensteinian experiment, Anne "creates" her mother when she invites her to resume the role she had abandoned eighteen years earlier. Desolate at her desertion by Chris Fenno, Kate is "born again" when she disembarks from the ship in New York (*MR* 56). As Kate explains to Fred Landers: " 'Anne has told me that her experiment has been a mistake.' 'What experiment?' 'Having me back.' 'Is that what she calls it—an experiment?' " (*MR* 164). Eventually, when Anne tries to relinquish Chris, she and Kate travel but like Furies their desolation accompanies them because Anne is now the Fury: "The girl stood before her like a blanched Fury" (*MR* 159).

Wharton's descriptions echo Victor Frankenstein's anguished journeys through the Alps: "Fantastic shapes of heavy, leaf-shadows on blinding whiteness. Torrents of blue and lilac and crimson foaming over the branches of unknown trees. Azure distances, snow-peaks, silver reefs, and an unbroken glare of dead-white sunshine merging into a moonlight hardly whiter. Was there never any night, real, black, obliterating, in all these dazzling latitudes in which two desperate women had sought refuge?" (*MR* 147). Finally, Fred Landers's comment about Lilla—which Kate's experiences all refute—that her family "all have a theory Lilla need only be happy to be good" (*MR* 113), alludes to the Creature: "Make me happy, and I shall again be virtuous. . . . it is in your power to recompense me."[7]

M. H. Abrams's statement that *Prometheus Unbound* expresses the theme of the human need for love but negates personal responsibility for the fulfillment of that need applies equally well to *Frankenstein* and *The Mother's Recompense.* In both novels the "theme of the human need for love fulfills what is incomplete and reintegrates what has been divided, both in the individual psyche and in the social order."[8]

The surface division between mother and daughter is caused by an unusual (and some say artificial) twist of plot that results in their shared lover. The psychologically complex "incest" theme develops this way: Kate must be responsible for the consequences of two major actions in her life, the decision to leave her husband and three-year-old daughter for a lover and, some years later, the decision to have a secret affair with Chris Fenno. The result of the first decision is that Kate feels severely the "insatiable longing to be back on the nursery floor with Anne." She suffers the deprivation of her baby's love (*MR* 58) so attempts to supply it through her affair with Fenno. Chris, with his appropriately androgynous name, is a dozen years younger than Kate, who is old enough to be, if not his mother, at least his mother-in-law. Though he awakens her mature sexuality, her mind fuses the idea of his love with the idea of her love for her child: "Why, in the very act of thinking of her daughter, had she suddenly strayed away into thinking of Chris? It was the first time it had happened to her to confront the two images, and she felt as if she had committed a sort of profanation" (*MR* 73).

The "father-daughter" (Chris-Anne) "incest" branches to a "mother-child" incest theme. In so closely associating her love for Anne with her love for Chris, Kate has psychologically "committed" incest with her own child, an idea that naturally she cannot face consciously: "And of course she'd never been that dreadful kind of woman they called a 'baby-snatcher'. . . . " (*MR* 9, Wharton's ellipses). Furthermore, she is disgusted by Lilla, who wants a key to Anne's studio to bring her "little boys" to the "kindergarten" (*MR* 79).

When remembering her anguish at separation from her child, Kate recalls attempting "a midnight visit (inspired by *Anna Karénine*)" (*MR* 15). The midnight visit hints at mother-child incest, for in Tolstoy's novel Anna sneaks a visit to her eldest child, Serezha, on his birthday, but when confronted there by Karenin, she rushes away. "Upon the first child, though by an unloved man, all Anna's unsatisfied capacity for loving was lavished."[9] Like Kate Clephane, Anna Karenina does not share her feelings about her child with her lover: "She herself had hidden from him [Vronsky] all that concerned her son."[10] Tolstoy's novel ends with Anna Karenina throwing herself in the path of an oncoming train. In her agony, too, Kate is about to rush in front of a vehicle: "What else was there to do but to go straight to the river, or to some tram line with its mortal headlights bearing straight down on one? One didn't have to have a hat and cloak to go out in search of annihilation . . . " (*MR* 222, Wharton's ellipses). But fate works both ways—she is stopped by the doorbell.

Anna's surreptitious visit to her son (repeated in Kate's concealed attempt to see Anne in Canada) contains the subtlest hint of Anna's incestuous love for Serezha and a more overt case of erotic substitution of son for lover. Kate asks herself, "Why, in the very act of thinking of her daughter, had she suddenly strayed away into thinking of Chris?" (*MR* 73). The answer is that when Kate accepts her daughter's invitation to return home, Anne takes Chris's place and becomes like a lover providing all the things husbands do—flowers, jewelry, home, social position. In addition, Anne is tall, with an "air of boyish aloofness" (*MR* 54), and in being taller seems to hang above Kate (*MR* 45), like the portrait of Beatrice Cenci that hangs across the hall over the bed that she once shared with Anne's father (*MR* 36). "Kate was frightened, sometimes" by the likeness of her love for her daughter to "that other isolated and devouring emotion which her love for Chris had been" (*MR* 82).

As if all these "incestuous" associations were not enough, Anne becomes a "mother" to Kate, further intensifying the psychologically incestuous relationship by creating a "child-mother" incest theme: "It was so sweet to be compelled, to have things decided for one, to be told what one wanted and what was best for one. . . . She liked better still to be 'mothered' in that fond blundering way the young have of mothering their elders" (*MR* 46–47).

Here a new twist develops. The mother-child incest theme dissolves into a brother-sister incest theme. Since, psychologically, both Chris and Anne are her children and both are her lovers, Kate is "committing incest" with both, and they would be committing sibling incest by marrying, a theme that occurs in *Frankenstein* when Victor plans to marry Elizabeth, who, though unrelated by blood, has been raised as his sister.

The result of Kate's second decision, the decision to have an affair with Fenno, is the intervention of the Furies, another name Wharton sometimes uses for the Fates that cause coincidences and accidents like Anne's engagement to Chris. In choosing her conclusion, Wharton seems to indicate that, unfair as it may seem, Kate's moral obligation is to take responsibility for the unexpected results of her actions, as well as those that can be foreseen, regardless that those actions are motivated by deep personal need.

Wharton creates a "ghastly labyrinth" (*MR* 155) of incestuous relationships in which this and other ideas filtering up from the subconscious, fusing past and present, blurring sexual and generational identities, are ghosts that Kate (like Newland Archer in his situation) is not endowed with the gift of seeing. At the beginning of the novel she is blind to them in much the same way that people can be "haunted" by the Furies of guilt, fear of the past, memories, or fear of an unknown future.

In the familiar genre, the ghost is often the spirit of a departed person who has one important secret to communicate before its soul can rest. This is also the case for Kate Clephane, whose secret is sexual. As the novel opens, she receives a telegram: " 'Mrs. Clephane dead—.' A shiver ran over her. *Mrs. Clephane dead?* Not if Mrs. Clephane knew it! Never more alive than today. . . . What was the meaning of this grim joke?" (*MR* 7–8). But the telegram announces the death of her mother-in-law, a fact that blurs the difference between illusion and reality, "effacing even Chris as though he were the thinnest of ghosts, and the cable in her hand a cockrow" (*MR* 8). When she decides to go home, it "seemed a part of the general unreal rapture that even the money-worry should have vanished" (*MR* 17). But the secret of her affair with Chris is not effaced, and she cannot find a way to explain it to either her daughter or her old family friend, Fred Landers. Still, in her happy new life it seems not to matter.

As book 1 closes, however, Kate sees the "objectionable person," Lilla Gates, "lingering in that deserted path [that] had called up old associations. She remembered meetings of the same kind—but was it her own young figure she saw fading down these far-off perspectives? Well—if it were, let it go! She owned no kinship with that unhappy ghost. . . . she walked on again out of that vanishing past into the warm tangible present" (*MR* 84). Why does Kate object so strongly to Lilla? Because Lilla is Kate's doppleganger, a double whose love of "little boys" mirrors Kate's affair with Chris and even her concern for the little lame boy who, as the novel opens, sends her violets, a romantic gesture formerly reserved for Chris.

Time merges at the vision of Lilla, the intangible past, fading and vanishing as Kate watches: "The shock of the encounter still tingling in her, he [Chris] remained far off, almost imponderable, less close and importunate than her memories of him. It was as if his actual presence had exorcised his ghost. But now— He had not vanished" (*MR* 91).

When Kate unexpectedly meets Chris with Anne in Anne's art studio, the secret rises to the surface: "Silence fell. Kate struggled to break it, feeling that she was expected to speak, to say something, anything; but there was an obstruction in her throat, as if her voice were a ghost vainly struggling to raise its own grave-stone" (*MR* 103). Finally, secrecy assured by her stunned inability to speak, she herself fades away when she accidentally encounters Chris and Anne in a lovers' embrace: "Kate Clephane stood behind them like a ghost" (*MR* 221). The "real self" that Kate claims developed from her relationship with Chris is canceled by his love for her daughter, and it fades into a shade.

The secrecy into which she finds herself forced by her moral and social scruples also serves to contribute to the inadequacy of her sense of identity. "It made her feel like a ghost to be so invisible and inaudible" (*MR* 221). In explaining to Fred Landers her feelings about being with Anne, Kate comments (like Ellen Olenska) that returning to New York was "like dying and going to heaven" (*MR* 256).

She feared finding the "key to the mystery" because it would dissolve her sense of identity as a youthful, desirable woman and as a mother. In her love for Chris, she stands on the line between generations, an aging lover, a banished mother, uncertain who she is. The latchkey becomes a symbol for the prison of an uncertain identity. Kate hates the sound of her overbearing husband's latchkey and tries to escape it on her lover's yacht. She is angered when Lilla wants a latchkey to the studio that symbolizes Anne's identity, and whenever she uses her own key to Anne's studio, she fears finding Chris present, an integral part of Anne. Kate has a final chance to create an identity as Fred Landers's wife, but inexplicably returns to Europe and continually refuses his renewed proposals.

This denouement has puzzled and dismayed readers past and present. A review of a recent edition of *The Mother's Recompense* expresses typical annoyance: "Mrs. Wharton demonstrates little compassion for her heroine in the end—using a complicated succession of plot twists to sacrifice her, quite unnecessarily, to some abstract sense of tragedy that has little to do with the compelling novel that went before."[11] And Kate's failure to marry the kind, suitable Fred Landers, who loves her even knowing the truth about her past, has irritated critics like Auchincloss, who comments in his introduction, "I impenitently fail to see why Fred Landers and Kate Clephane would not have happier and better lives married to each other" (*MR* xii). The ending, however, has nothing to do with an "abstract sense of tragedy" but everything to do with the "novel that went before."

Wharton was equally annoyed at some readers. She knew that in the context of allusions to incest themes the conclusion makes perfect sense. In May, 1925 she wrote to John Hugh-Smith that "one reviewer . . . explained the title . . . by saying that Kate's reward for sparing her daughter useless pain is 'the love of a good man'!" As Wolff interprets this comment, Wharton was upset because the reviewer in question was "dangerously close to the mark."[12] In allusions to brother-sister incest in Shakespeare and uncle-niece incest in the Bible, however, clues to the meaning of this conclusion show that Wharton's indignation was justified.

First of all, Kate cannot marry Fred Landers, so quick with his wallet, because she feels that the Furies cannot be bought and that trying to marry him would reduce to ghostliness whatever sense of identity she has left: "With the little wood-fire playing on the hearth, and this honest kindly man looking down at her, how safe and homelike the room seemed! Yet her real self was not in it at all, but blown about on a lonely wind of anguish, outside in the night" (*MR* 166–67). Second, Fred is too fraternal. "As he blinked at [Kate] with kindly brotherly eyes she saw in their ingenuous depths the terror of the man who has tried to buy off fate by one optimistic evasion after another" (*MR* 40). He gives her a "sense of a brotherly reassuring presence" (*MR* 165). To reinforce the sense of Fred as a brother, Anne calls him "Uncle" and flirts with him in "half-daughterly, half-feminine ways" (*MR* 62). Psychologically, marriage to Fred would seem like sibling incest, impossible for Kate to bear.

Referring to Anne's coming marriage to Chris, Fred worries that between

Anne's "violence of feeling" and Chris's determination to marry her, Chris might succeed in winning over Kate's opposition by "taking advantage" of Anne—by making her pregnant. Kate thinks not. "Well, all's well that end's well," he says (*MR* 199). Here Wharton's nearly limitless sense of literary depth and irony arises from Helena's speech in Shakespeare's play:

> You are my mother, madam; would you were—
> So that my lord, your son, were not my brother—
> Indeed my mother! Or were you both our mothers
> I care no more for than I do for heaven,
> So I were not his sister. Can't no other
> But, I your daughter, he must be my brother?
>
> [*All's Well*, act 1, scene 3, lines 162–67]

To Kate the lawful marriage to Fred would be as much a "sinful fact" as if they were actually related by blood:

> Let us assay our plot, which, if it speed,
> Is wicked meaning in a lawful deed,
> And lawful meaning in a lawful act,
> Where both not sin, and yet a sinful fact.
>
> [*All's Well*, act 3, scene 7, lines 44–47]

The entire set of thematic clusters of literary allusions to incestual relationships is held together by an "umbrella allusion" that includes all forms of sinful facts. Emphasis on the sinful incestuousness of nonblood family relationships, and an additional reason Kate cannot marry Fred, can be found in the Old Testament tradition of Leviticus 18:7–18, including the commandment that a man like Fred "shall not have intercourse with [his] sister," and a man like Chris "shall not have intercourse with a woman and also with her daughter." Marriage as well as intercourse is forbidden in the various incestuous relationships described, which include relationships by marriage as well as by blood. Such things are "abhorrent," "abominable," "defiling," and "shameful" to the authors of Leviticus. This is the tradition into which Kate had been indoctrinated as a member of Episcopalian old New York society: "Nothing shocks the young people nowadays—not even the Bible," remarks Kate's sister-in-law (*MR* 77).

Biblical allusions abound. As in Ruth 1:16, Kate had gone from her mother-in-law's house, saying to herself, "Thy gods shall *not* be my gods" (*MR* 106) and, as in Leviticus 16:8 "cast her lot elsewhere" (*MR* 165). Now she must live with the consequences of that decision. Dr. Arklow said it "as positively as if he were handing down a commandment from Sinai: 'The daughter must be told' " (*MR* 214). But it is Leviticus that Dr. Arklow echoes when he tells Kate that the situation is an "abomination" (*MR* 211, 214). The author recognizes the good intentions of the priest and is sympathetic, but like Camillo, the priest in *The Cenci*, he is impotent in the matter just because he is a Christian. But even though the arc of his spiritual light is low, the cleric suddenly modifies his position: The daughter must be told unless Kate has "the courage to *keep silence—always*." Sometimes there must be compromises—"adjustments in the balance of evil," he says, and "the thing in the world I'm most afraid of is sterile pain" (*MR* 211-12, italics added). As a mother who had labored to give birth—fertile pain—Kate Clephane intuitively understands. He has raised "The Sphinx," Emerson's "under pain pleasure / Under pleasure pain lies / Love works at the center" (*Sphinx*, stanza 13, ll. 99-100), so she chooses a life in Europe where she needs neither to disclose the truth nor live a lie. Kate chooses to suffer pain because of the pleasure of her love for her daughter. This sacrifice of mother for the sake of her daughter's fertility is an important development among the clues to the code. When the novel concludes with Kate living on the Riviera, she does have a recompense, one thing she didn't have before, a bridge between Europe and America. Fred had "held out his hand" to Kate, creating a bridge "across the whole width of his traditions and convictions; and she had blessed him for it, and stood fast on her own side" (*MR* 272).

In the world of Kate Clephane's Riviera, cast off Americans play at bridge. Only the indomitable Mrs. Minity has American connections that satisfy her, in particular a niece from Bridgeport who sends her brandied peaches (a delicacy also favored by Miss Painter in *The Reef*). In fact, Kate's transporting symbol is the view of the Brooklyn Bridge from Anne's studio: "A single wide window overlooking the reaches of the Sound all jewelled and netted with lights, the fairy span of the Brooklyn Bridge, and the dark roof-forest of the intervening city. It all seemed strangely significant and mysterious in that disguising dusk—full of shadows, distances, invitations. Kate leaned in the window, surprised at this brush of the wings of poetry" (*MR* 78).

Kate's view exactly describes two famous paintings by Joseph Stella (1877-1946), *The Bridge*, a stained glass window interpretation of the Brooklyn Bridge on the fifth panel of *New York Interpreted* (1922), and *Brooklyn Bridge* (1918-1919), both abstract in mode. These paintings of Stella's, as well as his *Battle of Lights, Coney Island* (1903) and *Luna Park at Night* (1913-1914), for example, burst with kaleidoscopic illumination.[13] Wharton probably saw his paintings either in Paris or in New York on the trip she made just prior to the composition of *The Mother's Recompense*.

After Kate absorbs the beauty of the view, Anne responds to a comment of Lilla's as to the sparsity of furniture: "Oh, the furniture's all outside—and the pictures too" (*MR* 79), a comment that reflects the minimalist approach of the new generation of modern artists and interior designers such as the decorator Elsie de Wolfe, who transformed the principles of Wharton and Codman's *Decoration of Houses* into practical reality in the fashionable drawing rooms of New York.

Although forgiving people like Kate's relatives, the *Tressleton's*, have provided the framework for the bridge, only Anne has managed to span Europe and America (even Asia by choosing Oriental decor) by combining her modern art with her old-fashioned graceful manners: "If this were indeed a mannerless age, how miraculously Anne's manners had been preserved!" (*MR* 52).

Stella's stained glass illuminations create a bridge between the impressionists and the cubists, but the fragmentation represented by modern abstract art is not as well reflected in the fragmented communication between generations in *The Mother's Recompense*. Of Anne's friends, Kate thinks, "They had all . . . far more interests and ideas than had scantily furnished her own youth, but all so broken up, scattered, and perpetually interrupted" (*MR* 53). Their indecipherible ideas and actions lead to a sense of kaleidoscopic unreality: "The group was so continually breaking up and reshaping itself, with the addition of new elements, and the departing scattered in so many different directions, and towards destinations so unguessable, that once out of sight they seemed to have no more substance or permanence than figures twitching by on a film" (*MR* 262).

Kate realizes that in part the fragmentation has something to do with the newly "altered world" (*MR* 43) caused by the Great War. Apparently commenting on modernism, as she would again in *Hudson River Bracketed*, Wharton emphasizes Emerson's themes of "eterne alteration" when Kate recalls how Chris and others his age "thought it their duty as 'artists' or 'thinkers' to ignore the barbarian commotion. It was only in 1915, when Chris's own attitude was mysteriously altered. . . . He often said that his opinions hadn't altered, but that there were times when opinions didn't count . . . when a fellow just had to *act*. It was her own secret thought . . . but with Chris—could one ever tell?" (*MR* 43, Second ellipses Wharton's).

With him she is a "little less sure of her speech than her thoughts . . . the smile in his eyes used to break up her words into little meaningless splinters that she could never put together again till he was gone" (*MR* 87). Something was missing in their common understanding of literary or other allusions: "It was no use to murmur disjointed phrases to herself, conjure him away with the language of her new life, with allusions and incantations unknown to him; he just stood there and waited. . . . she would have liked to draw the old tattered glamour over him; but there must always have been rents and cracks in it" (*MR* 91–92).

Thus the allusions of the novel perform three functions: structural, thematic, and "umbrella." The shade of Grace Aguilar and her angelic mother provide an exterior structural allusion for the mother-daughter plot, and a second structural allusion to Percy Shelley's *Prometheus Unbound* provides an internal frame for the interior psychological plot. Like most of the other allusive techniques discussed here, it is Wharton's alone. Thematic allusions to *The Cenci* and the *Portrait of Beatrice Cenci* set up the father-daughter incest, *Frankenstein* the brother-sister incest, *Anna Karenina* the hint of "mother-son" incest, and Leviticus contains all other possible combinations, including uncle-niece.

The "incestuous horror" is an Oedipal accident that seems to leave only two choices for Kate; one is the tortuous lovelessness experienced by Frankenstein's creature, and the other is a symbiotic incest that gives birth to further psychological monsters. Instead, however, Wharton suggests an oxymoronic compromise, a connected separateness between generations and traditions: "Often two people still in the act of exchanging tender or violent words are in reality at the opposite ends of the earth . . . the *centre* of her wretchedness seemed the point at which they were meant to meet" (*MR* 258, emphasis mine). If Fred crosses all the way over to the Riviera, there is no longer a bridge; together he and Kate would become outcasts in Europe. If Kate returns all the way to America, they become conspirators in lies. Kate's choice creates a bridge by which to compromise. Her Sphinx-like retreat from the psychological Furies of incest may not provide opportunities for intimate family love, but neither does it impose "sterile pain."

The novel reinforces clues already planted in the themes of *The House of Mirth* and *The Reef*. Like them, *The Mother's Recompense* ends (to readers) in an unsatisfactorily solved dilemma. Like *The House of Mirth* and *The Custom of the Country*, it features a suicide motif. Undine's childhood training was neglected when her parents relinquished their authority. By spoiling her, they indirectly destroyed the lives of those with whom she came in contact, like their grandson, Paul, and Ralph Marvell, who killed himself. This extreme is no more desirable than that of Grace Aguilar's controlling Mrs. Hamilton.

Like *The Reef, The Mother's Recompense* features pain and incest themes. Its plot, growing in part from the circumstances of abandonment, strengthens the "neglected child" theme: "It was eighteen years ago—that she had 'lost' Anne: 'lost' was the euphemism she had invented (as people called the Furies The Amiable Ones), because a mother couldn't confess, even to her most secret self, that she had willingly deserted her child" (*MR* 13). With the "fertile" pain of separation modified by a bridge of sacrifice and reconciliation between generations, Emerson's poem begins to seem like an umbrella over all of these novels.

Eterne alteration
    Now follows, now flies;
And under pain, pleasure—
    Under pleasure, pain lies.

    [*Sphinx,* stanza 13, ll. 99–100]

Next Wharton turns to *Twilight Sleep,* in which she drops the themes of insoluble dilemma and the bridge temporarily but adds further pieces to the neglected child puzzle and again highlights an important theme touched upon in *The Mother's Recompense,* the acceptance versus the refusal of pain.

# 7 | *Twilight Sleep*
## Generic Allusions

For critics eternally dissatisfied with the conclusions of Wharton's novels, whether the dilemma of *The Reef* or the "hackneyed," romantic ending of *The Glimpses of the Moon*, the indeterminate conclusion of *Twilight Sleep* is exasperating.[1] Readers complain of melodrama, of failed tragedy.[2] On the contrary, this ending makes a masterful use of a generic allusion to the detective story. Wharton, who kept a close eye on business, must have been fully aware of the contemporary popularity of detective stories, for *Twilight Sleep* was high on the best-seller list, "well ahead of Sir Arthur Conan Doyle's *The Casebook of Sherlock Holmes.*"[3]

We saw that *The Mother's Recompense* is constructed of a set of clustered allusions to categories of incest, held together by a generic allusion to the ghost story under an umbrella allusion to incest. *Twilight Sleep* refines the technique. This novel builds on a set of clustered allusions to religion (broadly defined), with branches to pain and sacrifice held together by a generic allusion to the detective story under a broader umbrella, a search for meaning.

What meaning can there be, for instance, in the sacrifice of children represented by the cluster of allusions to sacrificial daughters like Iphigenia, whose father attempts to sacrifice her at the behest of the gods? When he closes his eyes to stab her, the goddess Artemis substitutes a deer and whisks Iphigenia to an Aegean island. There Iphigenia serves as priestess in a temple in which foreigners are sacrificed. One day soldiers capture Iphigenia's brother, Orestes. A masterfully joyous recognition scene between brother and sister is followed by their escape for home. The allusion to *Iphigenia in Taurus* constitutes part of a cluster of thematic allusions to the sacrifice of children. Maisie Bruss's name is an allusion to Henry James's *What Maisie Knew,* a daughter sacrificed by parents pursuing sexual pleasure. (Ironically, Wharton's Maisie is a daughter who sacrifices for a mother dying of cancer.) A tale from Washington Irving's *The Alhambra,* and the story of Lucrezia Borgia (sacrificed by her father, an ignominious Pope, for political gain) form two more members of the cluster.

Furthermore, Wharton created a "cross-word puzzle" of names (*TW* 29), one solution to which is that PAIN is part of *PAulINe*'s name. Pain is part of the human condition, and Pauline's faddish reliance on sundry "religious heal-ers" has led her into a concept in conflict with Genesis 3:16: "Unto the woman he said, I will greatly multiply thy sorrow and thy conception, in sorrow thou shalt bring forth children." Later Pauline has the insight to note "how wicked she had been ever to doubt the designs of Providence," for Whom there is meaning in pain (*TW* 143). Most characters in *Twilight Sleep* adopt artificial methods to avoid pain, but in the world of the novel, death of the soul can be the only result of the avoidances of pain and sorrow because they are part of the plan of God—unless there is redeeming intervention.

Edith Wharton's novels never propose simple solutions to the problems presented, and *Twilight Sleep* is no exception, but the literary Sherlock finds that the solutions to the novel and the social problems Edith Wharton presents are similar. A line from *The Glimpses of the Moon* illustrates the particular detective metaphor that originates with Wharton: Susy had "grown interested in her charges . . . and the search for a clue to their methods . . . was as excit-ing to her as the development of a detective story" (*GM* 296). In fact, from this point forward, dilemmas are not quite so paradoxical, and the author begins to offer at least partial solutions culminating in *The Gods Arrive,* in which the first direct message emerges.

At the climax of the formula detective story, the main characters are gath-ered together at the scene of the crime. Likewise, at the conclusion of *Twilight Sleep,* Pauline Manford opens the door to her daughter-in-law's bedroom to find her son's wife, Lita, her husband, Dexter, and her ex-husband, Arthur Wyant, hovering stricken over the body of her daughter, Nona. Furthermore, in the earlier Dawnside episode, Wharton employs the language of the Perry Mason detective story. An attorney, Dexter agrees to take the "case" for the Lindons and conduct an "investigation" into the matter: "The Lindons have got their proofs" (*TW* 64). Pauline objects. "And how shall you feel if Nona is called as a witness—or Lita?" (*TW* 65). Readers become detectives, ex-pected to solve the deadly mystery as presented through the frightened eyes of Pauline Manford, whose concern during the entire novel has been, ironically, for "safety first." Yet the conclusion is not an actual "solution" but a puzzle to be solved. The dilemma is exactly who did what to whom? How? And why? And the answer is hiding under the cluster of literary allusions to *Faust.*

The general theme of *Faust* is Faust's willingness to sell his soul for magic rather than true wisdom. Allusions to Faust's dialogue with Care, a character in Goethe's *Faust* (part 2, act 5), "Twilight Sleep," "Safety First," and Euri-pides' *Iphigenia in Taurus* become a casebook of clues with which to begin solving the detective story we could call "The Mystery of the Sacrificial Daugh-ter." The novel focuses again on neglected children, incest, pain, poison, drugs, and hints of suicide, and the dilemma is a search for meaning, a puzzle that, this time, can be partially resolved.

Under the "umbrella" of the search for the meaning of life, a series of clusters of allusions to types of religion attempt to raise questions about the "mystery" of existential pain and how various denominations propose to "cure" or bear it. In particular, the novel discusses nature religions, Roman Catholicism, Oriental healers, deism, the idolization of fads, and religions of popular science. The novel also develops issues of atheism, Puritanism, and Kierkegaardian existentialism. The clusters join thematically in such a way as to suggest that Wharton believed—or at least the novel believes—that none of them is a solution in itself but that if all could unite ecumenically, they might have a dynamic impact.

The novel's climactic scene is preceded by a complex plot centering on Pauline Manford and her daughter, Nona. Pauline has been married twice, first to Arthur Wyant, whom she divorced when she found him "immoral," but by whom she had her first son, Jim. Her second husband is Dexter Manford, a successful attorney by whom she had her daughter, Nona. An intelligent, efficient, energetic woman, Pauline runs her life from the boudoir her children jokingly call her "office." The kind of woman who should be running a major corporation, she instead keeps herself so busy chasing fads promising worry-free eternal youth that her children must make appointments to see her. Because she loses touch with her family, she doesn't realize that Jim and Lita are on the verge of divorce, that Nona is clinically depressed, and that her husband is having an affair with his daughter-in-law, a biblically incestuous relationship that threatens the family's very foundation.

Three family "emergencies" occur at once. The first, Nona's emergency, is her fear for her brother's marriage combined with the breakup of her own love affair. The second emergency is the scandal that Lita and Nona's cousin, Bee, have been photographed dancing nude at "Dawnside," the "religious retreat" of one of Pauline's "healers," the Mahatma. Third, Arthur Wyant's cousin, Amalasuntha, who married into Italian royalty, has arrived from Europe planning to reform her attractive playboy son and to solve his indebtedness by marrying him to the beautiful Lita (already married to Jim) then sending them to Hollywood to get rich. Pauline begs Dexter to drop the Dawnside case, bribes Amalasuntha to keep her son, Michelangelo, in Italy, then tries to talk Lita out of divorcing Jim. Meanwhile, unnoticed by her mother, Nona becomes listless, pale, and thin.

Pauline feels she can efficiently solve all problems at once by taking her entire family to the country environment of her Cedarledge home for the Easter holidays. Their "idyllic" life there, however, is disturbed by the unexpected arrivals of Amalasuntha, who demands a party for her friend, a Roman Catholic cardinal; by the alcoholic ex-husband, who roams the house mumbling incoherently about "honor"; and by the constant absence of Dexter and Lita. Then the shooting occurs, followed by a coverup, and the family members disperse to "travel." Nona stays home, claiming, in a "refusal" much like Kate Clephane's, that she wants to enter a convent where no one believes in anything.

The sleuth rereading the novel to decipher the clues planted in its literary allusions quickly discovers that the final climactic scene is the last of the mysteries, not the first. Mysteries surround most characters, even Pauline and Nona, the sympathetic mother and daughter with whom the novel opens.

Nona attempts to see Pauline, who is driven by Furies to frantic activity, for in a free hour she might be forced to face herself. She fills every moment with causes, even causes that contradict one another, like the Birth Control Committee and the Mother's Day Meetings. Her whirlwind life aims at an impossible task, to "set the houses of others in order," yet she fails to recognize that her own is in serious disrepair (*TW* 7). For instance, Nona is verging on suicide, Lucrezia Borgia is poisoning the entire family, and everyone is in the "twilight sleep" of some pain-killing addiction. Meanwhile, in a reversal of *The Custom of the Country*, dangerous Goths threaten to invade, and perhaps destroy, American civilization.

Material for a plethora of the religious positions is found in the cluster of related allusions that comprise Dexter Manford's reading:

> He had got together a little library of his own in which Robert Ingersoll's lectures represented science, the sermons of the Reverend Frank Gunsaulus of Chicago, theology, John Burroughs, natural history, and Jared Sparks and Bancroft almost the whole of history. He had gradually discovered the inadequacy of these guides, but without ever having done much to replace them. . . . Mrs. Tallentyre's "Voltaire" had been a revelation. . . . After that, Manford decided to start in on a course of European history, and got as far as taking the first volume of Macaulay up to bed. [*TW* 58]

The allusion to Ingersoll is a layered allusion to an antireligious man who writes in praise of Voltaire's deist response to Pascal's Roman Catholic *Pensées*. Mrs. Tallentyre wrote a biography of Voltaire that emphasizes his stance against the Pope and the Jesuits. Gunsaulus was a Congregationalist Protestant whose collection of Japanese art is possibly Wharton's source for Lita's decor. Burroughs's God is Nature, and he writes about Whitman, to whom Wharton also alludes. Sparks and Bancroft both discuss Benjamin Franklin, a deist and American idol of hard work and self-sufficiency, while Macaulay's first volume contains an essay about Machiavelli, who was a rival of Cesare Borgia. This cluster of allusions to religion relates to the novel's theme of pain, which people often turn to religion to alleviate. The thematic allusion to *Faust* on the title page sets up motifs of religion, pain, sorrow, and sin and serves as a source for the novel's food, digestion, and sleep imagery.

Perhaps the primary question asked of religious and philosophical systems is how they propose to explain human pain, sorrow, and death. The lines quoted by Wharton on the title page translate as follows—(*Sorge,* the German word for "care," can also mean "sorrow"):

FAUST.     Und du, wer bist du?
SORGE.    Bin einmal da.
FAUST.     Entferne dich!
SORGE.    Ich bin am rechten Ort.

             [*Faust,* part 2, act 5, ll. 11421–24]

FAUST.     And you, who are you then?
CARE.     But here I am.
FAUST.     Go back, then!
CARE.     I am in my proper station.[4]

Care asks Faust whether he has never known worry, and Faust replies that he has always avoided it. Care says that nevertheless, he is always present, "Ever found though sought for never."

CARE.     One whom I can thus possess
             Finds the whole world profitless;
             . . . . . . . . . . . . . . . . . . . . . . . .
             He starves in plenty, and for him
             Weal and woe become mere whim;

Care says the man who avoids him is in a twilight sleep,

             Semi-sleeping with no rest,
             He is fixed in place and groomed
             For the hell to which he's doomed.

             [*Faust,* part 2, act 5, ll. 11420–86]

Like Faust, Pauline tries to avoid care, sorrow, pain, and the Furies, "to ignore sorrow and evil, 'think them away' as superannuated bogies, survivals of some obsolete European superstition unworthy of enlightened Americans, to whom plumbing and dentistry had given higher standards, and bi-focal glasses a clearer view of the universe—as if the demons the elder generation ignored, baulked of their natural prey, had cast their hungry shadow over the young" (*TW* 47–48).

Busy refusing pain, escaping the Furies of conscience and worry, Pauline is unable to learn, as readers may from another allusion to Faust, that Nona's world has shattered because of separate actions by her father and lover—her lover's refusal to divorce his Catholic wife, and Nona's ironic disgust about her father's affair with Lita. "The silence which had enclosed them as in a crystal globe had been splintered to atoms, and had left them stammering and exposed" (*TW* 175). This sense of Nona's disaster deepens when Wharton alludes to the following passage from *Faust:*

(The young monkeys have been playing with a large globe and now roll it forward):

> That is the world;
> Spun and twirled,
> It never ceases;
> It rings like glass,
> But hollow, alas,

[*Faust*, part 1, ll. 2402-2407]

At this moment Nona has experienced death and loss—death of a love affair, loss of respect for her father, and loss of access to her mother, all ingredients of clinical depression. As guardian of the family, Pauline not only misses a chance to comfort her daughter but also deprives herself of painful but important information about matters threatening the family unit.

Her confused explanation for her evidence is embedded in scrambled biblical dogma preached by Pauline Manford. Pauline advises avoiding pain because "being prepared to suffer is really the way to create suffering. And creating suffering is creating sin, because sin and suffering are really one. We ought to refuse ourselves to pain" (*TW* 324). Her theory includes the pain of childbirth: " 'Of course there ought to be no Pain . . . nothing but Beauty . . . It ought to be one of the loveliest, most poetic things in the world to have a baby,' Mrs. Manford declared, in that bright efficient voice which made loveliness and poetry sound like the attributes of an advanced industrialism, and babies something to be turned out in series like Fords" (*TW* 14, Wharton's ellipses). Pauline establishes her daughter-in-law in a "twilight sleep" maternity ward where the birth of Lita's son occurs in the half-drugged state recommended by the doctors who wrote the book of the novel's titular allusion, *Twilight Sleep*.[5]

In refusing pain Pauline also refuses to recognize her children's pain and by analogy the fallen state of mankind, the subject of Milton's *Paradise Lost*, a further source for the themes of pain and safety. In book 2, after the fallen angels have been cast into hell and the war council has been convened, Beliel debates Moloch's proposal to wage eternal war on heaven, saying in part that such a move could infuriate the Almighty into dispensing with them altogether:

> Thus repuls'd, our final hope
> Is flat despair: we must exasperate
> Th' Almighty Victor to spend all his rage,
> To be no more; sad cure; for who would lose,
> Though full of pain, this intellectual being

[*Paradise Lost*, book 2, ll. 143-45]

Mammon refutes this, however, proposing instead that they create a heaven in hell, "and work ease out of pain / Through labor and endurance," learn to "remove / The sensible of pain" (*Paradise Lost,* book 2, ll. 277–78) and "in safety best" . . . / Compose our present evils (*Paradise Lost,* book 2, ll. 280–81). Like Mammon, Pauline tries to create a kind of heaven on earth, a form of blasphemy against God's command that the fallen shall bear pain. So the price of Pauline's "heaven" is the well-being of her daughter as made clear by the cluster of thematic allusions to sacrificed daughters—Maisie, Iphigenia, Lucrezia Borgia, and Washington Irving's three princesses.

When Nona tries to warn her mother of problems in Jim's and Lita's marriage, she is turned away kindly by Maisie Bruss, Pauline's omniscient secretary. In discussion with Maisie, Nona learns that she and her mother had planned to visit Arthur Wyant at the same hour, but because her husband informs her of a public scandal that implicates the family, Pauline's visit must be postponed so that she can confer with Dexter instead.

"Well, then—for once 'A' must be sacrificed" (*TW* 23). A Victorian museum piece affectionately called "Exhibit A," Wyant is Pauline Manford's ailing first husband, for whom she has come to feel so "responsible" that he figures as "See A" on her crowded list. Nona prefers to visit Arthur separately, since she has begun meeting her married lover at Arthur's apartment. So Nona Manford and Arthur Wyant are both sacrificed by Pauline that day, and nineteen-year-old Nona is left with the responsibility for Wyant, a Fury that pursues her throughout the remainder of the novel:

> There were moments when Nona felt oppressed by responsibilities and anxieties not of her age, apprehensions that she could not shake off and yet had not enough experience of life to know how to meet. . . . the demons the elder generation ignored, baulked of their natural prey, had cast their hungry shadow over the young. After all, somebody in every family had to remember now and then that such things as wickedness, suffering and death had not yet been banished from the earth; and . . . perhaps [the] children had to serve as vicarious sacrifices. There were hours when Nona Manford, bewildered little Iphigenia, uneasily argued in this way. [*TW* 47–8]

Of course, this is the passage quoted by critics who find *Twilight Sleep* an unsatisfactory tragedy. They overlook that Euripides' play is not actually a tragedy, as Edith Wharton would have been fully aware.[6] Furthermore, the allusion to Iphigenia is only one of several allusions to sacrificed children.

Dexter's name and his relationship to Nona, Lita, and Bee come from the story that follows "The Tower of Las Infantas," "The Legend of the Three Beautiful Princesses" in Irving's *The Alhambra* (*TW* 152). The story is about Mohamad El Hayzari, "The Left-handed": "Some say he was so called on account of his being really more expert with his sinister than his dexter hand;

others, because he was prone to take everything by the wrong end, or, in other words, to mar wherever he meddled."[7] Mohamad El Hayzari's worst mistake is imprisoning his three beautiful daughters in a tower to keep them from men. Naturally, two of them run away, while the third dies young, so he loses them completely. Allegorically the same thing is about to happen in Wharton's story, so the allusion is also structural. It also raises a question, however, about Dexter's intentions with Lita. Are they "dexter," right, as they seem to Pauline, or are they "sinister," as they seem to Nona? On the novel's surface, Nona seems sacrificed by her mother, but the choice of these particular child sacrifice allusions is especially interesting. In each case a female child is sacrificed by a father figure, part of the mystery to be solved in light of Pauline's "sacrifices." Nevertheless, one variation occurs in the cluster in the several allusions to Herod's massacre of the innocents, whom Herod expected to include Christ. The meaning of that allusion becomes clear at the climactic conclusion.

The emergency that forced Pauline to "sacrifice" Nona and Arthur Wyant is created by the *Looker On*, a scandal sheet featuring a front-page picture of female nudes dancing at "Dawnside." Dawnside is the religious retreat of "the Mahatma," one of Pauline's favorite healers.[8] Among the dancers Dexter recognized Nona's cousin, Bee Lindon, and Lita Wyant, his step daughter-in-law. The headline, "Dawnside Co-Eds," suggests that the nude dancing was performed for a male audience. The mention of "veils" hints that the girls were doing the dance of the seven veils that Salome performed for Herod before claiming the head of John the Baptist. This story, in turn, is part of the "Herodias" for which a Hollywood producer entices Lita to audition (*TW* 86, 159).

The literary detective realizes that Nona was also among the dancers, though her parents are too detached from their daughter to form the inference. First, Nona's mother's example and her father's words had taught her to "revere activity as a virtue in itself" (*TW* 6). Second, the three girls' names are linked as dancers. As Maisie remarks, Nona dances away the nights with Lita (*TW* 9), and discussing the situation with her husband, Pauline remembers that "Bee and Nona have been intimate since they were babies, and Bee is always at Lita's" (*TW* 65). She also casually recalls taking Nona to see the Mahatma: " 'Nona has attended his eurythmic classes at our house, and gone to his lectures with me: at one time they interested her intensely. . . . I mean to take a rest-cure at Dawnside in March.' She gave the little playful laugh with which she had been used, in old times, to ridicule the naughtiness of her children" (*TW* 65–6). Ironically, Dexter Manford thinks, "Fancy comparing that degenerate fool of a Bee Lindon to his Nona, and imagining that 'bringing-up' made the difference!" (*TW* 62). Nevertheless, after visiting Arthur Wyant, Nona decides to go dancing: "After an hour's dancing she would feel better, more alive and competent" (*TW* 54). But "dancing" at the cabaret involves drinking, drugs, and degeneracy. In a later scene a Hollywood producer suggests that

Nona remove her clothes to audition: "Don't this lady dance?" . . . "Miss Manford? Bet she does! Come along, Nona; shed your togs and let's show Mr. Klawhammer here present that Lita's not the only peb—" (*TW* 90).

Dexter Manford resolves to "look after Lita" to deflect her attention from Dawnside. Though she must grope "for a careless voice" (*TW* 124), Nona tells her lover that her father is "looking after Lita. He probably found out at the last minute that Jim couldn't come, and made up his mind to replace him. Isn't it splendid, how he's helping us? I know he loathes this sort of place—and the people she's with. But he told me we oughtn't to lose our influence on her, we ought to keep tight hold of her—" (*TW* 175). Of course, Nona has already deciphered several clues to the fact that Dexter and Lita are having an affair, leaving her to carry not only her own burdens but also those of Pauline, Jim, and Arthur Wyant.

Arthur "had developed, rather early, a queer sort of nervous hypochondria —[a] cousin came downstairs and nursed him" (*TW* 41). Nona meets the usually invisible cousin Eleanor: "Poor Exhibit A! I'm sorry he's ill again." "He's been—imprudent. But the worst of it's over" (*TW* 41). After visiting Arthur, Nona and Stanley Heuston leave together. Stan wants to discuss Arthur, but Nona becomes apprehensive. " 'Why; what's the matter?' . . . 'Haven't you noticed? He looks like the devil. He's been drinking again'. . . . There it was—all the responsibilities and worries always closed in on Nona! But this one, after all, was relatively bearable" (*TW* 51). For all of her "sense of responsibility" to Arthur, Pauline has not focused on his drinking, so this burden, too, falls on Nona who, at nineteen, is too young for it: "All these tangled cross-threads of life, inextricably and fatally interwoven; how were a girl's hands to unravel them?" (*TW* 217). The responsibilities pile too high, leading Nona to subtle, easily missed thoughts of suicide. But the suicide theme is supported by a literary allusion to the atheistic Ingersoll.

Now besides worrying about Jim and Lita, her father's infidelities, the Dawnside scandal in which she may be implicated, and Arthur's drinking, Nona also worries about her affair with a married man. She and Stanley go to the cabaret, where first Nona is shocked to spot her father with Lita, then argues with Stanley about her unwillingness to sleep with him as long as he is married, so in retribution he announces that he will live publicly with Cleo Merrick. The name of that amorata can be understood as an allusion to the suicide of Cleopatra in *Antony and Cleopatra*. As a consequence Nona ends the affair: "She had made her great, her final, refusal. She had sacrificed herself, sacrificed [Stanley] Heuston, to the stupid ideal of an obstinate woman [his wife, Agnes] who managed to impress people by dressing up her egotism in formulas of philanthropy and piety" (*TW* 210).

But Nona has not made her final sacrifice. The combinations of burdens, fears, and losses—her entanglement in the "fatally interwoven" cross-threads of life—has resulted in suicidal depression: "The fact that she judged and still loved showed that her malady was mortal. 'Oh, well—it won't last; nothing lasts for our lot,' she murmured to herself without conviction. 'Or at the worst it will only last as long as I do; and that's a date I can fix as I choose' " (*TW* 167). Wharton's earlier allusion to Ingersoll is pertinent here. Ingersoll was the well-known atheist who (in his essay "Is Suicide a Sin?") argued that it is not: "The old idea was that 'God' made us and placed us here for a purpose, and that it was our duty to remain until He called us. The world is outgrowing this absurdity. What pleasure can it give 'God' to see a man devoured by a cancer? . . . If 'God' determined all births and deaths, of what use is medicine, and why should doctors defy, with pills and powders, the decrees of 'God'?"[9]

Ingersoll's point is emphasized by Pauline's avoidance of Maisie's mother, who has cancer (though Nona visits), and by the novel's language of medicine and healing: "What ails Nona?"

Of course the illnesses are moral, but the novel is supporting neither an atheistic suicidal point of view nor the Puritan hellfire and brimstone that so frighten Pauline. Ingersoll describes it: "Deny the dogma [hell] that fills the endless years with pain. They ought to know now that this dogma is utterly inconsistent with the wisdom, the justice, the goodness of their God. They ought to know that their belief in hell, gives to the Holy Ghost—the Dove—the beak of a vulture, and fills the mouth of the Lamb of God with the fangs of a viper."[10] When Nona is summoned by her lover's wife, Aggie (Agnes, from L. *agnus*, lamb), she is in a kind of hell: "Nona's nerves were beginning to jump and squirm like a bundle of young vipers" (*TW* 238). Pauline finally notices something not quite right with Nona, that she is becoming thin and drawn, and wonders vaguely whether the change has some connection with Stanley Heuston's disgraceful behavior, but she fails to understand the extremely dangerous nature of Nona's situation or that it is caused by parental neglect. A cluster of thematic allusions to the search for relief from life's anguish, in religions like Puritanism and Roman Catholicism and in pseudoreligions like atheism and science, make the point.

Pauline's inability to face her own pain and that of her family stems from psychological repression of her own fallenness, of sex, and of death (represented by her own aging and Maisie's dying mother). Always she is associated with wintry, end-of-life colors: silver, blue, white, and mauve, the coolness of which seems to suggest frigidity. In the words of Emerson's "The Sphinx," "cold shuddered the sphere" of her world, but Pauline continues to hope for warmth. When Dexter asks Pauline to cancel an important dinner party to spend time alone with him, she thinks he wants an intimate evening, so she dresses carefully in "the mauve tea-gown, the Chinese amethysts, and those silver sandals that made her feet so slender. She looked at herself with a sigh of pleasure" and ordered dinner in the boudoir (*TW* 198). Pauline is not frigid,

merely paralyzed by ignorance: "If only she had known how to reveal the secret tremors that were rippling through her! There were women not half as
clever and tactful—not younger, either, nor even as good-looking—who
would have known at once what to say, or how to spell the mute syllables of
soul-telegraphy. . . . Intimacy, to her, meant the tireless discussion of facts. . . .
What paralyzed her was the sense that, apart from his profession, her husband
didn't care for facts" (*TW* 199–200). It evolves that Dexter is not interested in
a romantic evening. Rather, he wants to talk about "that fool Amalasuntha"
(*TW* 200) and her son Michelangelo, whose debts Dexter had committed
Pauline to pay on the condition that Amalasuntha keep him in Italy, away from
Lita and Hollywood. In the course of their conversation Pauline also realizes
that her husband has dropped the Dawnside investigation "for Jim's sake and
Lita's" (*TW* 206).

In this novel Amalasuntha, a Goth invader returning from Europe, is as
much a genuine threat as the uncouth invaders from the midwest in *The Custom of the Country*. Allusions to the Vikings, and to Sigmund Freud and Havelock Ellis (the best-known sexual behaviorists of the day), combine to suggest
that a preoccupation with science as religion leaves society vulnerable to an
attack by the "Goths," with their gods of sex, money, and the glamor represented by Hollywood. Shown a picture of Michelangelo in revealing bathing
trunks, she thinks how "such things disgusted her!" (*TW* 103).

Symptomatic of Pauline's repression is a preoccupation with the benefits
of science—plumbing, bathing, and cleanliness. She uses the word "disgust"
indiscriminately for both personal and moral dirt. She surveys Lita's filthy
nursery "with an air of ineffable disgust" (*TW* 34), lending irony to Emerson's
romantic depiction of the pure and innocent infant:

> The babe by its mother
>   Lies bathed in joy
> Glide its hours uncounted,
>   The sun is its toy
>     [*Sphinx*, stanza 6, ll. 41–44]

The concept of science as religion was being expressed in the 1920s in publi-
cations like Havelock Ellis's *The Task of Social Hygiene*, an intraauthorial allusion.[11]

"Existence is realized in its perfection under whatever aspect it is manifested. . . . Or, as Whitman put it, 'There will never be any more perfection
than there is now' " (*Task*, vii). Social hygiene focuses on perfection of the
environment: "Create the right environment and you have done all that is necessary" (*Task*, 392): "It is the task of this hygiene not only to make sewers, but
to re-make love. . . . At the one end social hygiene may be regarded as simply

the extension of an elementary sanitary code; at the other end it seems to some to have in it the glorious freedom of a new religion" (*Task,* vii). Dexter, hiding his plan to keep Lita convenient for an affair, pleads to try to "save" Lita using the same environmental argument of social hygienists: "A sudden light glared out at [Pauline]. It was for Jim's sake and Lita's that he had dropped the case— sacrificed his convictions, his sense of the duty of exposing a social evil!" Manford said of Lita's aunt, "Swine—! And that's the rotten atmosphere [Lita] was brought up in. But she's not bad, Pauline . . . there's something still to be done with her . . . give me time . . . time . . . " (*TW* 206, Wharton's ellipses).

This new "religion" of hygiene, plumbing, and sewers is a perfect outlet for Pauline and Dexter's Freudian repressions. Pauline's frantic activity serves to distract her from her marriage, while Dexter's repressions erupt in infidelities. Repression explains the couple's constant concern with plumbing, Dexter having installed a bathroom in his mother's house (*TW* 68). Pauline's worry about health is often expressed in terms of biological plumbing: "Standing before the tall threefold mirror in her dressing-room, she glanced into the huge bathroom beyond—which looked like a biological laboratory, with its white tiles, polished pipes, weighing machines, mysterious appliances for douches, gymnastics and 'physical culture' " (*TW* 20). She was terribly concerned that her son Jim adopt "regular habits. Not that Jim's irregularities had ever been such as the phrase habitually suggests" (*TW* 28). "Echoes of the Freudian doctrine, perhaps rather confusedly apprehended, had strengthened her faith in the salutariness of 'talking things over,' and she longed to urge this remedy again on Dexter; but the last time she had done so he had wounded her by replying that he prefered an aperient" (*TW* 134). Dexter's preference for a laxative and his decision to pay Michelangelo's debts are ways "to relieve himself" (*TW* 204) of responsibility, more indications of faith in purification by plumbing, that religion of science reinforced the allusion to Pontius Pilate's "washing his hands of the affair" (*TW* 203).

The care Pauline gives the environment of Cedarledge and her disgusted reaction to the misguided "Purist" environment of the house of Kitty Landish, Lita's aunt, are also part of the "religion" of scientific social hygiene. Pauline and Dexter encounter one another at Kitty's, each planning to discuss with her how to avoid a divorce between Jim and Lita. Like Pauline, Aunt Kitty tries to create a pure environment, but she interprets this ideal to mean that she should live exactly as science has shown the Vikings lived. Kitty is not intelligent enough to master even that strange concept, so that the "gods of Viking Court" turn out to be the money, sex, and glamor reflected in Lita's home. Visiting there, Dexter thinks, "That was the air in which Lita had grown up, those were the gods of Viking Court!" (*TW* 195). Kitty Landish offers no hope for Lita and Jim, because she is under the influence of Amalasuntha, and The

Vikings are uniting, for the original Amalasuntha was a Goth princess.[12] In this allusion history repeats itself by posing a serious threat to social stability.

Meanwhile Pauline decides that the solution to the marital problems between Jim and Lita is to entice them to Cedarledge (Pauline's country house in Connecticut) for Easter while Jim and Arthur go fishing for meaning in Nature. Dexter chooses vacation at Cedarledge to help "look after" Lita. If environment alone could solve moral problems as Havelock Ellis believed, the idyllic gardens of Cedarledge in spring would indeed represent a solution, and the climactic scene would not be possible. But "nature religion" also fails.

Another failure is self-medication for moral and psychological pain by busyness, drugs, alcohol, and promiscuous sex. Everyone in the novel is addicted to one or more of these poisons, to which a major clue is Wharton's allusion to the Borgias.

During the stay at Cedarledge, Pauline finds herself forced to throw a party for Amalasuntha because she discovers that in spite of bribery, her cousin is "importing" Michelangelo to act in a movie about Cesare Borgia. Amalasuntha brags about her son as Lita listens intently: "It's the type, you see: between ourselves, there's always been a rumour of Borgia blood on the San Fedele side. A naughty ancestress! Perhaps you've noticed the likeness? You remember that wonderful profile portrait of Caesar Borgia in black velvet? . . . it came out in 'Vogue'!" (*TW* 294–95). She continues, "Yes! I see Lita listening, and I know she agrees with me. . . . Lita! What a Lucrezia for his Caesar! But why look shocked, dear Dexter? Of course you know that Lucrezia Borgia has been entirely rehabilitated? I saw that also in 'Vogue.' She was a perfectly pure woman—and her hair was exactly the colour of Lita's" (*TW* 296).[13]

The Borgia legend was romanticized in part by Victor Hugo, but Amalasuntha is correct that at the time Wharton wrote *Twilight Sleep,* Lucrezia's part in the political poisonings had been "rehabilitated." The Borgia reputation was based on a ubiquitous phial of poison, "the famous Borgia 'powder' " used as a convenient way to dispatch political enemies.[14] The *un*rehabilitated legend combined with the allusions to hand washing suggests Rossetti's painting of Lucrezia Borgia: "Dante Gabriel Rossetti's *Lucrezia Borgia* (1860–1) depicted a dark-haired, purposeful Lucrezia, attired in heavy robes, her large black eyes directed to the front, washing her hands in a basin after having administered a fatal dose of poison to her husband, Duke Alfonzo Bisceglie." In the repainted rendition, "her eyes are directed to her husband whom she has just poisoned, being walked up and down the room on crutches by her father, Pope Alexander IV, 'to settle the poison well into his system.' A mirror on the back wall reflects the participants in this grisly scene; below it stands a table on which are placed a decanter of wine and a poppy, sinister ingredients of the crime now being perpetrated."[15] Amalasuntha has associated Lita with

Lucrezia. In addition, the word root of both names means "light." The allusions to the Borgias suggest that like Cesare and Lucrezia, Dexter and Lita are poisoning their family *and* themselves. In this context Nona becomes her father's sacrificial victim.

Lita is the primary poisoner of herself and others, especially Dexter Manford: "Nona had rather feared that [Lita's] perpetual craving for new 'thrills' might lead to some insidious form of time-killing—some of the drinking or drugging that went on among the young women of their set" (*TW* 14).

One of the main themes of the novel is that characters use all kinds of drugs to avoid feeling pain and to avoid the search for meaning. Clues to Lita's alcohol and drug addiction begin with an offhand comment when Lita appears too late for lunch: "I had a sandwich and a cocktail after my exercises" (*TW* 33). On another midday occasion, Lita offers Pauline a cocktail instead of tea (*TW* 228). Her behavior is symptomatic. Her energy vacillates between stupefied apathy and frenetic dancing. Her appetite fluctuates wildly: "She either nibbled languidly at new health foods, or made ravenous inroads into the most indigestible dish presented to her" (*TW* 36). Nona's fear was well founded.

Her parents, Pauline and Dexter Manford, are work addicted. Early in his marriage Dexter employs the language of addiction about his and Pauline's hectic social life: "The endless going out had . . . gradually grown to be a soothing routine, a sort of mild drug-taking after the high pressure of professional hours," but he persisted because "Pauline could not live without it" (*TW* 59). Recently, he "had stopped to see his doctor and been told that he was over-working, and needed a nerve-tonic and a change of scene" (*TW* 56). Consciously or not, the nerve tonic and change of scene he chooses are Lita and her black boudoir: "[Manford] had been absorbing a slow poison, the poison emanating from this dusky self-conscious room, with all its pernicious implications" (*TW* 127). In one of his moments of disgust with Lita, "the relief of being quiet, of avoiding a conflict, of settling everything [about Lita's divorce] without effusion of blood, stole over him like the spell of the drug-taker's syringe" (*TW* 191).

The "poison" spreads insidiously to the rest of the family. Manford is not wrong. Pauline *is* addicted to activity and a frantic grasping at new ideas. To Pauline a "familiar word used as if it had some unsuspected and occult significance . . . fascinated her like a phial containing a new remedy" (*TW* 138), and she had "managed . . . to squeeze in a daily *séance,* and had come to depend on it as 'addicts' do on their morphia" (*TW* 179).

At the same time, Arthur Wyant had gradually become an alcoholic: "It was one of his father's usual attacks of 'nervousness'; cousin Eleanor had seen it coming, and tried to cut down the whiskies-and-sodas" (*TW* 256–57). Wyant's poison spreads metaphorically to his son Jim: "Nona felt a sudden exasperation against Wyant for trying to poison Jim's holiday by absurd insinuations and silly swagger" (*TW* 316), and when Jim Wyant sees Lita enter the room, he "drank the vision thirstily" (*TW* 85).

Even Nona is affected: "Since her talk with Aggie Heuston a sort of *curare* had entered into her veins. She was sharply aware of everything that was going on about her, but she felt unable to rouse herself" (*TW* 281). Under these pernicious influences, the entire family falls drugged into "twilight sleep." So when she arranges for the Easter vacation at Cedarledge, Pauline Manford does not recognize the danger for her family, or for the family of mankind.

Wharton remarkably forecasts contemporary social problems in which drugs and other poisons, "waking dreams," threaten internally, while Michelangelo, representing the Goths or any foreign power (including money), threatens war externally: "Nona herself felt more and more like one of the trench-watchers pictured in the war-time papers. . . . She had often wondered what those men thought about during the endless hours of watching, the days and weeks when nothing happened, when no faintest shadow of a skulking enemy crossed their span of no-man's land. What kept them from falling asleep, or from losing themselves in waking dreams, and failing to give warning when the attack impended?" (*TW* 280).

Everything explodes in the climactic scene in which Nona lies shot on the floor of Lita's bedroom, the disaster Edmund Wilson regarded as "not significant enough in itself to serve as the catastrophe toward which the whole novel builds."[16] But since the novel is built on thematic allusions to religions and the significance of Easter, the celebration of pain and sacrifice faced and redeemed, rather than avoided, the disaster is most significant under the encompassing idea of the search for meaning.

Pauline's largest mistake is misunderstanding the nature of pain. She tries to explain her position to Nona: " 'Being prepared to suffer is really the way to create suffering. And creating suffering is creating sin, because sin and suffering are really one. We ought to refuse ourselves to pain. All the great Healers have taught us that!' Nona lifted her eyebrows in the slightly disturbing way she had. 'Did Christ?' " (*TW* 324–25). But Edith Wharton has made clear by her allusions to Faust, Genesis, and *Paradise Lost* that the death of the soul will result from avoidance of "care" and sorrow because pain is ordained by God for fallen man—unless there is redeeming intervention. To state the matter secularly, the pain of parental sacrifice is necessary for the survival of the next generation: "Poor Nona—her mother had long been aware that she had no enthusiasm, no transports of faith. She took after her father" (*TW* 147).

The father she takes after, Dexter Manford, had "suffered the thousand irritations inseparable from a hard-working life . . . the fools who consume one's patience . . . , the endless labour of rolling human stupidity up the steep hill of understanding" (*TW* 57). The allusion is, of course, to the Greek myth of Sisyphus, who chained Death in a dungeon, then returned from the Underworld to live to great age. He was caught and punished, however, by being forced to roll a heavy rock up a mountain, a rock that perpetually rolled to the bottom just as it reached the summit. Sisyphus had become a symbol of the existential position even before Camus's *Le mythe de Sisyphe* (1942).

It is important to remember that Nona is suicidal. In spite of the fact that she is personally not religious, her "murder" is a deliberate Christ-like sacrifice on her part, appropriately staged at Easter. Nona thinks: "All her life [Pauline] had been used to buying off suffering with money, or denying its existence with words, and her moral muscles had become so atrophied that only some great shock would restore their natural strength . . . 'Great shock! People like mother never have great shocks,' Nona mused . . . 'Unless I were to give her one' . . . she added with an inward smile" (*TW* 307, first and last ellipses Wharton's). Nona's sacrifice, then, becomes a combination of Christianity and existentialism that suggests a Kierkegaardian stance. While Nona's position is to embrace no particular religion while holding Christianity as a possibility, Pauline's position is to embrace all religions at once and attempt to bring them together.

But how did Nona stage the "sacrifice," and what happened in Lita's bedroom? The day after Nona decided a shock might be helpful, she visits Maisie and her mother in the hospital. Afterward a "resurrection" occurs when Nona goes "out into the April freshness with the sense of relief that the healthy feel when they escape back to life after a glimpse of death" (*TW* 310). Meanwhile, in his alcoholic haze, Arthur has emerged planning to take "honorable" action, but Pauline is too rushed to notice. "And when I told him I couldn't [visit] he said that if I didn't he'd come out" to Cedarledge where he had lived when married to Pauline: "Nona gave an impatient shrug. 'How absurd! but of course he won't. I don't exactly see dear old Exhibit walking up to the front door of Cedarledge. . . . There were certain things, as he was always saying, that a man didn't do: that was all" (*TW* 328). The phrase echoes Judge Brack after Hedda Gabler pulls the trigger: "People don't do such things." But then Nona takes over. She realizes that if Arthur does come she can stage her "shock": "Nona was still pondering. 'I wouldn't go to town to see him, mother; why should you? As long as we're here he'll never come, and when this mood passes off he won't even remember what it was about. If you like I'll write and tell him that you'll see him as soon as we get back' " (*TW* 328). The comments that Arthur is in a "mood" and "won't remember" suggest that she knows that if she doesn't write, Arthur will arrive drunk at Cedarledge. And he does. Pauline's furtive glance at Nona is meant to ask, "Didn't you write?"

Upset, Arthur wanders around the house looking, oddly, for Lita's room. As Pauline falls asleep she hears "her husband" come in and undress, but when she checks after the shots, she finds his bed unslept in: "Was it the burglars she had heard, looting his room?" (*TW* 353). Of course it *was* her husband—her first husband, Arthur, looking for a gun. Since everything in the house had remained unchanged, Arthur would know where guns were hidden.

When the shot is fired, Pauline finds four people in the room: Arthur, Dexter, Lita, and Nona. The literary Sherlock deduces that King Arthur, like Don Quixote, has come to the rescue. He must have shot at Manford because a gentleman of old New York would never fire at a lady. Nona, expecting Arthur to respond to threats to his "honor," waited in Lita's bedroom, then threw herself suicidally in the path of the bullet.

As Nona predicted, the shock forced Pauline to face the truth. Luckily, Nona is merely an angel "winged." Two weeks later she is beginning to recover from the fever that accompanied the wound. "Shock, the doctors said, chiefly . . . " (*TW* 357, Wharton's ellipses). Ironically, though, the shock was meant for Pauline.

Nona forgives her father but tells her mother she wants to enter a convent: "Nona watched, with a faint smile, the old Puritan terror of gliding priests and incense and idolatry rise to the surface of her mother's face. Perhaps that terror was the only solid fibre left in her. . . . 'Oh, but I mean a convent where nobody believes in anything' " (*TW* 373).

There are several results from Nona's sacrifice. "Sick to nausea" (*TW* 362), Nona adopts an existentialist stance toward life. Meanwhile, Pauline whips efficiently into action, sending Arthur to an "inebriate asylum." Dexter sends Jim and Lita to Paris together, and Pauline and Dexter will leave immediately on a long trip to Canada and Japan. Critics who have objected to the apparent frivolity of this solution fail to recognize that it in this case splitting the family rather than keeping it together represents a restoration of social order. Pauline cares for Nona and the others and reunites the married couples. Even Amalasuntha has been deflected—temporarily.

Another matter that has seemed "frivolous" is that Pauline gives her party for the Cardinal in spite of Nona's "accident": "But it had come off on the appointed day—only the fourth after the burglary—and Pauline had made it a success. . . . Every one had been there, all the official and ecclesiastical dignitaries, including the Bishop of New York and the Chief Rabbi—yes, even the Scientific Initiate . . . in some half-priestly dress . . . , and yet there had been no crush, no confusion, nothing to detract from the dignity and amenity of the evening" (*TW* 366). In Nona's opinion, the significance of the party is not that it unites "celebrities for a social 'draw,' as a selfish child might gather all its toys into one heap" but that it's a kind of ecumenical council meant "to bring together the representatives of the conflicting creeds, the bearers of the multiple messages, in the hope of drawing from their contact the flash of revelation for which the whole creation groaned" (*TW* 323).

Because of Nona's sacrifice Pauline has made the party happen on the fourth day, the day after the "resurrection." Her sacrifice has made new life possible: "Pauline's face looked younger and fresher than ever, and as smooth and empty as if she had just been born again—'And she *has*, after all,' Nona concluded" (*TW* 364). "My broken arm saved her" (*TW* 363). Pauline must now face the question of the Sphinx in regard to Nona: "Who, with sadness and madness / Has turned my child's head?" (stanza 13). Neither eurythmic exercises nor psychoanalysis provides escape from the human dilemma. She must recognize the truth of existence: "Under pain pleasure—, / Under pleasure, pain lies."

We now know it was the mother who "drugged my boy's [and girl's] cup." As in Wharton's allusion to Faust, cold and fear shuddered Pauline's hollow sphere and shattered it. Someone "dies," but families can be reborn. Even so, the "ecumenical council" combined with Nona's sacrifice has been insufficient to banish evil. Care is back in his "proper station." Amalasuntha awaits Lita's return, and Michelangelo, "like a bombshell on that precarious roof" (*TW* 151), has been idolized as the star of the party. The invasion of the "Goths" has begun, but thanks to Nona's sacrifice, Pauline is girded for war.

In this novel's allusion to the detective genre, Edith Wharton emphasizes child neglect (Nona and Lita's son), pain, suicide, drugs, and poison that produce a "twilight sleep" in spite of an increasing need for social and familial vigilance. Emerson envisions the innocent child in the care of its mother playing with the sun as the monkeys play with the glass globe in Goethe's *Faust*:

> The babe by its mother
> Lies bathed in joy;
> Glide its hours uncounted,
> The sun is its toy—
>
> [*Sphinx*, stanza 6, ll. 41–44]

But Wharton is not misguided by romanticism. Anything can happen, and the "Herodias" motif of the "slaughtered innocents" recurs in *The Children*, a novel that focuses on mythic monsters like those of *The Custom of the Country*. These monsters, however, stalk children when parental vigilance is absent.

# 8 | *The Children*
## Metaphysical Allusions

IT WOULD SEEM hard to surpass the sadness of a novel like *Twilight Sleep* in which children are sacrificed to the gods of youth,[1] but "this is the saddest novel that Wharton ever wrote," claims one of the rare critical examiners of *The Children*.[2] The novel apparently "describes the unsuccessful efforts of a good man to rescue seven children, neglected by their parents and corrupted by their environment."[3] "Martin Boyne . . . develops affection for the Wheater children after a chance encounter with them on board ship. Before many weeks he finds himself the guardian of the children, who are fighting to remain together without parental supervision."[4] But *The Children* is the saddest novel Edith Wharton ever wrote only in that it is the most shocking.

The story lulls the reader into a reassuring sense that the children are at last safe. Forty-six-year-old Martin Boyne is on leave from his South American engineering job after an illness, sailing to Europe in order to marry an old love, Rose Sellars, now widowed. On the ship he notices seven stepbrothers and sisters traveling alone. Bored, Boyne becomes curious, soon discovering that these are the neglected children of often divorced acquaintances. As a "friend of the family" he responds to the pleas of the eldest to keep the children together. Boyne seeks legal guardianship. When he is reunited with Rose, she feels Boyne fails to understand the responsibility he has assumed and further suspects that he is in love with Judith, the eldest. Unable to agree, ostensibly about the adoption of the children, they break their engagement. When Boyne afterward proposes to Judith, she laughs. Broken-hearted, he sails for South America. In an epilogue he returns three years later and learns the fate of the children.

Wharton creates sympathy for Boyne by using an ironic surface of appearances that keeps readers from recognizing that Boyne's rationalizing mind is untrustworthy, even though Wharton has slyly chosen to use his point of view. First, he has no sense of the most basic needs of children. Second, he lies to himself and to friends, denying his less attractive qualities. Third, he projects his own psychological responses onto others, and fourth, he uses people for his own pleasure.

The neglected children are in physical and moral danger because of their separation from their parents, however promiscuous and sybaritic. When approached through literary allusion, Boyne emerges quite unlike the "good man" he seems. The children's danger is not from incest but from a different sexual perversion, pedophilia. Contained inside a structural allusion to the "family circus" of Margaret Kennedy's popular novel, thematic allusions to Goethe, Robert Louis Stevenson, Milton, and Tennyson work together as metaphysical conceits or metaphors, bending, remolding, and transmuting images and ideas, so that Boyne is transformed from a mere busybody to a scholar who has retreated from life, to a seductive sorcerer, to a madman and denizen of hell, to a pedophile. In forty-six-year-old Martin Boyne Wharton anticipates Humbert Humbert. Fifteen-year-old Judith prefigures Lolita, a rebellious adolescent and seductive nymphet. The children metamorphose from charming innocents to destructive animals. On the other hand, Rose and Mr. Dobree emerge as heavenly representatives of cool reason, order, and peace.

Wharton uncannily anticipates Nabokov with such adroit psychology and such allusive sleight-of-hand that the novel has not only never been censored but has never been suspected, an amazing accomplishment, considering that later *The Gods Arrive* was rejected by several publishers because of out-of-wedlock cohabitation, which seems almost trivial to today's readers.

A sharp-eyed reviewer noted a certain resemblance of *The Children* to *The Constant Nymph* (1925) by Margaret Kennedy, accidentally stumbling on the novel's structural allusion, the source of Wharton's circus imagery and the first of a cluster of allusions to children as animals and seductive nymphs.[5] Book 1 of Kennedy's story is entitled "Sanger's Circus"; book 2, "Nymphs and Shepherds." In *The Constant Nymph,* Albert Sanger is a famous musician and the father of seven undisciplined children from several marriages: "They were, in their own orbit, known collectively as 'Sanger's Circus,' a nickname earned for them by their wandering existence, their vulgarity, their conspicuous brilliance, the noise they made. . . . They had received no sort of regular education, but . . . could abuse each other most profanely in the *argot* of four languages."[6] One of the children is called "a posturing little monkey [who] should have been trained for a tight-rope dancer."[7] Tessa, the fourteen-year-old, falls in love with Lewis Dodd, who is about twenty-one. After their father's death the children are separated by guardians, and the rest of the story centers on the efforts of Tessa and Lewis to reunite.

Wharton's children also number seven. Besides Judith, there are Terry and Blanca, eleven-year-old twins, five-year-old Zinnie, their half sister, Bun and Beechy, five- and six-year-old Italian stepsister and stepbrother unrelated to the rest by blood, and two-year-old Chip, all products of their parents' assorted marriages. Bun and Beechy were the "offspring of the unscrupulous Prince Buondelmonte and a vile woman—a circus performer" (*CH* 24). Bun does "his menagerie-tricks [for] . . . his mother was a lion-tamer" (*CH* 14). They, too, are undisciplined, exuberant nomads who have had no regular education and are capable of abusing one another in Italian, French, or English. Their leader is their eldest sister, Judith, who has made them swear to stay together by taking an oath on their nurse Scopy's " 'Cyclopedia of Nursery Remedies."

On the ship Boyne falls into his own "twilight sleep," supported, of course, by a cluster of allusions to sleep and forgetfulness. Bored and melancholy, he seeks diversion in the form of the "luck" of an "adventure." He recalls his Uncle Edward, who was always meeting famous people and having "adventures" that resulted in gifts of attractive invitations and free opera tickets.[8] According to Boyne, "adventure worthy of the name perpetually eluded him" (*CH* 2). He attributes this misfortune to the shape of his nose: "It did not thrust itself forward far into other people's affairs" (*CH* 3).

Boyne's entire life has been "a sleep and a forgetting," going to the Lethe of his work as a civil engineer, avoiding the art of living. Allusions to "Rip Van Winkle," "Sleeping Beauty," and the dreams of "The Witch of Atlas" create a cluster of thematic allusions to boredom, sleep, and dreams. "He didn't want to come into contact with life again, and life always wooed him when he was not at work" (*CH* 336). But the man whose nose "did not thrust itself far forward into other people's affairs" awakens from his sleep long enough to seek "cloudy trophies" through passionate interference in the Wheater family's business. For indeed "Rip van Winkle," as Joyce Wheater calls Boyne (*CH* 54), interferes from boredom with the same expectation of reward that the children have in their constant clamoring for gifts, and further, he interferes without regard to consequences.

Boyne's delusive mood is supported by an allusion to Keats's "Ode on Melancholy": if *he* had had an adventure, "he would have burst all the grapes against his palate" (*CH* 2).

> Aye, in the very temple of Delight
> Veiled Melancholy has her sovran shrine,
> Though seen of none save him whose strenuous tongue
> Can burst Joy's grape against his palate fine;
> His soul shall taste the sadness of her might,
> And be among her cloudy trophies hung
>
> > [*Ode on Melancholy*, ll. 25–30]

The poem suggests that melancholy is to be sought for its intensity of feeling and its relationship to transitory beauty as a way of extracting the most from life.[9] It admonishes "go not to Lethe," to forgetfulness through sleep or death. Furthermore, Boyne's description of Judith's round "poppy-red lips" (*CH* 8) echoes the sleep and spell-inducing opiate images of Keats's poem (Wolf's-bane, nightshade, yew berries) and provides a clue to his sexual attraction to the little girl who, in one of the three important garden scenes, is described as a "sleeping beauty" (*CH* 207).

The thematic allusion to "Ode on Melancholy" also emphasizes several of the novel's other themes—Boyne's search for diversion through the "adventure" of his attraction to Judith, his game playing, and his isolation from the world as reflected through images of dreams and sleep. Boyne is an educated man who fails to use his imaginative or human capacities.

After he recites a stanza of poetry, Judith remarks, "The words you find are not like anybody else's" (*CH* 185). The lines Boyne had quoted were not his own but those Rose Sellers had read to *him,* lines he heard, ironically, without any sense of their application to himself:

All the peaks soar, but one the rest excels;
   Clouds overcome it;
No, yonder sparkle is the citadel's
   Circling its summit—

"I'd rather hear you talk than anybody who's dead," declares Judith when she finally discovers the lines are not Boyne's (*CH* 185). The comment is ironic because Boyne is dead to life, a point underscored by this allusion to "The Grammarian's Funeral," by Robert Browning (*CH* 191), a poem that reinforces the theme of Boyne's mental slumber.

In the poem the grammarian has died. His students, who revere him, carry his coffin up the mountain to bury him on the top described as "Crowded with culture!" They praise the scholar's life, telling how he had determined "that before living he'd learn how to live— / No end to learning." The poem is ironic, for of course the grammarian never does take time away from his studies to live: "This man decided not to Live but Know." Similarly, Boyne's history is one of gradual detachment from ordinary life. When he does go up Rose's mountain to culture and therefore "life," the life of the imagination, he goes as a dreaming corpse projecting his own ideas and fantasies onto others.

Boyne finds it psychologically convenient to impose his fantasies, which perfectly fit Judith, onto Miss Scope, the children's homely nurse: "He suspected that Miss Scope, like the Witch of Atlas, was used to racing on platforms of the wind, and laughed to hear the fire-balls roar behind" (*CH* 112).

Percy Shelley's "The Witch of Atlas" is another thematic allusion to sleep and dreams. The description of Miss Scope is similar to that of Miss Painter, the powerless deity of *The Reef*. She is a Puritanical gray-haired woman whose "sturdy weather-beaten face, which looked like a cliff on whose top a hermit had built a precarious refuge—her hat" (*CH* 21)—may have affinities to Halloween witches, and in her irresponsible care for the children, the description fits. But it certainly does not fit the Witch of Atlas:

A lovely lady garmented in light
    From her own beauty-deep her eyes, as are
Two openings of unfathomable night
    Seen through a Temple's cloven roof—her hair
Dark—the dim brain whirls dizzy with delight
    Picturing her form—her soft smiles shone afar,
And her low voice was heard like love, and drew
    All living things toward this wonder new.
    [*The Witch of Atlas,* ll. 81–88]

The beautiful Witch of Atlas is a sorceress who flies around the earth at night, entering people's dreams as a lighthearted and well-meant prank in order to do "good deeds." The witch's pranks have drastic results for the hapless victims because, as a goddess, the Witch does not understand the human ramifications of her actions. So, for example, when she casts a spell to allow a young couple to enjoy a night of love (which they each believe is a dream), she does them no favor because the result is a pregnancy nine months before the couple can marry. These pranks, like Boyne's, are games blindly played at the expense of others, a theme underscored by a cluster of allusions to games.

Again, one of the most important characteristics of Boyne's point of view is that he plays the psychological "game" of projecting his own wishes, desires, thoughts, and associations onto other people. The allusion to "The Witch of Atlas" performs a dual, "metaphysical" function as a thematic allusion to games when it combines with the allusion to the biblical story of Judith's war games. "Metaphysical allusions" bend and twist sinuously until they metamorphose, much like the reptilian Lamia of *The Custom of the Country.* Such allusions function like the sampling of "conceits" shown in *The Glimpses of the Moon,* the metaphors of seventeenth-century "metaphysical poetry."

Boyne has projected the Witch of Atlas's characteristics onto the least likely of the novel's characters, the haggish, gossipy, hypocritically Puritan Miss Scope. In the playing of games Boyne, too, is a "Witch of Atlas" and in the witch's—or warlock's—game-playing role, Boyne creates opportunities for physical contact with little girls. He joins in the children's games on the yacht, the descriptions of which bring to mind small animals. Like Gerald Ormerod, the tutor, he "proved unexpectedly good at games which involved scampering, hiding and pouncing, especially when Joyce and Judith took part, and could be caught and wrestled with" (*CH* 80).

As a young adolescent Judith has not outgrown games, but her games have metamorphosed into sophisticated war games with sexual overtones. Boyne's psychological confusion between Judith-as-child and Judith-as-woman derives in part from her seemingly mature leadership of her siblings, whom she calls "my children" (*CH* 18). Boyne "let his hand fall on hers with a faint laugh. What a child she became as soon as she was away from the other children!" (*CH* 35). "He was disappointed," but instead of resolving to teach her, "he was already busy at the masculine task of endowing the woman of the moment with every quality which made life interesting to himself. Woman—but she's not a woman! She's a child" (*CH* 35).

Boyne joins Judith's major game. The biblical Judith led and won a battle, "dressed to kill." She won it by beheading General Holofernes. "Here they all come, Judy in the lead as usual," notes her father (*CH* 49). Whether Judith ensnares Boyne or vice versa is not entirely clear, but she is active, Boyne passive. Nevertheless, as the adult, Boyne is ultimately responsible for deciding to join Judith in her rebellious adolescent war game, a game that might be entitled "Keep the Children Together and Away from Parents."

When Boyne first sees Judith, she not only is in the lead but literally has a chip on her shoulder: "His attention had been drawn to a young woman—a slip of a girl, rather—with a round flushed baby on her shoulder" (*CH* 3). The baby, of course, is her brother, Chip. The children are a "terrible army with banners" (an allusion to Kipling) (*CH* 192), and when Boyne returns victorious from his primary "battle," Rose notes that "Judith's a young lady who is eminently capable of fighting her own battles" (*CH* 171). But Boyne sees himself as the general:

> He pictured all these grown up powers and principalities leagued together against the handful of babes he commanded, and the bitterness of surrender entered into him. It was not that any of these parents really wanted their children. If they had, the break-up of Judith's dream [to keep the children together], though tragic, would have been too natural to struggle against. But it was simply that the poor little things had become a bone of contention, that the taking or keeping possession of them was a matter of pride or expediency, like fighting for a goal in some exciting game, or clinging to all one's points in an acrimoniously-disputed law-suit. [*CH* 301]

Judith's war game is not inconsistent with adolescent developmental rebelliousness. She is, in essence, a runaway: "Games have such a profound psychological significance," explains the scientific child psychologist, the newest Princess Buondelmonte, who eventually arrives to claim her stepchildren, Beechy and Bun (*CH* 281). "Telling a child that an older person will kill it seems to me so unspeakably wicked . . . This perpetuating of the old militarist instinct . . . 'Kill' is one of the words we have entirely eliminated" (*CH* 282, Wharton's ellipses). After every encounter with the Princess, Boyne and Judith ask each other, "Victory or defeat?" (*CH* 297).

At the reverse extreme, the Princess takes the brunt of Wharton's satire on contemporary educational psychology, which insists that "studies and games

[be] selected with a view to their particular moral, alimentary, dental and glandular heredity" and that "games, for instance, should be quite as carefully supervised as studies . . . " (*CH* 278, Wharton's ellipses). The irony is that at least where Judith's war games are concerned, the Princess Buondelmonte is quite correct. Parental supervision is needed, not Boyne's dubious cooperation. At this point the children's games, which have evolved into war, become associated with hell, and that, in Wharton's symbolic language, is associated with southern and hot places like Morocco and Boyne's South America. "The mere fact of gaining time was nine tenths of the battle," Boyne plots (*CH* 171). Aloud he recounts his "adventure" to Rose: "My battle royal was over Chipstone" (*CH* 176). This "battle royal" had taken place on the beach at the Lido under a Moroccan tent, a scene that refers back to Scopy's comment that "marriages [are] just like tents—folded up and thrown away when you've done with them" (*CH* 23).

In the world of this novel, cool, high places represent heaven, while hot, low places like the Lido and Morocco represent hell. Here Wharton again indulges in autoallusion, as noted in *The Glimpses of the Moon*. The direct allusion to her own travel book, *In Morocco,* functions to provide nomadic and animal imagery.[10] The Moslems are not, she notes there, "like the Arabs, wholly nomadic; but the tent, the flock, the tribe always entered in to their conception of life" (*MC* 179). The "little tribe generically known as the Wheaters" (*CH* 44), also referred to as Judith's "flock" (*CH* 60, 118), was at times "shepherded out by Nanny and the nursemaid to the downs above the valley" (*CH* 112).

*In Morocco* contains descriptions of animal sacrifice, flagellation ceremonies, and the induction of nine-year-old little girls into harems reminiscent of the sacrificial daughter allusions of *Twilight Sleep*. The experience had a profound effect on Edith Wharton. It is not surprising that because of its heat, its primitiveness, and its lust and other evils, Morocco becomes a hell, and Boyne descends into it.[11]

On the beach at the Lido, Boyne had intended to get the two Wheaters alone under the Moroccan tent for a discussion of the welfare of their children. But one by one the Wheaters invite in all of the parents and stepparents, past, present, and future. Nevertheless, Boyne succeeds in becoming "trial guardian" for the seven children whom he first met as they boarded the ship in the Bay of Algiers—near Morocco. That warm region is familiar territory, for he has just ascended from the hot regions of Australia, South America, and Africa: "How long he must have lived out of the world, on his engineering jobs, first in the Argentine, then in Australia, and since the war in Egypt—how out of step he must have become" (*CH* 4, 5). In addition, on Rose's wall hang watercolors and sketches by Sargent. The subjects of Sargent's sketches and watercolors include Venice, Arabs, Moroccan goatherds and black tents, and

John Singer Sargent, *Bedouin Camp* (1905–06). Watercolor on paper 25.4 × 35.7 (10 × 14 1/16) The Brooklyn Museum 09.811. Purchased by special subscription. Associative Allusion: *The Children*. A sample of Sargent's Moroccan watercolors.

portraits of Robert Louis Stevenson, allusions that combine "metaphysically" with allusions to Stevenson's *The Ebb Tide* and Wharton's *In Morocco* to emphasize themes of seductive madmen from hot places who behave like animals. Boyne's character shifts "metaphysically" once again.

Wharton alludes to insanity, particularly through *The Ebb Tide, Faust,* and *Maud.* The allusion to *The Ebb Tide* occurs when, with dismay and concern, Rose learns from her visiting family lawyer, Mr. Dobree, that Judith's best friend committed suicide during a period of neglect by her mother. She explains to Boyne: " 'She and Judith were together at Deauville the very summer that she killed herself. Both their mothers had gone off heaven knows where. Judith proclaims the fact to every one, as you know.' Boyne . . . was staring out at the familiar outline of the great crimson mountains beyond the balcony. A phrase of Stevenson's about 'the lovely and detested scene' (from 'The Ebb-tide,' he thought?) strayed through his mind as he gazed" (*CH* 202–203).[12] Boyne has been reminded of *The Ebb Tide* by Robert Louis Stevenson and Lloyd Osbourne (1893). Ironically, Stevenson is most famous for his children's stories. In the story, a ship docks at a port ruled by a murderous madman who

> Of his own volumes intervolved;—all gaunt
> And sanguine beasts her gentle looks made tame—
> They drank before her at her sacred fount—
> And every beast of beating heart grew bold,
> Such gentleness and power even to behold.
>
> [*The Witch of Atlas* 6, ll. 89–96]

Like the Sorceress, Judith is surrounded by her little "flock" who adore her, and it is with them that she plays her biggest "prank," or game, swearing to keep them together, then running away. These children are not just innocents. They are also small animals, a menagerie, a "pack of savages" who need to be socialized (*CH* 282). Boyne remarks that "the child is only half a person" (*CH* 9). But to the detriment of civilization, these children have so far been educated only by the example of adult behavior so seamy that Boyne seems saintly by comparison. Thus his purported good deeds are rendered so much more insidious.

Boyne begins to visualize the children as animals: "He had been gradually penetrated by the warm animal life which proceeds from a troop of happy, healthy children" (*CH* 45). Listening to Judith describe the behavior of her parents, which, to Boyne, "had leagued her little tribe against the recurrence of such moves[,] he had the sick feeling with which a powerless looker-on sees the torture of an animal" (*CH* 46). There is Bun "on all fours, emitting strange animal barks and crowings" (*CH* 13), shouting "I'm a pony" (*CH* 33). Chip is a lion "with Bun as lion tamer" (*CH* 305), Judith calls Zinnie a "little viper" (*CH* 67). They become battling goats during an altercation: "Some were screaming, some vituperating, some doing both, and butting at each other, head down, at the same time" (*CH* 281). On another occasion, Boyne jokes with Judith—"Have the wild animals left a morsel for me?" (*CH* 244). And one of Boyne's favorite adjectives is "beastly." Then the animals evolve metaphysically into little devils. Boyne is attracted to red—Judith's red lips and her "scarlet figure" (*CH* 141), Zinnie's red hair ("the little red devil" [*CH* 19]), and Bun's "scarlet jumper" (*CH* 13).

Judith alone seems exempt from animal imagery. Her charming spontaneity and openness, like Sophy Viner's, have captivated readers. But Judith steals five thousand dollars from her father (about fifty thousand dollars in today's funds), kidnaps six children and runs away with them, and is present when her best friend commits suicide partly because of drugs. (Did she encourage the suicide? Why didn't she prevent it? Was she, too, taking drugs? Was she endangered by the example?)

At fifteen Judith smokes and drinks, and Boyne most often supplies the cocktails and cigarettes. The oath the children take to stay together, which at first seems so touching, is urged by Judith as part of her war game. The children are too young to know what an oath is. Furthermore, Judith is involved with Gerald Ormerod, who, she says, wants to marry her in spite of being in the process of seducing her mother: "There had been, in Judith's language, an all-round circus, complicated by the fact that what Gerald really wanted was to marry *her*—" (*CH* 126). In addition, she acts seductively toward Boyne, calling him "Darling," throwing her arms around his neck and kissing him and inviting herself into his bedroom.

Boyne's attraction to a child is again emphasized by an allusion to the madness of Faust: Rose "was out when he reached the *châlet,* and his conviction [that he was right to be the guardian of the children] strengthened as he sat awaiting her. It drew its strength from the very atmosphere of the place— its self-sufficing harmony. '*Willkommen, suesser Daemmerschein!*' " (*CH* 169). Translated, this allusion to Goethe's *Faust* reads:

Welcome, lovely twilight glow,
How you pervade this sacred shrine!
    [*Faust,* part 1, ll. 2687–88]

The "sacred shrine" to which Faust refers is Gretchen's bedroom: "A sense of peace breathes in this room, / of order and contentment!" (*Faust,* part 1, ll. 2691–92). But Boyne is fooling himself again. This is the same Faustian sensation he shares with the Witch of Atlas and the madman in *The Ebb Tide:* "The fact of having reassured [Judith] so quickly awed Boyne a little, as if he had meddled with destiny. But it was pleasant, for once, to play the god, and he let himself drift away into visions of a vague millennium" (*CH* 187).

Later he thinks that it was "folly to indulge the illusion that he could really direct or control their fate" (*CH* 223), but he goes right on as if he had not had the thought. "It was all the result of idling and lack of hard exercise; when a working man has had too long a holiday, and resting has become dawdling, Satan proverbially intervenes" (*CH* 222). In a touch that is further suggestive of Satan, of idle hands doing the devil's work, most of Boyne's scenes take place at sunset, after dark, or in the shadows, as in one scene where he had "drawn back into the dusk of the passage, as if disclaiming any part in the impending drama" (*CH* 284).

The Princess Buondelmonte senses this darkness in Boyne. Despite the stinging satire Wharton directs at her, the Princess is quite often right. Her effort to win a point in an argument with Boyne becomes a Faustian battle for souls:

> "Mr. Boyne—I'm sorry. I can see that you're fond of the children. But fondness is not everything . . . it may even be a source of moral danger. I'm afraid we shouldn't altogether agree as to the choice of the persons Mrs. Wheater has left in care of them—not even as to her own daughter. [This

refs to Boyne.] The soul of a child—"

"Yes," Boyne acquiesced; "that's the very thing I'm pleading for." [*CH* 280; Wharton's ellipses]

The pleading for a soul, however, would seem to require a persistence Boyne lacks, as illustrated by another allusion to *Faust* (part 2, act 5, scene 6): "And all the while [he listened] there echoed in his ears, more insistently than anything [Judith] was saying, a line or two from the chorus of Lemures, in 'Faust,' which Rose had read aloud one evening at Cortina.

Who made the room so mean and bare—
Where are the chairs, the tables where?
It was lent for a moment only—

A moment only: not a bad title for the history of his last few months! A moment only; and he had always known it" (*CH* 331–32).

The lines further point out the irony of children's being lent to their parents for a moment only, a fact dramatized at the conclusion of the story when Boyne returns three years later. He finds that Chip, the robust and healthy favorite of his father, who depends on him to be the family heir rather than the sickly Terry, has suddenly died of meningitis. Cliffe Wheater had missed the baby's short time on earth. And so had Boyne.

At his first reunion with Wheater, Cliffe had recalled their "great old times" at college, where Boyne had been active among the girls: " 'Member that Cambridge girl you used to read poetry to? *Poetry!* She was a looker, too! 'Come into the garden, Maud' . . . *Garden* they used to call it in those days!" (*CH* 49, Wharton's ellipses).

The allusion to the mad poet of Tennyson's *Maud,* who mistakes the garden for the pit where his father committed suicide, clusters with the allusion to Stevenson's madman. The garden image and, by association, nymphs and nymphets, bring us back to Wharton's allusion to *The Constant Nymph,* the anticipation of *Lolita,* and the Princess's comment that "fondness is not everything . . . it may even be a source of moral danger" (*CH* 280, Wharton's ellipses).

Indeed, Boyne has a history of sexual seduction. The girl from Cambridge to whom he used to read Tennyson's *Maud* had been succeeded by Joyce Mervin of New York (now Mrs. Wheater), whom "Boyne himself had danced and flirted with through a remote winter not long after Harvard" (*CH* 5). Other references to Boyne's love life seem to arise in the context of Rose, but the reflections fit Judith, too: "So much easy love had come his way, he had grown so weary of nights without a morrow, that he needed to feel there was one woman in the world whom he was half-afraid to make love to" (*CH* 84). The need to be "half-afraid" and the fact that his "other amorous episodes had been too brief and simple for any great amount of manoeuvering" (*CH* 226) hint of the desire for the adventure of "one night stands" or prostitution as well as an inability to commit to anyone, adult or child.

As a structural thematic allusion, Tennyson's lines, like parts of Stevenson's novel, evoke madness, seduction, and Boyne's nocturnal habits and help focus on the three mythlike garden scenes structured at the beginning, middle, and end of *The Children*:

> Come into the garden, Maud,
>   For the black bat, night, has flown,
> Come into the garden, Maud,
>   I am here at the gate alone;
> And the woodbine spices are wafted abroad,
>   And the musk of the rose is blown.
>
>     [*Maud*, 23, ll. 850–55]

The invitation into the garden is an invitation to seduction.

Margaret Kennedy's nymphs may be "constant," but to Martin Boyne Judith is transitory. When he first meets her, the "imponderable and elusive creature" is described in imagery suggestive not only of the Witch of Atlas but also of the nymph: "Her mouth became a flame, her eyes fountains of laughter, her thin frail body a quiver of light—he didn't know how else to put it. Whatever she was, she was only intermittently; as if her body were the mere vehicle of her moods, the projection of successive fears, hopes, ardours, with hardly any material identity of its own" (*CH* 36–37). She was "like a young Daphne, half emerging into reality, half caught in the foliage of fairyland" (*CH* 265). The image is reinforced by three pastoral garden scenes each of which revolves around a picnic for the children.

The first picnic takes place in a kind of Eden, "a wonderful ducal garden containing ever so many acres of orange-trees always full of flowers and fruit" (*CH* 28–29). It is the "lavender-scented cathedral garden" of Monreale, where Boyne supplies "golden bales" of oranges (*CH* 31). It is in these garden settings that the seduction of the nymph stands out. As we have seen, Judith had become "the woman of the moment." Or had she? " 'Child!' He let his hand fall on hers" (*CH* 35).

Boyne emerges more prominently as seducer and pedophile in the second garden scene, Mr. Dobree's picnic. Recalling the "Antiope" paintings discussed in the chapter on *The Glimpses of the Moon*, Boyne is observing the sleeping Judith: "She looks almost grown up—she looks kissable" (*CH* 205). Meanwhile, Mr. Dobree is reddening as he observes Boyne:

> But with whom was Mr. Dobree angry? Why, with himself, manifestly. His eyes still rested on the dreaming Judith. . . . "He's frightened—he's fright-

ened at himself," Boyne thought, calling to mind—with a faint recoil from the reminder—that he also, once or twice, had been vaguely afraid of himself when he had looked too long at Judith. Had his eyes been like that, he wondered? And the muscles of his face been stretched in the effort to detach the eyes? The thing was not pleasant to visualise; and he disliked Mr. Dobree the more for serving as his mirror . . . [CH 206, final ellipses Wharton's]

After Boyne accuses Dobree of lusting after Judith, which is, of course, a projection of his own desires, Rose reveals that Dobree has proposed to her. Boyne laughs aloud at the idea of Rose with Dobree. His mirthful incredulity leads to another of his altercations with Rose but one in which he comes close to self-knowledge: "His laugh had simply mocked his own power of self-deception, and uttered his relief at finding himself so deceived" (CH 217). Rose tells him Dobree was "convinced that you were in love with Judith Wheater" (CH 219): "Shows what kind of a mind he must have. Thinking in that way about a child—a mere child—and about any man, any *decent* man; regarding it as possible, perhaps as natural . . . worst of all, suggesting it of some one standing in my position toward these children; as if I might take advantage of my opportunities to—to fall in love with a child in the schoolroom!" (CH 219, Wharton's ellipses). "Martin . . . , but you *are* in love with her! . . . I believe I've always known it" (CH 220, first ellipses Wharton's). This revelation leads ultimately to the breaking of their engagement, leaving Boyne free to consider that by marrying Judith he might keep the children. He comments tentatively to Judy that he knows a way the group can stay together: "Her eyes still bathed him in their radiance. 'My darling, my darling.' She leaned close as she said it, and he dared not move, in his new awe of her nearness—so subtly had she changed from the child of his familiar endearments to the woman he passionately longed for . . . " (CH 308–309, Wharton's ellipses).

The third garden scene occurs in Boyne's shipboard dream of the promised picnic at Versailles, which he has deserted without a word. In the dream Versailles becomes a "lordly pleasure-grounds," a phrase that echoes Coleridge's "Kubla Khan." He and Judith wander into the shadows of a bosquet. "The place seemed the ghostly setting of dead days. Boyne looked down at Judith, and even her face was ghostly . . . 'Come,' he said with a shiver, 'let's get back into the sun—' " (CH 334, Wharton's ellipses). By returning Judith to the light, part of Boyne, his human part, is unwilling to "kill" Judith's youthful spirit by seducing her, a conclusion that is reinforced by the scene three years later in which Boyne sees Judith for the last time.

Is there any antidote to the evils of sinful parents and seductive "guardians"? What will become of the children? The question is asked three times in the novel, once by the children themselves in the context of their parents' divorce, once by Boyne in the context of his engagement to Rose, and once by Rose, who asks what business it is of his what becomes of them (CH 62, 208,

233). The question recalls Boyne's intrusive nose. Will the children stay together? Supposing, as the Princess Buondelmonte suggests, that is not best for them? (*CH* 285).

The answer of the novel is that it is *not* best for these children to stay together. The reason becomes clear in two ways, both of which center on a Darwinian metaphor of evolution. The first clarification derives from an examination of individual children through their parentage and their names, and the second, through understanding the scene in which the children fight like goats over the aquarium.

Judith Wheater, as already shown, is a fighter of battles and as such is a survivor, but she is uneducated and belongs in school. The twins, Terry and Blanca Wheater, are a more complex case. Blanca is described as having given half of herself to make Terry. Terry, whose name derives from *terra*, earth, is always ill with a fever unless he is in high or "heavenly" altitudes. He craves books and education, and his father says he is "cut out to be a Doctor of Divinity; or President of a University, maybe! Talk of heredity—" (*CH* 50). His role in the novel is as the children's conscience, but his very survival is in question. Blanca, on the other hand, is interested only in clothes and fashions—things of the earth, yet her name, "white," suggests things of the clouds or spirit. Presumably her spiritual half is the half that went into the making of Terry. Terry needs to be brought down, so to speak, and Blanca raised up. She, too, needs to be educated.

The younger children are less well defined, but Zinnie—Zinnia—is a flower, Beechy a tree, and Bun an agile rabbit who wishes to become an acrobat or athlete. Chipstone is mineral, a chip off Cliffe Wheater's "old block." Animal, vegetable, mineral, earth, and air—each requires a different environment in order to flourish.

At the end of the novel, partly through fate and partly through the intervention of Mr. Dobree, some of the children are properly placed. Terry is in school high in the mountains of Switzerland, and Blanca is being educated in a convent after nearly getting into "trouble" (a euphemism for "pregnant") with an elevator boy. Beechy and Bun are under the supervision of their father and stepmother, the Princess. However odd or inadequate her scientific theories may be, they at least result in attention for the children, and Bun was to be provided with gymnastic equipment that may also help Beechy slim down. Chip, now dead, has returned to the earth.

The "aquarium scene" enlightens the matter further. Judy and Boyne tell the Princess Buondelmonte, who has grave doubts about the welfare of the children, how beautifully they get along together. As a demonstration, they throw open a door, only to reveal a screaming battle: "Boyne had never before seen [the children] engaged in so fierce a conflict" (*CH* 281). One of them, apparently Bun, had decided to find out whether a rabbit could survive in an aquarium, thereby nearly drowning the rabbit then breaking the water tank.

The rabbit, representing Bun, was placed in the wrong environment, as was the fish when the tank broke, resulting in further damage—a brilliant scenic pun on the cliché about fish out of water.

Furthermore, Bun and Beechy Buondelmonte are the Italian "steps" (whom Scopy insists on calling "foreigners," even on their native soil). "The 'steps,' in fact, had the definiteness of what the botanists call species." They are unrelated by blood to any of the "hybrids" (*CH* 20). Their real names are Astorre (star) and Beatrice (blessing), and their surname translates roughly "of the good mountain." Similar mountain imagery surrounds Rose. It becomes apparent also that the story of Bun and Beechy's "evil" father has all been second- or thirdhand hearsay passed on by Judith, who has her own motives, and by Scopy, who is prone to gossip. The Princess has quite another version (and perspective) that could just as easily be true. In any case, as Mrs. Wheater is made to say, "If the new Princess Buondelmonte was so full of good intentions, and so determined to have her own way, the two children might get a fairly decent bringing-up" (*CH* 326).

For Judith it seems to have been too late. She is now grown up, dating Peruvians (from a hot, "primitive" country), looking "sad as an autumn twilight" (*CH* 347), and wearing a black band around her wrist that suggests mourning. Zinnie, still only eight years old, is unsupervised, riding the elevators, wrestling with "lift boys," the same activity that caused Blanca's enrollment in a convent. Zinnie is in constant danger, taking candy from strangers: "One fat old gentleman in spats produced a bag of sweets, and pinched her bare arm as he gave it to her" (*CH* 339). The candy has liqueur centers; Boyne does not object. Zinnie asks Boyne for cigarettes; he gives them to her. She takes "his neck in her embrace, as Judith used to" (*CH* 340).

Wharton has restrained herself from making Boyne unmitigatedly evil, and her restraint serves to make him more believable. The final time Boyne sees Judith, the "heaven" of the ballroom and her presence is not available to him. She is in the light; he is lurking in the dark. He has tried to engage a table, but tables are all "bespoken" (*CH* 338). (Wharton uses the biblical term.) After dinner at a restaurant, Boyne "walked up through the warm dark night to the *Mirasol.* . . . as he reached the terrace a drizzling rain began to fall" (*CH* 344). He thinks he sees Judith and "moved away again into the darkness," speculating about her dress and wondering whether she is in love (*CH* 345). "He drew back into an unlit corner of the terrace, and sat there a long time in the dark. . . . Then he got up and walked away into the night" (*CH* 347).

A dozen other themes enrich *The Children,* but they must be discussed elsewhere. Surely, however, it is by now apparent that to read *The Children* as a novel about a good man attempting to rescue seven neglected children is no more accurate than to read *Lolita* as the story of Humbert's vacation with his daughter.

"Why, it's barbarous; it ought to be against the law!" Boyne thinks when he first sees Judith and assumes that the children are hers. As Boyne is forty-six and Judith is fifteen, chances are quite good that Boyne would be violating a statutory rape law should he become involved with her. In fact, at one point (*CH* 138) Cliff Wheater has a police warrant on Boyne for abduction, of which, of course, he is guilty.

Altogether, Wharton's choices of literary allusions serve to increase the reader's understanding of Martin Boyne's necessary exile to hot climes—necessary because evil must be controlled if, as in *Twilight Sleep,* it cannot be conquered. The image of him that emerges from the conceits of the metaphysical allusions shows him as the Grammarian who chooses learning over living, the Sorcerer who transforms people into animals and seduces virgins, a Faustian character in love with a child, the Satanic inhabitant of Moroccan and other hot climes, and the insane ruler of a tropical island who plays God with the children's destinies. In the context of all of these, Boyne's "boyishness" is reduced to mad self-delusion.

The nature of unrestrained children is revealed through clusters of thematic allusions to animals in the family circus of *The Constant Nymph,* the metamorphosed animals of *Comus,* the adoring animals of *The Witch of Atlas,* and the nomadic herd of sheep or goats that originally boards the ship at Algiers, a hellish place. *The Constant Nymph* becomes a kind of structural outline for the plot, while *Comus* sets up the main themes. Judith is portrayed as the nymph, the prank-playing Witch of Atlas, the Sleeping Beauty. Rose represents Milton's "lovely Logic" (*CH* 172) who, when she leaves Boyne, takes "her soul with her" (*CH* 242).

The novel does not end on the pessimistic note that readers have traditionally perceived. The last line, "On her deck stood Boyne, a lonely man," is ironic. Loneliness may be the least of what Boyne, as Emerson's fallen man, deserves:

> But man crouches and blushes
> >    Absconds and conceals;
> He creepeth and peepeth,
> >    He palters and steals;
> Inform, melancholy,
> >    Jealous glancing around,
> An oaf, an accomplice,
> >    He poisons the ground.
> >        [*The Sphinx,* stanza 8, ll. 49–56]

The insidious source of danger is on his way back to the hot places from whence he came, Rose has saved her soul, most of the children are safe, social order is more or less restored, and the theme of the pedophile has been added to the list of clues to Edith Wharton's code. Once again the novel features neglected children and hints of drugs and suicide reinforcing the thematic allusions of previous novels. Because of lack of vigilance, the "Invaders" of *The Custom of the Country,* and the Goths of *Twilight Sleep,* have been joined by a pervert invading the lives of children, and the bridge of this novel is its author's attempt to span "the distance between Mrs. Sellars's conception of life, and Judith Wheater's experience of it" (*CH* 124).

In *The Children* the insoluble dilemma is not emphasized, but when Scopy says "everything's all right again—for the present," emphasizing the present for "fear of the Fates overhearing me . . . " (*CH* 26–27, Wharton's ellipses), the irony strikes that she is confiding in a Fury who immediately pursues. Emerson's phrase "poisoning the ground" recalls the myth of the birth of the Furies, the poisonous reptiles of *The Custom of the Country,* and the mind-numbing distractions and poisons of *Twilight Sleep.*

Wharton's Sphinx, however, is present only symbolically in "the many thousand threads of association, strung with stored images of eye and brain, memories of books, of pictures, of great names and deeds" and "allusive symbolism" (*CH* 35) to "elucidate the mystery and fill in the gaps" (*CH* 23). As Emerson's Sphinx says, "Through a thousand voices / Spoke the universal dame." Again the author hints she has a message for us (*CH* 291), a message intended to shatter the "dream-paradise" of men like Martin Boyne (*CH* 135).

In *Hudson River Bracketed* topics of sexual perversion and suicide resurface, although they are subordinated to the theme of the development of artists, and once again Wharton takes up the subject of American education, in *The Children* addressed as a side issue through Bun and Beechy's atrocious spelling and Terry's interest in books. The clues to the code are now for the most part in place, and the last two novels Edith Wharton completed before she died, *Hudson River Bracketed* and its sequel, *The Gods Arrive,* offer intellectual and sexual education as partial solutions to social and moral dilemmas.

# 9 | *Hudson River Bracketed*
## Layered Allusions

*THE CHILDREN* explored the gulf between generations caused by parents selfishly absorbed in their own pleasures. So *Hudson River Bracketed* and *The Gods Arrive* attempt to establish a bridge across gulfs between past and present, New World and Old.[1] Edith Wharton's effort focused on perfecting the "layered" allusions with which she had previously experimented. Unlike "reverberating allusions," which reecho the same allusion, each "layered allusion" contains a reference to a poem, say, that itself alludes to an earlier poem, and so on. For example, in *Twilight Sleep,* Wharton alludes to *Paradise Lost,* which alludes to Genesis. If the allusions begin with older works and progress toward the present of the novel, they are called "reverse layered allusions." If they were charted, layered allusions would look like "branching thematic allusions" except that the "root tips" branch down to deeper allusions rather than up to new themes, literal roots to the past for the rootless American culture dramatized in *The House of Mirth* and *The Custom of the Country.*

In order to create or appreciate the beauty of such allusions, mind and spirit must be deeply educated, a major theme of *Hudson River Bracketed.* Vance Weston begins by learning to ask questions as Emerson suggests, and "take his quest through nature" represented by British and American romantics, though he finds their answers incomplete. Wharton starts her artist on architecture, with allusions to the architect Andrew Jackson Downing and an autoallusion to her structural allusions in *The House of Mirth.* Her analogy is the architecture of the creative imagination in *Hudson River Bracketed* and the architecture of the spirit in its sequel.

Most negative criticism of *Hudson River Bracketed* seems summarized by Blake Nevius's observation that "there is no single view of the action that will satisfactorily explain all its parts."[2] What must have precipitated the remark is that the novel's opening satirizes Vance Weston's education, his religious ideas, and his father's questionable business deals, but the topic of Vance's midwestern background seems to disappear as the novel goes on to satirize New York publishers and modernist art and literature. *Hudson River Bracketed,* however, was always intended to be the first of two parts, which fact immediately explains reviewers' perceptions of "lack of symmetry" and "definiteness of design"; they could not have known that it was half of a whole. Several of the characters and topics that disappear from *Hudson River Bracketed* resurface in *The Gods Arrive.*

*Hudson River Bracketed* is about Vance Weston's rudimentary education of mind and soul. Analogically, the "single view of the action" that explains the novel's parts is that art must be built on tradition—in Wharton's case allusion—a dictum that requires an education based on the "architecture," or roots, of cultural history. Vance builds his artistic education on American art: Hudson River painters, poets, and architects; the transcendentalists; jazz; and the modernists. Eventually he adds the skills of the romantics, neoclassicists, naturalists, and realists. Like Wharton herself, he begins by writing imitative poetry and progresses first to a slice-of-life short story, then to a historical novel of manners.

The story begins when Vance Weston becomes ill from typhoid. Lounging near a river, he discovered his grandfather in a liaison with his girlfriend, Floss Delaney. Like Ralph in *The Custom of the Country,* also victimized by a combination of psychological shock and poisoned water, he considers suicide but instead writes a cathartic short story about the experience. To speed his recovery, his parents send him to stay with cousins, the Tracys, who are caretakers of the old Lorburn house on the Hudson River. Vance becomes interested in the Willows, which is preserved exactly as it was when its owner died. Halo Spear, a relative of the owner, having come to check on the housekeeping, surprises Vance reading in the library, lost in the imaginative architecture of "Kubla Khan." Halo promises Vance access to the library at the Willows if he will clean and dust the books, but he becomes so absorbed that he allows them to fall into such disorder that some valuable Americana is stolen. The discovery of the theft occurs upon Vance's return from a three-day drunk at a house of prostitution (the wrong moral architecture). The episode was not entirely Vance's fault. Nevertheless, Mrs. Tracy accuses him of responsibility for both theft and debauch and banishes him not only from her home but also from Miss Lorburn's library at the Willows.

After nearly starving in New York, Vance is forced to return to Euphoria to work in journalism for three years before he can return. *The Hour,* the floundering literary magazine that published Vance's short story, has been bought by Lewis Tarrant, now Halo's husband. Tarrant, who depends completely on Halo's literary discernment, is searching for an exciting author to promote. After finding Vance's story in an old issue, and testing its promise on Halo, he hires Vance to write a column. Vance arrives in New York with barely enough time to keep his appointment with Tarrant. Yet he impulsively follows a lovely girl onto a bus, then recognizes her as his suddenly beautiful cousin Laura Lou Tracy, now engaged to Bunty Hayes.

Vance pursues her impetuously and insists that they elope. But since Vance is unable to provide for her, they live with Mrs. Tracy, who resents their presence. To secure a quiet place where he can write, away from his suspicious mother-in-law, Vance trespasses at the Willows but tells Laura Lou he is at his office. Halo discovers him there, they begin to work together, and they fall in love. Yet since both are married, they decide to part. Unfortunately, Mrs. Tracy discovers the deception, accuses Vance of adultery, and nearly persuades Laura Lou to divorce him. But the couple is reconciled and moves to New York.

After his nomination for the Pulsifer Prize, poverty-stricken Vance innocently attempts to borrow money from Mrs. Pulsifer, a mistake that costs him the prize and alienates Tarrant, his sponsor. Tarrant then refuses to release him from his contract with *The New Hour,* a document complexly tied to his book-publishing agreement, so he remains poor in spite of his successful novel. Meanwhile, Laura Lou is sickly, childlike, and unintelligent, so he reads his manuscripts to Halo. Next, Laura Lou contracts pneumonia and later dies of tuberculosis. Halo, who has inherited the Lorburn house, is on the verge of divorce from Tarrant. The novel ends with Vance and Halo reunited.

The "single view of the action" that explains the novel is encompassed in the novel's technique itself; Wharton's technique now features "layered" and "reverberating" allusions. "Reverberating" allusions echo literary phrases borrowed by generation after generation of authors with little change, like a biblical quotation that echoes faintly in every work of literature and art ever to use it but that alters it very little. The theme upon which *Hudson River Bracketed* focuses is "the architecture of education." Wharton begins with an "umbrella" allusion to education.

The reason the topic of Vance's background in the Midwest disappears so quickly is that the story is about overcoming that background, a somnolent, morally ill, culturally impoverished education by family, church, and school. Education and religion are not separate issues in the novel, though here treatment of them has been divided for clarity. Vance's religious grandmother, Mrs. Scrimser, has been the greatest early influence on him, but he rejects her version of God as the "Supreme Moralist of a great educational system" in favor of one he thinks he invented but is actually derivative of Emerson: "I don't exactly want to get near Him anyhow; what I want is to get way out beyond Him, out somewhere where He won't look any bigger than a speck, and the god in *me* can sort of walk all round Him" (*HRB* 17).

The novel's allusions indicate that to understand Vance's intellectual and spiritual education as it develops, it is important to know how the ideas of Ralph Waldo Emerson affected American education: "What [Vance] needed, no doubt, to enter that world [of books], was *education*—the very thing he thought he already had!" (*HRB* 117). Wharton incorporates that subject into a "reverse layered allusion"—an indirect layered allusion that moves forward in time rather than backward—starting with Emerson, who strongly influenced Dewey, and progressing to the victory of Dewey's theories of practical vocational education over Irving K. Babbitt's theories of classical education.

Halo reflects Babbitt's classical theory when she mocks Dewey's theoretical application of Emerson to education: "I wasn't laughing at you, but at the intelligence of our national educators—no, educationists, I think they call themselves nowadays—who manage to take the bloom off our greatest treasures by giving them to young savages to maul. I see, for instance, that they've spoilt 'The Ancient Mariner' for you" (*HRB* 64).

One critic takes strong exception to the truth behind Wharton's mockery of early twentieth-century education. She asks how it can be that Vance has graduated from college by age nineteen, commenting that it's "difficult to defend [Wharton's] snobbish treatment of Vance's Midwestern background and his lack of literary sophistication": "For a college graduate interested in the arts, [Vance] is impossibly ignorant of literature; American colleges could not have been so provincial as Mrs. Wharton makes them out to be. So his remark to Halo . . . , 'Why did no one ever tell me about the Past before' is totally false. American education would have done better in those days by Vance." Was midwestern literary education "doing better than that" by students?[3] Both internal and external evidence suggest not.[4]

Vance remembers that "he had been nurtured on: James Whitcomb Riley, Ella Wheeler Wilcox, Bliss Carman's 'Songs from Vagabondia'; hackneyed old 'pieces' from Whittier and Longfellow, in the *Sixth Reader;* Lowell's 'Ode'— there were fine bits in that—Whitman's 'Pioneers' (good too, but rather jiggy)" (*HRB* 61). The preface of one actual *Sixth Reader* makes clear its attempt to be "modern" and practical—in short, to reflect the theories of Dewey. It states that the student is entering upon a "definite period of noble impulses and exalted ideals. . . . Much distinctly new matter has been used, in which ethical ideas are clothed in the concrete forms to which we are best accustomed in this age. On the other hand, a few standard pieces are used."[5] The table of contents of this reader includes weak works by popular American authors: "Robert Burns" and "Sandalphon" by Longfellow and "A Winter Evening" and "Education" by Whittier, not the best of either poet. When Emerson wrote, "I think I will never read any but the commonest books,—the Bible, Homer, Dante, Shakespeare and Milton," then continued (slyly alluding to Cooper's *The Prairie*), the "imagination delights in the woodcraft of Indians, trappers and beehunters,"[6] he could hardly have suspected that the Bible, Homer, Dante, Shakespeare, and Milton would be dropped from curricula on the basis of his philosophy. Altogether, Wharton appears quite justified in having Vance ask, "Why wasn't I ever told about the Past before?" (*HRB* 59). But as hard as she is on American education, satirizing collegiate emphasis on sports and fraternities and an inadequate curriculum, Wharton is ultimately optimistic about possibilities for the individual and the nation. She makes the point through a layered allusion to education: Emerson alludes to Milton, who alludes to the Bible.

Vance educates himself as Wharton did, by voraciously reading great literature under the guidance of classically educated friends. In the process he discovers "the mighty shock of English prose": "Methinks I see in my mind a noble and puissant nation rousing herself like a strong man after sleep, and shaking her invincible locks; methinks I see her as an eagle nursing her mighty youth" (*HRB* 117). He has come across the "Areopagetica," Milton's famous essay against censorship which advocates free education. Even though later Bunty Hayes, making an intraauthorial allusion, comments that "literary people didn't seem to realize as yet that writing a good advertisement was just as much an art as turning out *Paradise Lost*" (*HRB* 510), the extract becomes a perfect metaphor for Vance's intellectual awakening.

*Paradise Lost,* structured upon Genesis, is also an important part of the architecture of *Hudson River Bracketed.* During Vance's visit to his grandparents' house, with its lilacs blooming in the dooryard, the earth is in Paradisiacal resurrection, but like Adam, Vance has sinned. In fact, Vance and his grandfather are guilty of the same "original sin," sexual promiscuity with Floss Delaney. She is Eve whom Vance literally picks out of the mud where she has fallen. The scene demonstrates Wharton's disagreement with Matthew Arnold about the innocence of instinct. On one occasion, for instance, the "instinct of self-protection stirred [Vance] to cruelty" (*HRB* 414). In this and several subsequent episodes, Wharton dramatizes Numbers 14:18: The Lord forgives but "by no means clearing the guilty, visiting the iniquity of the fathers upon the children unto the third and fourth generation."

Vance is unforgiving of his grandfather, further failing to realize he has committed the same sin. The sins of the fathers are visited upon the children. Therefore, especially since the Lord does not necessarily forgive immediately, Vance must fall again and suffer purgatory before achieving true salvation as an artist and as a person. This difficult process of moral education begins with sin (death), recognition of sin, contrition, expiation, and forgiveness (both the ability to forgive and to be forgiven). The question of whether there is salvation at the end of the process is left open. Vance does not achieve all of it, but by the end of *The Gods Arrive,* he seems on a correct path to new moral and creative life.

Forgiveness is an important theme involving the ineluctable interdependence of moral and intellectual development. The discovery of his grandfather's sin and Vance's adamant refusal to forgive it recalls the eating of the tree of the fruit of knowledge. It provides the psychological blow that causes Vance's symbolic death of soul when he falls ill of typhoid and nearly commits suicide. This "gratuitous" episode is an important part of the "fall" of the artist, who must become Man redeemed by shriving and absolution derived from trans-forming the experience into fiction.

The first paragraph of *Hudson River Bracketed* uses an unmarked (no quotation marks or italics), unattributed (no author mentioned) layered allu-sion to the Hudson River School of painters to satirize American concepts of the past and present and to introduce the four medieval elements. Two nov-els and a dozen years educate Vance with knowledge (earth), spirituality (air), passion (fire), and reproductive love, both physical and imaginative (water). "By the time he was nineteen Vance Weston had graduated from the College of Euphoria, Illinois, where his parents then lived, had spent a week in Chicago [earth], invented a new religion [air], and edited for a few months a college magazine called *Getting There,* to which he had contributed several love poems and a series of iconoclastic essays [water]. He had also been engaged for a whole week to the inspirer of the poems [fire]. . . . " (*HRB* 3, Wharton's ellipses).

*Hudson River Bracketed* focuses on earth and water; *The Gods Arrive* on water and fire. Air is a hope by the end of the sequel. Earth in Euphoria, Illi-nois, like Apex in *The Custom of the Country,* is literally being sold down the river, commodified as real estate, the water poisoned by typhoid because people cheated on plumbing and drainage systems. Fire is replaced by cold fur-naces, and Vance's trip east for "the good country air" (*HRB* 33) implies that the atmosphere is culturally and morally unhealthy. First, he needs experience of earth—satisfaction of basic physical needs—food, clothing, shelter, and a living wage; second, experience of air; satisfaction of the intellectual and spiri-tual needs Wharton calls "life-stuff," including morality.

The developing artist, especially, needs grounding in place and past, char-acteristics Vance lacks until he discovers the Willows, the "very old house" in the Hudson River Bracketed style that is the novel's centering symbol for the arts of writing, painting, landscape gardening, and architecture. Its emanating atmosphere is a crucial influence on Vance, and its location on the Hudson River places it in the cradle of indigenous Euro-American art. Built in 1830, the fictional house was owned by the deceased Miss Emily Lorburn. But it made Vance's "mind [strike] root deep down in accumulated layers of experi-ence . . . —so that this absurd house, the joke of Halo's childhood, was to him the very emblem of man's long effort, was Chartres, the Parthenon, the Pyra-mids" (*HRB* 338).

In the first of the layered allusions, Halo describes the origin and architec-ture of the Willows:

"I perceive," she continued, "that you are not familiar with the epoch-mak-ing work of A. J. Downing, Esq. on Landscape Gardening in America. . . .
Here—here's the place. It's too long to read aloud; but the point is that Mr.

Downing, who was the great authority of the period, sums up the principal architectural styles as the Grecian, the Chinese, the Gothic, the Tuscan or Italian villa, and—Hudson River Bracketed. Unless I'm mistaken, he cites the Willows as one of the most perfect examples of Hudson River Bracketed (this was in 1842), and—yes, here's the place: 'The seat of Ambrose Lorburn Esq., the Willows, near Paul's Landing, Dutchess County, N.Y., is one of the most successful instances of etc., etc. . . . architectural elements ingeniously combined from the Chinese and the Tuscan.' " [*HRB* 66–67]

The paragraph Halo reads is not in Downing, though Wharton successfully mimics his style. Downing does say that a rural architectural modification, "partaking somewhat of the Italian and Swiss features, is what we have described more fully in our 'Cottage Residences' as the Bracketed mode. . . . We hope to see this Bracketed style becoming every day more common in the United States."[7] In *Victorian Cottage Residences* Downing devotes a chapter to "a cottage villa in the Bracketed mode." Yet only under one engraving does Downing actually use the label "Hudson River Bracketed."

Furthermore, Downing remarks: "There is scarcely a building or place more replete with interest in America, than the cottage of Washington Irving near Tarrytown. . . . The 'Legend of Sleepy Hollow,' so delightfully told in the Sketch-Book, has made every one acquainted with this neighborhood."[8] Wharton alludes to Downing, who alludes to himself and to Washington Irving, a layered allusion to a "Hudson River writer." The book goes on to explain the Dutch-English origin of the Van Tassel House in the Hudson River Bracketed style, thus merging two traditions into an indigenous mode of American domestic architecture.

But there is another layer. Halo continues: "And here's the picture, willows and all! How lovely these old steel engravings were . . . and look at my great-uncle and aunt on the lawn, pointing out to each other with pride and admiration their fairly obvious copper beech . . . 'one of the first ever planted in a gentleman's grounds in the United States' " (*HRB* 67, Wharton's ellipses). They bend over the engraving, "which reproduced the house exactly as Vance had just beheld it, except that the willows were then slender young trees, and the lawns mown, that striped awnings shaded the lower windows, and that a gentleman in a tall hat and a stock was calling the attention of a lady in bonnet and cashmere shawl to the celebrated copper beech" (*HRB* 67). Both of Downing's books are illustrated with steel engravings, but the picture Wharton describes may be a painting by Frederic Rondel, one of the members of the "Hudson River School," entitled *The Hudson River, Viewed from Lovat, the Fraser Home:* "The Lovat home, which still exists, was built in the popular 'Hudson River Bracketed' style, a term based upon the enthusiastic acceptance of the style in the Hudson River area."[9]

This Downing-Irving-Rondel allusion, however, with those below to Bryant,

Whitman, and Irving collectively, locates the birthplace of American architecture, landscape gardening, literature, and painting on the Hudson River. The "ghosts" in the historic atmosphere of the Willows combine with Halo's practical help to inspire Vance Weston's first successful novel, *Instead*, a title that seems to echo "homestead" but also foreshadows his self-destructive impulsiveness.

Halo herself lives with her relatively impoverished old New York family at Eaglewood, a "low-studded old house of gray stone" on a mountainside above the "great sweep of the Hudson" (*HRB* 69), undoubtedly similar to the illustration from Downing's *Victorian Cottage Residences*. There is history in that house, too, but like the family money, it has not been preserved. "The poets have sung us," brags Mr. Spear:

"You remember Bryant's 'Eyrie'? Yes—that's the Eaglewood view. He used to stay here with my wife's great-grandfather. And Washington Irving, in his *Sketch Book*. And Whitman—it's generally supposed . . . " (*HRB* 70, Wharton's ellipses). But "Mr. Spear's past was full of the dateless blur of the remarkable things he had not jotted down" (*HRB* 70). Furthermore, because it is not written down, his memory errs. No "Eyrie" appears in the complete works of William Cullen Bryant.[10]

Vance's future begins with typhoid contracted on a visit down the river to Crampton, where his grandparents temporarily occupy property owned by Mr. Weston. He arrives on a day "when the lilacs in his grandmother's dooryard were bursting . . . , when the earth throbbed with renewal. . . . He was irritated by the fact that he did not know the name of the bird, or of the yellow flowers. 'I should like to give everything its right name, and to know why that name *was* the right one. . . . ' There were botany manuals . . . ; but what he wanted to get at was something deeper" (*HRB* 12–13).

Here Wharton uses layered allusion to Whitman's "When Lilacs Last in the Dooryard Bloom'd," which alludes to American history and the death of Abraham Lincoln, and the subject of "names" seems to refer to Emerson's "Blight" (Emerson being important to this novel), which includes an allusion to Genesis:

But these young scholars, who invade our hills,
Bold as the engineer who fells the wood,
And travelling often in the cut he makes,
Love not the flower they pluck, and know it not,
And all their botany is Latin names

[*Blight*, ll. 17–21]

If Vance is to name nature like an American Adam, he must know its essence, the "something deeper" that is not included in even "aristocratic" college education. The above lines of Emerson's (1867), however, echo Matthew Arnold's "Scholar-Gipsy" (1853), who haunted the "green-muffled Cumner hills," and Tennyson's "Flower in the Crannied Wall" (1869), in which the plucked flower represents the mysteries of God and man. Both of these poems are directly mentioned in *The Gods Arrive* (*GA* 45, 175).

Vance's education in physical survival and Americana—things of Earth—is complete by the time he and Halo sail from New York to Spain. He receives modest royalties from his novels, and Halo has inherited the Willows. In Spain Vance becomes friends with Alders, a man whose intellect he considers impressive but whom Halo immediately recognizes as a dilettante: Alders suggested that "among his friends (he implied that they were few but illustrious) he was known as 'The Scholar Gypsy'—adding that the name (taken, he smilingly explained, from a poem by Matthew Arnold) had been conferred on him because of his nomadic habits; perhaps also, he concluded, of his scholarly tastes. . . . [Halo discovered] Alders possessed a miscellaneous accumulation of facts and anecdotes about places and people. His mind was like the inside of one of the humble curiosity-shops on the way up to the Alhambra, where nothing was worth more than a few pesetas" (*GA* 45).

First, the passage shows why Wharton chose to set the early scenes of *The Gods Arrive* in Spain, for her allusion to Washington Irving's *The Alhambra*, part of a layered allusion to Irving, Arnold, and Tennyson, connects Spain with the United States. Irving's European education significantly influenced his writing. Obviously, neither memorizing botanical names nor aimless gypsying is sufficient for Vance's education, and Alders's mention of his "scholarly tastes" is a hint of an intraauthorial allusion to Arnold's "Literature and Science," an essay Arnold delivered to audiences on an American tour in which, like Irving K. Babbitt, he defended the study of humanities against the forces of scientific and vocational education advocated by Dewey:

> This desire in men that good should be forever present to them—which acts in us when we feel the *impulse* for relating our *knowledge* to our sense for *conduct* and to our sense for *beauty*. At any rate, with men in general the *instinct* exists. Such is human nature. And the instinct, it will be admitted, is *innocent*, and human nature is preserved by our following the lead of its innocent instincts. Therefore, in seeking to gratify this instinct in question, we are following the instinct of self-preservation in humanity. But, no doubt, some kinds of knowledge cannot be made to directly serve the instinct in question, cannot be directly related to the sense for beauty, to the sense for conduct. These are *instrument* knowledges; they lead on to other knowledges. [Italics mine][11]

This is a key passage to which we will return, but one of the seven italicized words that help explain Vance's educational Odyssey is "impulse," for Sirens of literary and sexual experiment (harking back to *The Reef*) sing on every side path. Vance constantly acts impulsively in spite of the advice Frenside gives when Vance wonders about the subject of a second novel:

> "Follow your impulse" is no use when you have a hundred impulses tugging at you from the inside, and all that clatter of contradictory opinion from the outside, eh? . . . Well, you've got to stuff cotton in your ears and go ahead. . . .
>
> Ahead, you say? But where? Well, Nature abhors a void, and to fill it she's wasteful—wildly wasteful. In the abstract, my advice would be: follow her example. Be as wasteful as she is. Her darlings always are. Chase after one impulse and another . . . ; [but] let your masterpieces die off by the dozen without seeing the light. [*HRB* 376–77]

Similarly in *The Gods Arrive,* Vance tells Churley, a new friend, why he once wrote a novel on a subject he now considers inappropriate: "What's that thing in Tennyson, about 'little flower in the crannied wall,' if I knew what put you there, I'd know all there is to know; or something of that sort. Well, I was in Spain, and the subject caught me. What I call one of the siren-subjects . . . I never stir now without cotton in my ears" (*GA* 175, Wharton's ellipses). Vance is beginning to get the experience that Arnold mentions in "Literature and Science": "The appeal [of poetry] is to experience. Experience shows that for the vast majority of men, for mankind in general, they have the power. Next, do they exercise it? They do. But then, *how* do they exercise it so as to affect man's sense for conduct, his sense for beauty? . . . With patience," Arnold answers himself, quoting Homer: "for an enduring heart have the destinies appointed to the children of men," and quoting Spinoza, "Man's happiness consists in his being able to preserve his own essence" (Arnold 963). In contrast to Dewey's concept of immediate empirical experience, Arnold insists that people receive the best education through the experience of knowing "the best that has been thought and uttered in the world" (Arnold 958).

Ironically, Halo gets Arnold's kind of experience while Vance darts impulsively after what Tennyson describes in "Flower in the Crannied Wall" (1869):

> Flower in the crannied wall.
> I pluck you out of the crannies,
> I hold you here, root and all, in my hand,
> Little flower—but *if* I could understand
> What you are, root and all, and all in all,
> I should know what God and man is.

Like the romantics parodied in this poem, Vance greedily plucks the flower of his subject, examines it, and tosses it away, still hungry for knowledge.

The complex set of layered allusions just explicated began with a "double branched," or rooted, layered allusion to Whitman and Emerson. One branching root led from Whitman to Lincoln to the New Testament (resurrection). The other path led from Emerson to Genesis and to another double branching root, Arnold and Tennyson. The Arnold path led to "The Scholar-Gipsy" and "Literature and Science," which in turn led to a key word in both *Hudson River Bracketed* and *The Gods Arrive*: "impulse." That led particularly to a passage in *Hudson River Bracketed,* which alluded to an episode in the *Odyssey,* and anticipated a similar passage in *The Gods Arrive* that looped back to Tennyson. The effect of Wharton's labyrinthine layering of allusions has been to contrast American ideas of education with European ideas. As the story continues, she layers allusions to American transcendentalists as well, in the next example—Whitman, Hawthorne, and Thoreau—she also includes Irving.

After his aborted suicide, Vance arrives at Paul's Landing on the Hudson River to discover symbols of resurrection, lilacs "blooming more richly than Grandma Scrimser's" (*HRB* 38) in Mrs. Tracy's "overshaded dooryard." He finds the community so quiet that it "seems as if they'd all slept right round the clock." The Tracy house was "not an isolated phenomenon but part of some huge geological accident. 'As if they'd been caught centuries ago under a landslide, and just gone on living there, like those toads they find alive inside a stone— and on this confused analogy the young traveller fell asleep" (*HRB* 42). Vance, still ill, sleeps "nearly as long as he had metaphorically accused the inhabitants of Paul's Landing of doing" (*HRB* 43).

Wharton here has created an "associative allusion," an indirect "layered" allusion that juxtaposes literary bricks rather than stacking them. Vance has confusedly jumbled together Irving's "Rip Van Winkle," and Hawthorne's "Ambitious Guest" (in which a traveler is buried in a landslide), awakening to find the lilac, a hint of Whitman's resurrection theme in "When Lilacs Last in a Dooryard Bloom'd." He spends the morning writing a poem about a "mysterious city built of leaves" in which "his own soul was like a forest" (echoing the "architectural foliage" of Thoreau's *Walden*) and like a "mysterious stranger" (the title of Mark Twain's novel) within himself.

Vance's poem features Christ likening the Magdalen's gesture of breaking a box of lilac ointment over his feet to the "perfume of holiness" (*HRB* 45). This allusion is to Luke 7:38 and John 11, so that Magdalen, the forgiven prostitute, ironically refers back to the strangely unaccused Floss Delaney and the unforgiven Grandpa Scrimser. John, however, may be the source of another layered allusion, for that episode recorded in John is followed by another, John 11:2-4: "(It was that Mary which anointed the Lord with ointment and wiped his feet with her hair, whose brother Lazarus was sick). . . . When Jesus heard *that,* he said, 'This sickness is not unto death.' " This is a reverse layered allusion to Kierkegaard's existential work on despair, *Sickness Unto Death,* and is related to the resurrection theme of the novel represented by clusters of allusions to Genesis, sin, death, atonement, and resurrection.

The first resurrection from illness occurs in Euphoria when Vance writes his short story. The second occurs at the Tracys' when he writes the Magdalen-lilac poem. Finally, Wharton allows America to awaken. That awakening is reinforced by Halo's influence and the view of the Hudson River at sunrise from Thundertop—ironically a mountain named after the eerie peak overlooking the Hudson where, under "rolling peals, like distant thunder," Rip Van Winkle fell asleep. There Vance awakens to his literary genius; he becomes a storyteller as Rip did. But allegorically America also awakens to art, for at the Willows below Thundertop, Wharton gathers together a description of the first bloom of several American arts—Hudson River Bracketed architecture, the allusions to the poetry, novels, stories, and essays of Whitman, Thoreau, Hawthorne, Irving, and Emerson, the landscape architecture and etchings of Downing, the Hudson River School paintings, and the anonymous colonial painting of Miss Lorburn over the fireplace at the Willows. The reference to Bryant spreads the allusions to the arts because, as editor of the *Atlantic Monthly*, Bryant was the influential patron of the Hudson River artists and the friend and patron of Downing. This combination of allusions to the arts suggests when and where Wharton places the beginnings of non–Native American art. The third awakening occurs at the conclusion to *The Gods Arrive,* when Vance recovers from pneumonia and takes up his responsibilities.

Vance also has three falls, the first with Floss Delaney and his near suicide, the second with Upton Tracy at the house of prostitution, and the third, which occurs in *The Gods Arrive,* again involves Floss Delaney but includes the suicide of Chris Churley. But at nineteen, as he writes "One Day" about his grandfather, Vance discovers that writing is a "way of reconciling his soul to its experiences" (*HRB* 31), and "reconciliation" can be another word for forgiveness. Writing is a way to cleanse the soul and live on. Yet while writing may cleanse the soul of sin, it requires life experience in which, paradoxically, the trap of sinfulness is inherent. At the Tracys', Vance was disappointed, "feeling that he was somehow being cheated out of hoped-for experiences" (*HRB* 46–47). In an autoallusion to a letter Edith Wharton once wrote, Wharton says Vance felt that "if his mind contained more of the stuff of experience, words would have flocked of their own accord for its expression. He supposed it must take a good deal of experience to furnish the material for even a few lines of poetry" (*HRB* 47–48).

Vance's second fall results from experiences that begin with his literary education under Halo's tutelage. The artist needs experience in order to write, but Wharton means experience of what she calls "life-stuff" (*HRB* 216), part of which is sexuality, as shown in *The Reef.* And by now Vance has begun to waken to his inexperience: "And he felt also increasingly, as his life widened, how small his provision of experience was. He needed time for himself—time to let his mind ripen. . . . everything he saw, and took into himself, came with a breaking away of tendrils, a rending of filaments to which the soil of life still clung—and he was familiar, as yet, with so few inches of that soil" (*HRB* 258). Vance is mistaken about rootlessness, but experience here is not the structured empirical experience of Dewey's formal education, nor just learning, nor just the observation of Nature advocated by Emerson in "Experience," although those are included. It is "life-stuff," absorbed and digested, and that "stuff" is the ineluctable and inseparable combination of the physical, psychological, moral and intellectual. To dramatize this Fury-like hunger for the experience of life stuff, Wharton makes Vance into the "starving artist" and implicitly compares him to Tarrant, an incompetent editor who is finicky about food, incapable of digesting even an egg, another resurrection symbol, which *he* claims is "slow death" (*HRB* 207).

Vance's experiences of life invariably arise from impulsive satisfactions of ravenous hungers. Emerson called impulsiveness "spontaneity" and approved of it: "So in this great society wide lying around us, a critical analysis would find very few spontaneous actions."[12] But Babbitt felt that for a student to follow his "spontaneous inclinations, natural preferences, and easiest habitual activities" was absurd and for that reason strongly resisted college courses on the elective system: "The elective system's self-evident absurdity called only for Babbitt's satiric restatement: 'The wisdom of all the ages is to be as naught compared with the inclination of a sophomore.' "[13] Vance *learned* to be impulsive in school, and his impulses invariably lead to disaster.

In almost every case of Vance's impulsive behavior someone is hurt. Take, for instance, the "theft" of Laura Lou from her fiancé, Bunty Hayes. Bunty gets drunk and violently accosts Vance in his office for the "theft" of his fiancée. Yet Vance "was not in the least sorry for what they had done to Bunty Hayes" (*HRB* 288). He has yet to learn that where there is no repentance, there is no forgiveness and no redemption.

Vance's next ethical error is negotiating with a second publisher while under contract to "Dreck and Saltzer" (an apparent allusion to Carlyle's *Sartor Resartus*). Wharton is merciless in her satire of the shallow commercialization of art, including the practice of buying literary prizes: "The whole subject of the Pulsifer Prize, with its half-confessed background of wire-pulling and influencing, was particularly distasteful" (*HRB* 330). She criticizes the use of art to promote merchandise; the indentured slavery of artists to unfair contracts; the sculptress who "does" popular artists, hoping to cash in on their successes; and commercial use of artists to write book jackets, advertising, or "pot boilers." But in another layered allusion, this one to Carlyle, Keats, and Shakespeare, Wharton admits the practical truths that the artist is entitled to a living wage on the one hand, but that Vance must learn to deal with commercialism on the other. He must learn in emotional *and* practical matters to "load every rift with gold."

When Halo and Vance discover they are in love, Halo insists they part: "He had an idea she would be very conscientious, full of scruples he wasn't sure he wholly understood. For if she hadn't cared as much as he did, why should she have devoted all those hours to helping him? If it was just for the good of the *New Hour,* she was indeed the ideal wife for an editor! But no: those afternoons had been as full for her as for him. What was that phrase she had pointed out, in the volume of Keats's *Letters* she had given him—about loading every rift with gold? That was what they had done to their hours together" (*HRB* 350).

The allusion is to Keats's letter to Percy Bysshe Shelley of 16 August 1820, in which he suggests that the artist deserves to be paid, that there is an element of slavery to discipline, and that the purpose of art must have density of meaning: "A modern work it is said must have a purpose, which may be the God— *an artist* must serve Mammon—he must have 'self-concentration' selfishness perhaps. You I am sure will forgive me for sincerely remarking that you might curb your magnanimity and be more of an artist, and 'load every rift' of your subject with ore. The thought of such discipline must fall like cold chains upon you, who perhaps never sat with your wings furl'd for six Months together."[14]

In turn, Keats was alluding to exploring the rough architecture of the caves of Mammon in Spenser's *Faerie Queene,* II.vii.28:

That houses forme within was rude and strong,
Like an huge cave hewne out of rocky clift,
From whose rough vaut the ragged breaches hong,
Embost with massy gold of glorious gift,
And with rich metall loaded every rift,
That heavy ruine they did seeme to threat;
And over them Arachne high did lift
Her cunning web, and spred her subtile net,
Enwrapped in fowle smoke and clouds more blacke then
    Jet.

The *Faerie Queene,* then, is Wharton's source for Jet Pulsifer, the golden-clad spider's first name (" 'Jet'. . . . she had such a queer name" [*HRB* 298]), and for the scene where she seduces Vance, the unwary fly, in the circular parlor of her mansion where he is "enchanted" by "shadowy hangings full of figures and trees and colonnaded architecture" (*HRB* 299). Thus, using a layered allusion rooted in the past, Wharton returns to her major themes, the architecture of the creative imagination, the interweaving of the arts, the education that "weaving" requires, and the dangers of commercialization.

Wharton entwines matters of physical and economic survival with education about the poets and artists of American landscape to demonstrate the foundation necessary for the intellectual and spiritual maturation of the American artist. So after Mrs. Tracy's machinations, Vance lives with Laura Lou in a New York rooming house, thinking, writing, and reading: "The foundations of his being had been shaken; . . . But all the while he was rebuilding his soul" (*HRB* 487–88).

During his first stay in New York, Vance submits his poetry to *The Hour*. Frenside, its editor, responds cynically to his imitation of transcendentalism, the inevitable Whitman: " 'Vast enigmatic reaches of ocean beyond me'—just so. It *is* beyond you, my dear fellow, at least at present" (*HRB* 164–65). Vance's poem is imitative of Whitman's "As I Ebb'd with the Ocean of Life," in which the ocean symbolizes an eternal creative mother. Though the poetry is rejected, three days later, "One Day," the slice-of-life story about Grandfather Scrimser's revolting affair with Floss Delaney, is accepted.

With the money Vance can return to Euphoria, but first, Wharton establishes the bridge to *The Gods Arrive,* in which the elements of water (creativity) and fire (passion) predominate. " 'I want to go and see the ocean,' he suddenly said aloud. He didn't know where the words had come from, but the force of the impulse was overwhelming. Perhaps he had unconsciously recalled Frenside's sneer: 'Ever seen the ocean? Not even from Coney Island?' " (*HRB* 168). He goes there and finds "another surface, an unknown element":

> Vance stood and gazed, and felt for the first time the weight of the universe upon him. Even the open sky of the plains, bending to the horizon on all sides, and traceried and buttressed, up aloft, with the great structure of the stars, seemed less huge, less immemorial, less incomprehensible to the finite mind than this expanse which rested not yet moved not, except in a rhythmic sway as regular as the march of the heavens. . . . he scrambled across the dunes to the sands, reached the stones of the beach, knelt close to that long incoming curve, and plunged his hands into it, as if in dedication. [*HRB* 169–70]

Using the language of architecture and an expiatory washing of hands, Vance virtually dramatizes Whitman's line, "As the ocean so mysterious rolls toward me closer and closer" ("As I Ebb'd," line 21) with a ritual prayer to the symbol of eternity, the origin of life, universal creative mother.

Vance connects Laura Lou with watery creativity, with Venus coming out of the sea—the pinks, peaches, and pearls of shells. But he is mistaken in associating the passive and unintelligent Laura Lou with creativity. Nevertheless, she reminds him of poetry he read in Miss Lorburn's library, Christopher Marlowe's *Dr. Faustus:*

> "Is this the face that launched a thousand ships
> And burnt the topless towers of Ilium?" [*HRB* 115]

Wharton connects the ship/water/beauty imagery in Marlowe to Beddoes:

"When she moves, you see
Like water from a crystal overflowed,
Fresh beauty tremble out of her, and lave
Her fair sides to the ground . . . " [*HRB* 115–16, 247, Wharton's ellipses]

"There was something almost rigidly attentive in [Laura Lou's] look and attitude, as though she were a translucent vessel so brimming with happiness that
she feared to move or speak lest it should overflow" (*HRB* 228). The lines are
from Thomas Beddoes's verse drama, *Death's Jestbook,* a Gothic revenge
tragedy in which death and resurrection are the black comedy of fools. Beddoes wrote to a friend that he had written a play in which "Despair has married wildest mirth."[15] Laura Lou is Vance's "little creature, who seemed as
transparent as a crystal cup (his little cup, he had once called her)," yet she is
also "a painted veil over the unknown" (*HRB* 288). In actuality she is passion-
less, passive, and bland, a figment of Vance's poetic imagination and impulsive
response to empty beauty that deadens his creative forces. When Laura Lou
becomes ill the first time, Vance's thoughts echo the fragmented globe of
Goethe's *Faust* as he watches "the crystal splinters of his poem melt away one
after another, as the spring icicles were melting from the roof" (*HRB* 291).

Vance soon realizes that he has married "despair." Laura Lou is childlike
and sickly. Creative waters merely sustain her life. She sleeps constantly, is
nursed on liquids—milk and tonics. On the one hand "she was the vessel from
which he had drunk . . . divine reassurance," a "moment of union with the
universe" (*HRB* 238–39), but on the other she is also "a woman with a sealed
soul" (*HRB* 237), whose "mental limits" mean that "things that counted for
him would never count for her" (*HRB* 259). Intellectually and physically she
is a cold, empty shell who, having no life of her own, literally drains Vance.
He must waste creative energy by continually resurrecting her: "whenever he
returned, after an absence of a few hours, only her lovely ghost awaited him,
and his presence had to warm her back to life" (*HRB* 253–54).

Laura Lou is of earth ("a solid earthly fact" [*HRB* 253]), not water after
all, and theirs is not a fairy-tale marriage. "He knew that Laura Lou, the inspirer of this desire [to write], was also the insuperable obstacle to its ful-
filment" (*HRB* 239). Her jealousies and passive unintelligence cool both physical passion and the fire of inspiration.

Examples of reverberating allusions occur in Vance's three ritual awaken-
ings from his intellectual "twilight sleep." The first had occurred after "seeing
his grandfather by the river with Floss Delaney—he had been dragged back to
life by the need to work his anguish out in words" (*HRB* 516). The second was
signaled by a reverberating allusion to Shakespeare and Whitman. The lilac
Laura Lou places on Vance's pillow is Whitman's symbol of resurrection. In
"When Lilacs Last in the Dooryard Bloom'd," Whitman's phrase "lovely and

soothing death" (sec. 14) echoes "O, amiable, lovely Death" (Shakespeare, *King John*, act 3, scene 3, l. 25), which is spoken with ironic anguish by Constance, mother of the pretender to the throne. *King John* is about Prince Philip's political and moral education, a play linked thematically to Vance's moral education.

Vance's third awakening occurs after the cruel jest of Laura Lou's death: "She seemed to have been modelled by a sculptor who had no power of conveying the deeper emotions—or to have reached a region where they drop from the soul like a worn garment. . . . For a long while he stood gazing at the empty shell" (*HRB* 525).

The shell image recalls Oliver Wendell Holmes's poem "The Chambered Nautilus," which not only returns the reader to the theme of architecture, seen in Keats's chamber of maiden thought and mansion of many apartments, but also reflects the sea/water imagery Vance associates with Laura Lou:

> Build thee more stately mansions, O my soul,
> As the swift seasons roll!
> Leave thy low-vaulted past!
> Let each new temple, nobler than the last,
> Shut thee from heaven with a dome more vast,
> Till thou at length art free,
> Leaving thine outgrown shell by life's unresting sea!
>
> [*Chambered Nautilus*, ll. 29–35]

Vance's experience of death is strangely empty. In *Death's Jest Book*, Beddoes describes Wolfram's death as a vapor dissolving into the elements: "Aye, nobly doffed he his humanity. / The bodily cloud that veiled his majesty / Melted away into the elements" (*Fragments*, VIII). But for Vance "it was as if a door had quietly opened and shut in a room in which he was working—and when he looked up from his work he saw no change" (*HRB* 528). This image of a door closing on nothingness bounces back to Renaissance drama, especially the revenge tragedies. And Wharton's passage contains this "reverberating allusion": "Death hath so many doors to let out life" (Beaumont and Massinger, *Custom of the Country*, II.ii); "I know death hath ten thousand several doors / For men to take their exit" (John Webster, *The Duchess of Malfi*, IV.ii); "Death hath a thousand doors to let out life—" (Philip Massinger, *A Very Woman*, act 5 scene 4); "The thousand doors that let out death" (Thomas Browne, *Religio Medici*, part 1, sec. 46).

Possibly, when Wharton said that *Hudson River Bracketed* was her "best book," she had in mind this complex development of layered and reverberating allusions, while her sigh that "I have little hope that the public will think so" reflects her understanding that limited education would prevent Americans from recognizing its worth.[16] This deeply felt belief in education, experience, and culture is reflected in a letter of 19 October 1918, in which Wharton tells an aspiring poet, "It takes a great deal of the deepest kind of culture to write one little poem." She restates this judgment in 1929 when she makes Vance say in *Hudson River Bracketed*, "He supposed it must take a good deal of experience to furnish the material for even a few lines of poetry" (*HRB* 47–48).

With *Hudson River Bracketed*, Edith Wharton begins to summarize her creative techniques, even naming her own layered allusions, for Vance's awakening on Thundertop begins with an Emersonian sense of Nature but is "filled with layer upon layer of delicately drawn motionless leaves" (*HRB* 93). He writes a romantic poem about "a city of leaves," about "the soul's city being built of all the murmurs and rustlings of our impressions, emotions, instincts . . . " But Halo tries to inspire him past the tree leaves of transcendentalism, toward layers of leaves, layers of books, by telling the story about the temple at Delphi where Oedipus sought knowledge of his future (*HRB* 99, Wharton's ellipses). She fails just then, but Vance develops a "fury of intellectual hunger" at the Willows that prompts him to ask endless questions. As he begins to understand simple allusions to Lohengrin and Moses (*HRB* 317), Halo inculcates "principles of order," and in the library Vance begins to think, "This is the Past—if only I could get back into it. . . . " (*HRB* 317, Wharton's ellipses). Meanwhile the portrait of Miss Lorburn, as if Wharton herself, hovers over this writer of the next generation. "No one, apparently had . . . wanted to receive what she offered; yet instead of withering she had ripened. Her books, and some inner source of life, had kept her warm" (*HRB* 318). "Her long thin hands [were] full of gifts for someone . . . " "Suddenly a queer idea" came to Vance, and he spent the night writing. She had "known love" (*HRB* 318, Wharton's ellipses). Miss Lorburn, her portrait, and her library had the answer to the Sphinx's "unanswered question," a literary allusion: "I heard a poet answer. . . . Deep love lieth under / These pictures of time; / They fade in the light of their meaning sublime" (*The Sphinx*, stanza 9, ll. 65, 69–72).

Moreover, by the end of the novel Vance begins to realize that his grandmother, who preaches the religious sublime, is the "bearer of a message," but Grandmother Scrimser is disappointed, as Wharton must have been, that her "message didn't get over" (*HRB* 443). The theme of the encoded message is in place for *The Gods Arrive* to develop. Learning, education, the asking of questions, and experience have been stressed in *Hudson River Bracketed*, but themes of suicide, the neglected child, and awakening from sleep again hover in the background. In *The Gods Arrive*, Vance must travel, searching the world to awaken to language, literature, classical music, philosophy, art history, impressionist painting, Gothic architecture, theater, opera, and ballet before he is able to hear his grandmother's message and before we can solve the code.

# *The Gods Arrive*
## More Reverberating and Layered Allusions

T HE SEQUEL TO *Hudson River Bracketed, The Gods Arrive,* continues with European scenes, educating Vance in the arts, in passion, and spirituality (fire, air).[1] Problems of the earth—matters of basic survival—were solved in *Hudson River Bracketed,* where he floundered in the waters of creativity while drawn to the wrong fiery passions.[2] In sustaining these themes, Wharton continues using layered and reverberating allusions.

Water images provide a transition between the novels. In the opening scene Halo and Vance leave New York, crossing the ocean to live together in Europe until Tarrant divorces Halo to marry Jet Pulsifer. The decision that at first seems liberating becomes a lie, precipitating a string of events that eventually result in disastrous consequences Halo is too "short-sighted" to anticipate. Halo is ostracized by society for unmarried cohabitation, but Vance is not. Furthermore, Vance begins to wish for an intellectual life that is independent of Halo's. Her disappointment when he doesn't share his work with her, and his resentment of her expectations, gradually alienate them. The problems can be solved only when Vance learns to grow up, think of others, develop the "habit" of work, and take responsibility for his impulsive actions. In her turn, Halo needs to communicate her feelings and develop a creative outlet of her own. So Vance's education has not yet graduated to Fire and Air, to inspiration and spirituality.

At a party Vance accidentally discovers from Mrs. Glashier that Halo is being snubbed for "living in sin." The New York society matron tells Vance that Halo's husband, Lewis Tarrant, is no longer "engaged" to Mrs. Pulsifer and is in Paris. Vance dashes impulsively through a drenching rainstorm to talk Tarrant into divorcing Halo. Tarrant receives him coolly and in his "icy pride" refuses to discuss the situation, but afraid of a scene, he allows Vance into his sitting room with its "empty hearth." Suddenly Vance experiences compassion, possibly for the first time. This is a developmental moment, symbolized by Vance's overcoat drenched from his plunge into the psychological ocean of the Mothers: "The wetness of his overcoat began to penetrate to his skin, and he shivered slightly, and pulled the overcoat off" (*GA* 143). Symbolically stripping himself of the cold layer of literary naturalism, he is ready to face his Puritan heritage and build a firmer architectural foundation for mind and soul.

A quotation from *Hudson River Bracketed* is a structural allusion to the source of the surface design of both novels about the development of an artist. Wharton attributes an epigram on the title page to Charles Auchester: "All things make me glad, and sorry too." Charles Auchester is the title character of a Victorian novel by Sara Elizabeth Sheppard.[3] *Charles Auchester* (1853) was begun by its Jewish author when she was only sixteen. In a German music school the young violinist is influenced by the angellike Saraphael, a genius representing Mendelssohn. In *Charles Auchester* artists are always godly and morally superior. The characters are fifteen-year-old geniuses of angelic disposition who expire after major triumphs. When Charles tells Clara, "All things make me glad and sorry, too,"[4] he is alluding to the romantic idea that natural emotion is the source of individual artistic genius.

Much of Wharton's satire in *Hudson River Bracketed* and *The Gods Arrive* is contained in comparisons to *Charles Auchester,* representative of a tradition of sentimentalized romantic notions. Filtered through American transcendentalism into popular culture, those notions devalue tradition at the same time that they depend on it. Wharton demonstrates what happens to a genius educated in "nature" without tradition, who assumes that because he is "inspired" he is automatically morally superior. Wharton's informed opinion is that the artist needs strong feelings *balanced by* nature, education, experience, and discipline ("the habit of work"), and Vance Weston will not be a great American artist until he achieves them all.

The topic of *Charles Auchester* is classical music, and Wharton, like many nonmusicians in the 1920s, regards jazz as merely a fad in the Fitzgerald stories she satirizes as *Jerks and Jazzes* (HRB 224). To her there is no great American music yet. Nevertheless, music is an important part of the architecture of culture, so it's not incidental that Charles Auchester finds Spanish and German castles so inspirational (as does Vance in *The Gods Arrive*). Another reverberating allusion begins with Emerson's essay "Quotation and Originality," in which he attributes the phrase "architecture is frozen music" to Madame de Staël: "The sign of a monument is like a continuous and stationary music" (*Corina* [1807], book 4, chapter 3), a statement Madame de Staël borrowed from Goethe's "architecture is frozen music" (*Philosophie der Kunst* 576, 593).[5]

The umbrella theme of nearly all of the literary allusions of *The Gods Arrive* is spirit: air, love, heaven, God, gods or goddesses, the Mothers. An art allusion to Poussin's *The Inspiration of the Poet* (GA 114)[6] seems to sum it up, as does another stanza of Emerson's "The Sphinx":

Nicholas Poussin, *The Inspiration of the Poet* (c. 1636). Musée du Louvre, Cliché des Musée Nationaux—Paris. Thematic Allusion: *The Gods Arrive*. (This painting is probably the one Wharton meant by "Poet and Muse.")

The heavens that now draw him
    With sweetness untold
Once found,—for new heavens
    He spurneth the old.
    [*The Sphinx*, stanza 11, ll. 85–88]

Water imagery continues. After several months in Spain during which Vance publishes his second novel, *Puritan in Spain,* Halo and Vance move to Paris. When Vance looks into the Seine, recalling their friendless, monotonous life in Cadiz, images of fire and water recur: "The sight of the moving waters always arrested him, and he leaned on the parapet and watched the breeze crisp the river. . . . He had imagined that once he was at work Halo's presence would be the only stimulus he needed; and no doubt it was, since the book had been written. But he had not felt her imagination flaming through him as it had when they used to meet at the Willows. The dampening effect of habit seemed to have extinguished that flame" (*GA* 72). He disappoints Halo, however, by not reacting as she expects to glorious works of art—the architecture of air and fire—for which he is so unready. Furthermore, Vance finds that his old epistemology does not function with "celestial architecture":

> The monumental Spanish sky was full of cloud-architecture. Long azure perspectives between colonnades and towers stretched away majestically above an empty earth. The real Spain seemed to be overhead, heavy with history . . . splendours . . . stored in the air-palaces along those radiant avenues. The clouds peopled even the earth with their shadow-masses. . . . All that Vance had ever read about mirages and desert semblances rose in his mind . . . , with all those New Jerusalems building and re-building themselves overhead. [*GA* 20–21]

In this passage the heavy floats, and the substantial becomes a mirage. The epistemological confusion caused by Europe's plethora of unaccustomed sights and sounds throws Vance into a painfully sensitive psychological state.

In a rich scene that further reflects Vance's psychological disorientation, Halo takes him, as it seems, *down* into a cathedral. " 'The place is as big as that sky out there,' he murmured" (*GA* 21). Completely confused and overwhelmed, he is plunged into a world in which Einstein's theory of relativity seems at work: He "felt as if he had dropped over the brim of things into the mysterious world where straight lines loop themselves into curves." He can't bear it: "They were caught in a network of architectural forms, perpetually repeated abstractions of the relation between arch and shaft" (*GA* 21). "It's like the feel of poetry, just as it's beginning to be born" (*GA* 22). But he feels that he is lost in a "Cretan labyrinth," that he is Faust descending to the Mothers (*GA* 23). While he fears he "might never find the right door, but go on turning about forever at the dark heart of things," at the same time something seductive makes him long "to sit down at the foot of one of the glimmering shafts and let the immensity and the mystery sweep over him like the sea" (*GA* 23). The experience is a strange Freudian-Faustian struggle between the desire to procreate, symbolized by the arch and shaft, and the desire to die, to descend, to find the heart of darkness and never return. Heaven and hell, sex and death, are inextricably entangled. When at last "they found the right door. . . . Vance felt like a disembodied spirit coming back to earth" (*GA* 21–23). Before Vance can dive into a "vision profounder," as Emerson called it in "The Sphinx," a vision that suspends familiar modes of thinking, that permits parallel lines to

curve, and stone palaces to float, he must first understand the nature of creativity. Vance must "descend to the Mothers," the Faustian goddesses who live
beneath the ocean; alone he must negotiate the submarine maze and resurface
without drowning in the sea of self-knowledge.

He gets a hint of realization on an occasion after his overwhelming experience in the Spanish cathedral when Vance gazes into the river, recalling a
separation from his friends during a car trip through an unfamiliar town. During a rainstorm he had taken refuge in a church and was rewarded with fleeting
glimpses of heaven and hell, of air and fire for, as he sat in hellish darkness,
lightning flashes had briefly illuminated stunning stained glass windows.

On the Riviera, Vance and Halo meet Chris Churley, an aspiring writer
with a brain "uncertain as the sea" (*GA* 177). In Oubli Chris is constantly
depressed, complaining that he needs to get away from his family and experience the world before he can write. Chris is a youth with "flaming intelligence" (*GA* 172) who talks about writing but never writes. "Talk of ineffectual
angels—there were ineffectual devils too, and he was one of them," he tells
Vance in his depression.[7] "For his part, he'd rather give himself a hypo and be
done with it . . . " (*GA* 244, Wharton's ellipses). Now progressed to the position of mentor, Vance sympathetically lends him money to work for a London
literary journal, the *Windmill*. Chris vanishes.

In response to the worry of one of the Mothers, Mrs. Churley, Vance locates his friend in Monte Carlo gambling and otherwise living a dissolute life.
But Vance disrupts Chris's rescue when he succumbs to an impulse to pursue
the newly resurfaced Floss Delaney, the girl who slept with his grandfather by
the river at the beginning of *Hudson River Bracketed*. Without considering the
consequences of his actions, Vance abandons Chris without seeing him safely
home. Chris commits suicide. Once again Vance is forced to consider the
meanings of responsibility and death: he "understood that at that moment the
Furies only slept" (*GA* 189).

Guilt and renewed interest in Floss Delaney contribute to his decision to
leave Halo, but Floss rejects Vance, who then retreats into the woods where,
still "drowning," he contracts pneumonia. His recovery becomes a resurrection. Reborn and ready to "eat the food of the full grown," ready to accept
responsibility and pain, he returns to the Willows, unaware that Halo is living
there waiting for the birth of their child. She now has her own creative preoc-
cupations. The couple is reunited with hope for a fruitful future.

The allusions to the descent to the Mothers in Goethe's *Faust* are central
to these novels. As Vance reads his work to a hometown audience in *Hudson
River Bracketed*, he "could hear his voice flagging and groping as he hurried
on from fragment to fragment . . . Which was it now? Ah: the descent to the
Mothers, the crux, the centre of the book. He had put the whole of himself
into that scene—and his self had come out of Euphoria, been conceived and

fashioned there" (*GA* 380, Wharton's ellipses). In both novels, literally all of the women are "Mothers," whether or not they have children. Halo is described as maternal to Vance even before she marries Tarrant and gives birth to a baby that does not survive. Laura Lou is described as maternal when she tells Vance she is not pregnant. Even Mrs. Tracy has a glimmer of maternal light to offer as she leaves the flicker of a "candle at the upper landing" (*HRB* 52). Maternal characters include Grandmother Scrimser, "Mother Hubbard," "mother Glaisher," and Rebecca Stram's "Jewish mother." Some of the mothers are helpful, others are not.

Wharton's leitmotifs of experience, education, the elements, and architecture converge in *Faust*. They delve beneath the Mothers in layered allusions to creativity in Goethe, Marlowe, Plutarch, and Homer. Specifically, the layers include Goethe's *Faust*, which was based on Chrisopher Marlowe's *Dr. Faustus*. Both were based on Plutarch's *Lives*, which itself alludes to Homer. Since all contain the story of Helen of Troy, this is a layered cluster with a secondary thematic allusion like the cluster in *The Glimpses of the Moon* that contains a secondary thematic allusion to Cleopatra.

Goethe's use of the Mothers was inspired by an episode in Plutarch's *Lives*, specifically the life of Marcellus, but who are the Mothers and what do they represent? According to a study by Harold Jantz, "The Mothers . . . symbolize the original action of those elemental forces in Man, out of which grew the aesthetic development of the race. . . . the Idea of the Beautiful has a more mysterious origin, springs from a diviner necessity, and finds only hints, not perfect results in the operations of Nature."[8] Based on Wharton's extensive reading of Goethe, there can be little doubt that she was aware of Goethe's source and the idea of The Beautiful represented by Helen of Troy, to whom she has already connected Laura Lou through Marlowe's *Dr. Faustus*.

Halo, who from the beginning of *Hudson River Bracketed* has symbolized fire and air, intellectual inspiration, and spirituality, first suggested the hike up Thundertop to see the sunrise, which reminds her of certain lines from *Faust* that she quotes in German (*HRB* 85):

"Die Sonne tönt nach alter Weise
In Brudersphären Wettgesang.
Und ihre vorgeschriebene Reise
Vollendet sie mit Donnergang.
Ihr Anblick giebt den Engeln Stärke
Wenn keiner sie ergründen mag,
Die unbegreiflich hohen Werke
Sind herrlich wie am ersten Tag."

The passage is from Raphael's first speech in the Prologue of *Faust*, Part 1. Shelley's translation is especially beautiful:

The sun makes music as of old
Amid the rival spheres of Heaven,
In its predestined circle rolled
With thunder speed. The Angels even
Draw strength from gazing on its glance
Though none its meaning fathom may;
The world's unwithered countenance
Is bright as at creation's day.

Since Vance speaks no German, he can only appreciate the music of the poetry, and until he is educated in the Spirit he cannot be a true artist, for an artist must control "impulses," and risk the dive to inspirational sources, the paradoxical Mothers of creativity and destruction alluded to by Emerson:

To vision profounder,
    Man's spirit must dive;
His aye-rolling orb
    At no goal will arrive;
    [Emerson, "The Sphinx", stanza 11]

The same theme is expressed in *Faust:*

Whoever is ignorant
of the four elements
of the strength they wield
and of their quality
cannot master
the band of the spirits.
    [*Faust,* part 1, ll. 1278–83]

In Spain at the beginning of *The Gods Arrive,* Vance remains untrained in the language of architecture until he experiences his frightening psychosexual descent to the Mothers in the cathedral. That mythological experience must precede a symbolic rebirth. The author now begins to braid together Vance's experiences, and this novel, which seems so simple on the surface, becomes densely complex.

In the Spanish cathedral with Halo "Vance remembered a passage in the Second Faust which had always haunted him: the scene where Faust descends to the Mothers. 'He must have wound round and round like this,' he thought" (*GA* 22–23). In his mind he associates Faust's subterranean journey with the unique Cretan architectural invention, the labyrinth.

In the passage Vance recalls, Mephistopheles tells Faust he must seek the

Mothers, who hold secret the mystery necessary to make the symbol of beauty, Helen of Troy, materialize:

> Unwilling, I reveal a loftier mystery.—
>> In solitude are throned the Goddesses,
>> No Space around them, Place and Time, still
>>> less;
>> Only to speak of them embarrasses.
>> They are THE MOTHERS.
>> . . . . . . . . . . . . . . . . .
>> It is so. Goddesses, unknown to ye,
>> The Mortals,—named by us unwillingly.
>> Delve in the deepest depths must thou, to
>>> reach them:

Faust asks the way:

>> No way!—To the Unreachable,
>> Ne'er to be trodden! A Way to the
>> Unbeseechable, Never to be sought! Art thou
>> prepared? There are no locks, no latches to
>> be lifted; Through endless solitudes shalt
>> thou be drifted. Hast thou through solitudes
>> and deserts fared?
>> . . . . . . . . . . . . .
>> And hadst thou swum to farthest verge of
>>> ocean,
>> And there the boundless space beheld,
>> Still hadst thou seen wave after wave in
>>> motion,
>> Even though impending doom thy fear compelled.
>> Thou hadst seen something,—in the beryl dim
>> Of peace-lulled seas the sportive dolphins
>>> swim;
>> Hadst seen the flying clouds, sun, moon, and
>>> star:
>> Not hear thy footstep fall, nor meet
>> A stable spot to rest thy feet.
>
> [part 2, act 1, ll. 6212–49]

Goethe's realm of the Mothers (or the "Eternal-Feminine" [act 5, l. 12110]) is womblike: "The ultimate deep symbol of motherhood raised to the universal and the cosmic, of the birth, sending forth, death, and return of all things in an eternal cycle, is expressed in the Mothers, the matrices of all forms, at the timeless, placeless originating womb or hearth where chaos is transmuted into cosmos and whence the forms of creation issue forth into the world of place and time. . . . a realm of this kind is more a matter of continuous poetic tradition than has ever been realized" (Jantz 37).

Wharton connects the Mothers to the scene in the Spanish church through the architectural symbol of the labyrinth (supposedly designed in Crete by Daedalus—the "Daedalian plan" of Emerson's "The Sphinx"), which in these novels is always associated with moral, ethical, and artistic errors such as Vance's father's "labyrinth of . . . underground arrangements" (*HRB* 246). Vance's own ethical miscalculations over his literary contracts is a "blind labyrinth, a disconnected muddle" (*HRB* 388), his trip to London is a floating "labyrinthine adventure" of artistic misjudgments in which Goethe's dolphin image appears: "He felt the stealing temptation to dream his own books instead of writing them. What a row of masterpieces they would be! They die in the process of being written, he mused. And he thought what his life might have been if he could have drifted from one fancy to another, letting each scatter its dolphin-colours unseen as another replaced it" (*GA* 280).

One of the two most significant labyrinths was his mistaken marriage to Laura Lou: "This discovery of the frail limits of personality, of the transformation of what seemed closest and most fixed in the flux of life, dragged his brain down into a labyrinth of conjecture. . . . Unknown forces possessed her, she was wandering in ways he could not follow. . . . " (*HRB* 293, second ellipses Wharton's). The descent to the Mothers' labyrinth is always destructive unless the mortal traveler escapes and he almost never does. Mephistopheles gives Faust a sparkling magic key to help him find his way (the image of the key is recurrent in these novels) but wonders whether Faust will ever return. Faust understands that he is being sent into the void but says,

> Well, let us on! We'll plumb your deepest ground,
> For in your Nothing may the All be found.
>
> [*Faust,* part 2, act 1, ll. 6255–56]

Vance realizes, "You have to go plumb down to the Mothers to fish up the real thing" (*GA* 118).

So when, near the end of *The Gods Arrive,* Vance finds himself in an aimless maze after his disastrous experience with Floss Delaney, who is intensely interested in Mothers' Meetings, he luckily recalls a clue in the earlier advice of Frenside: "Well, now take hold of life as it lies around you; you remember Goethe: 'Wherever you take hold of it, it's interesting' ? So it is—but only in proportion as *you* are. . . . The artist has got to feed his offspring out of his own tissue" (*HRB* 377). Frenside, the friend who originally insisted that Vance needed to see the ocean, alludes to the Prologue in the Theater:

> Grasp the exhaustless life that all men live!
> Each shares therein, though few may comprehend
> Where'er you touch, there's interest without end.
>
> [*Faust,* part 1, Prologue in the Theater]

"Perhaps . . . 'God' was the same as what he called 'The Mothers'—that mysterious Sea of Being of which the dark reaches swayed and rumoured in his soul . . . perhaps one symbol was as good as another to figure the imperceptible point where the fleeting human consciousness touches Infinity. . . . " (*HRB* 429–30, Wharton's ellipses). In a perfect circle of Emersonian reason, the Mothers are life, life is experience, experience is God, God is the Mothers, the Mothers are life. God is where "human consciousness touches Infinity," or whatever experience the artist can plumb from his own tissue. From his descent to the Mothers, Vance learns of life forces, of connectedness, and of how actions have consequences. He accepts it when he returns to Halo, marriage, and fatherhood. He finds that he cannot live healthily or creatively outside the architecture of social institutions like marriage.

Plutarch's "Life of Marcellus," Goethe's inspiration for the Mothers, examines several ways in which the community insists on controlling the actions of individuals through social and religious structure. The story described there takes place at a temple built by the Cretans and dedicated by Ulysses to the goddesses called the Mothers. A political prisoner named Nician, knowing he was being watched, allowed himself to be overheard speaking blasphemously of the Mothers. Then, when he was about to be sentenced, he threw himself on the ground, ripping off his clothes, running mad, screaming that he was being driven by the wrath of the Mothers. That way he escaped because, fearing the Mothers, no one dared pursue him. Plutarch's Mothers seem remarkably similar to Aeschylus's Furies, and they represent the depth Wharton has plumbed through her layered allusion to Marlowe, Goethe, Plutarch, and Homer to demonstrate that human beings need positive and negative structures like heaven and hell, marriage, and the arts to nurture creativity. In Spain Vance experiences a partial untangling of his ideas of heaven and hell, but they are still not clearly divided:

> The church was empty, immense, and dark as night. . . . Vance sat down, and was listening absently to the roar of the storm when a flash illuminated the walls of glass, and celestial fields of azure and rose suddenly embowered him. In another instant all was dark, as if obliterated by the thunder following the flash; then the incandescence began again—a flowering of magical

sky-gardens in which every heavenly hue blossomed against a blue as dazzling as sunlight; and after each flowering came extinction. [*GA* 80]

In a thematic allusion, he is reminded of "alternate cantos of the Paradiso and the Inferno" (*GA* 80). Then, using a technique of which Alexander Pope was master, Wharton juxtaposes Vance's experience with his friends' talk about Bibles and billets-doux, about the "new experiments in painting and literature, about Eddington and Whitehead, Pure Poetry and Thomism, and the best trout-flies for the stream they were to fish . . . " (*GA* 80–81, Wharton's ellipses). "These memories flowed through Vance's mind as he sat on the parapet looking across the Seine. His months in Paris had been rich in experience; if his receptivity sometimes failed him when Halo had most counted on it, he had secreted treasures unsuspected by her, such as the sights and sounds of the river, or that fragment of heaven torn from the storm in the unknown church" (*GA* 81).

Vance's major failings are his inability to think ahead, to understand that actions and lapses, such as lack of consideration for Halo, have consequences. He had said that "his art and this woman were one" (*HRB* 420), that with her "maternal airs" Halo was "the goddess, the miracle, the unattainable being who haunted the peaks of his imagination" (*HRB* 421), that all his feelings for her were "merged in a rich deep communion; it was the element in which everything else in him lived: 'All thoughts, all motions, all delights, Whatever stirs this mortal frame—' " he thinks, quoting Coleridge's poem, "Love" (*HRB* 432).

Yet when he decides that he "no longer needed a companion in these explorations of the depths; what he most wanted . . . was to be alone," he dashes off suddenly without a word, inconsiderately leaving Halo alone to worry (*GA* 77). "After one of these plunges into the depths he always rose to the surface sore and bewildered; it was a relief to know that . . . explanations could be deferred till the morrow" (*GA* 119). Halo is afraid to ask what these absences mean, because the question might seem to restrict the "freedom" Vance supposedly retains as an unmarried man. And she blames herself: "Rain-clouds hung low on the Sierra; summer seemed to have passed with the passing of her unclouded hours. She recalled Vance's impulsiveness, his moody fits. What if he had taken the train and gone off, heaven knew where, away from her tears and her reproaches" (*GA* 58). She, and her spirit, search for him, "but a bleak wind blew over the ramparts, shaking the leaves from the elms, and she returned, chilled and discouraged" (*GA* 58). He had said that she was "the breath of life," that "if you cut off a fellow's oxygen he collapses. . . . " (*HRB* 418, Wharton's ellipses). But now "he would never say of her again that she was like the air he breathed!" (*GA* 59).

Halo's shortsighted mistake is in withholding some of her feelings on the one hand and believing Emersonian misinterpretation of Pope that the artist must be "free as air" on the other.[9] These mistakes are foreshadowed in the titular structural allusion that Wharton chose for *The Gods Arrive*. The title comes from Emerson's poem, "Give All to Love" (1846):

> Though thou loved her as thyself,
> As a self of purer clay,
> Though her parting dims the day,
> Stealing grace from all alive,
> Heartily know,
> When half-gods go,
> The gods arrive.

Paraphrased, Emerson's poem says: give all to love, your friends, kin, estate, good-fame, credit and the Muse. Love is a brave master; follow it utterly, but it is also a god that requires you to have the courage to leave it free. It will reward you by returning multiplied. But Frenside speaks for the author: "H'm— free as air. The untrammelled artist. Well, I don't believe it's the ideal state for the artist, any more than it is for the retail grocer. We all of us seem to need chains—and wings" (*GA* 312). "The Spirit bloweth where it listeth . . . , and genius *is* the Spirit, isn't it, Frenside?" (*HRB* 279). But "if you cut off a fellow's oxygen he collapses" (*HRB* 418). In context the allusion to John 3:8 regards inspiration by the Holy Spirit: "Ye must be born again. The wind bloweth where it listeth, and thou hearest the sound thereof, but canst not tell whence it cometh, and whither it goeth: so is every one that is born of the Spirit" (John 7–8).

Halo and Vance, furthermore, need to solve the conflict between the responsibilities to one another that have been created by living as married people, though unmarried. Halo thinks: "Before her own conscience and her lover's she was already irrevocably what she called herself: his wife. . . . she had to think of her own situation as binding her irrevocably, or else to assume that life, in its deepest essence, was as brittle as the glass globe which the monkeys shatter in the bitter scene of Faust's visit to the witch. If she were not Vance Weston's for always the future was already a handful of splinters" (*GA* 3,4).

The chant of the He-Monkies is a prognostication:

> The world's the ball:
> Doth rise and fall,
> And roll incessant:
> Like glass doth ring,
> A hollow thing,—
> . . . . . . . . . . . . . .
> Thy doom is spoken!

'Tis made of clay,
And will be broken.

[*Faust,* part 1, ll. 2402–15]

It seems a small world that is about to be fragmented. New York society arrives in Paris represented by the cold Mrs. Glaisher who holds the double standard. She "cuts" Halo but not Vance. Because of this they retreat to Oubli-sur-Mer in Southern France, a place for forgetting, yet there they find an exiled British population whose Mothers also shun Halo. A social person, she is completely isolated, especially in Vance's absences. Therefore, "seeing in a flash the desert distances of life without him," she forgets her "magnanimous resolve to respect his freedom" (*GA* 62).

Vance is willing to marry Halo, but he seldom thinks about it. Meanwhile, Halo has withheld information that Tarrant has vowed never to divorce her because, by living openly with Vance, she has embarrassed him in New York society. She feels that Vance would interpret the news as interference with his freedom.

Earlier, in *Hudson River Bracketed,* Vance had been driven to read Gogol's "The Cloak" (also translated "The Overcoat"). "All Tolstoy and Tchekov came out of 'The Cloak,' the advanced ones said" (*HRB* 274). Gogol's allegorical story about an anonymous bureaucrat victimized by his social environment is considered the first example of naturalist literature. It becomes a thematic allusion, a genre Vance had tried unsatisfactorily. "The thing had come too easily; he knew it had not been fetched up out of the depths" (*GA* 71). He had not yet experienced enough emotion like the compassion he feels for Tarrant in their confrontation scene.

As Vance sheds the overcoat, he symbolically sheds naturalism and takes personal responsibility for his fate if not yet for his impulsiveness. He studies Tarrant:

> The man opposite him, whose distress he recognized and could not help pitying, seemed to be struggling in vain to express his real self, in its helpless vanity, humiliation and self-deception. The studied attitude of composure which gave him a superficial advantage over an untutored antagonist was really only another bondage. When a man had disciplined himself out of all impulsiveness he stood powerless on the brink of the deeper feelings. If only, Vance thought, he could help Tarrant to break through those bonds! . . . Above all, he reminded himself, he must try not to be angry or impatient.
> [*GA* 145]

The two men are polar opposites. Tarrant is bone dry. He stands on the brink of the descent to the Mothers but will never dive because, emotionally bound, he has never learned to swim. Vance has jumped but flounders and nearly drowns. Tarrant is restrained; Vance is impulsive, just beginning to understand the need to control emotion, to overcome an education that stressed immediacy but not discipline. As Wharton hinted by using an epigram from Wordsworth's "Laodamia" on the flyleaf of *The Gods Arrive:* "The gods approve the depth and not the tumult of the soul"; each person is in a tumult that requires compromise.

In Wordsworth's poem, probably a structural allusion for Halo's subplot, Laodamia beseeches the gods to allow her dead husband to return to her. He appears temporarily, but when his time is up, Laodamia is so heartbroken that she dies. Faust's conjuring Helen of Troy, the Greek ideal of Beauty, from the Mothers nearly kills him as well. And Vance will nearly die from another water-related illness as a result of his second exploration of Floss Delaney's promiscuous world. That experience is followed by his third spiritual "resurrection," highlighted by another reverberating allusion that emphasizes the symbolic element, air.

" 'The wind on the heath?' Chris interpolated drily. 'Well, yes, damn it—the wind . . . " (*GA* 244, Wharton's ellipses). Chris alludes to a passage from "Gypsy Wisdom" by the winner of the 1919 Pulitzer Prize for poetry, Margaret Widdemer (1884–1978) that reverberates from the title of Arnold's "The Scholar-Gipsy":

He built life well, the gypsy-man
    In those days gone by—
There's the wind on the heath, brother,
    And a quiet sky. [stanza 1]

Widdemer also alludes to a passage from George Borrow's *Lavengro* (1851): "There's night and day, brother, both sweet things; sun, moon, and stars, brother, all sweet things; there's likewise a wind on the heath. Life is very sweet, brother; who would wish to die?" This reverberating allusion is relevant to Wharton's themes of education, experience, and the four elements. Borrow also wrote *The Bible in Spain,* which Vance had been reading during his first days in Seville (*GA* 26). George Henry Borrow wrote vivid autobiographical fiction based on his travels and his sufferings from manic-depressive disease, a disorder that also afflicts Chris Churley. " 'The wind on the heath, brother—' How Chris had shrugged away Vance's facile admonitions! Wind on the heath, wind in the palms, all the multiple murmurs of life—Chris Churley's ears were forever closed to them" (*GA* 255). The funeral takes place in a drenching downpour. "In the dry season the rattle of palms in the wind sounds just like rain. God, it gets up a fellow's thirst!" (*GA* 253). The service from the Book of Common Prayer echoes an earlier reverberating allusion, Vance's meditations on the death of Laura Lou: "Thou makest his beauty to consume away, like as it were a moth fretting a garment . . . " (*GA* 253, Wharton's ellipses). He reflects on his brotherhood with Chris: "He had not given it a thought when he shoved Chris into the train and dashed away. . . . What had he done with his brother?" (*GA* 255).

Vance had learned to forgive by the end of *Hudson River Bracketed*, he had begun to learn compassion in the scene with Tarrant, he had begun to consider Halo, but that he is his brother's keeper is the maturing lesson Vance learns from the episode of Chris Churley. He had been tempted away from his "brother" by the Siren spell of one of the Mothers, Floss Delaney, whose father had described her "inside" as a "combination of a [stock] ticker and a refrigerator" (*GA* 228). Unlike the "wind on the heath," she has "a still windless face" and a body "as light as a feather" (*GA* 207). Floss is insubstantial fluff, as indicated by the surname derived from the French "delaine," a light woolen fabric, according to the *Oxford English Dictionary*.

Wharton draws together imagery of water, air, and fire so that, in a beautiful passage reminiscent of a scene in *The Glimpses of the Moon*, Vance's viewing of fireworks with Floss becomes a vision of the realm of the Mothers. Up and down are again meaningless concepts. The sky is an airy ocean full of fire: "The night was mild and windless; the younger women . . . stood about in luminous groups of mother-of-pearl" (*GA* 218).

> Far below the villa sea and horizon became suddenly incandescent; then a dawn-like radiance effaced the fires, and when that vanished every corner of the night was arched with streamers and rainbows of flashing colour. Through them, as they shot up and crossed each other in celestial trellisings, the moon looked down in wonder. Now she seemed a silver fish caught in a golden net, now a great orange on a tree full of blossoms, or a bird of Paradise in a cage of sapphires and rubies—yet so aloof, so serenely remote, that she seemed to smile down goddess-like at the tangle of earthly lights. . . . Yet while she mused, he saw that she too changed colour with the change of lights, turning now blush-red, now gold, now pearl, like a goddess who reddens and pales because Actaeon has looked at her . . . Somehow that wondering moon, going her cool way alone, yet blushing and faltering in the tangle of earth-lights, suddenly reminded him of Halo. [*GA* 218-19, final ellipses Wharton's]

Vance doesn't understand Floss's attraction except that there was a "dumb subterranean power in her that corresponded with how own sense of the forces by which his inventive faculty was fed" (*GA* 378). And "to hold Floss Delaney was to plunge into a dark night, a hurrying river. It was as if her blood and his were the tide sweeping them away. Everything else was drowned in that wild current" (*GA* 296). All victims of the Mothers—George Darrow lured onto the reef by a Siren, Ralph Marvell drowned in the "*noyad* of marriage" to an Undine, and Vance tempted first by Laura Lou, the empty shell, then Floss, a cold, insubstantial Siren-Mother—all must resurface without drowning. Some do. Some do not.

Halo has a better idea than Vance of these tempting forces. She knew the "starving artist" of *Hudson River Bracketed,* and now that his physical hungers are satisfied, she knows the Furies, the "irresistible force[s] which drove him in pursuit of the food his imagination required. . . . the hunger of his mind was perpetual and insatiable" (*GA* 27). Floss represents a dead-end detour in the subterranean labyrinth, a return to physical hungers. With Floss "he felt ravenous for food" (*GA* 206). *The Gods Arrive* is about Vance's pursuit of the food of the imagination and he is "as hungry as a cannibal" (*GA* 24).

Back in America, Vance emerges into creative oxygen, inspiration, literally "beautiful air," an outcome foreshadowed by the scene with Frenside in *Hudson River Bracketed:* "Two days later he was on his way to Lake Belair. After a day's journey the train left him at dusk at a wayside station, and as he got out the icy air caught him by the throat and then suddenly swung him up on wings" (*GA* 405). His retreat has been purgatorial and serves to reconnect Vance to his national inheritance. Wharton's description of Vance's life at Lake Belair echoes Whitman, for instance, "Out of a Cradle Endlessly Rocking." Vance stays with laborers who "lived unconsciously in those cosmic hands in which he felt himself cradled, and as vigour of mind and body returned he began to crave for a conscious intelligence, an intelligence not complicated or sophisticated but moulded on the large quiet lines of the landscape" (*GA* 408). Poetic consonance shows the care Wharton took with this passage, suggesting the importance of her concern that European-educated artists develop an American intelligence, a creativity true to their heritage and reflected in the landscape of their souls.

Through memory and the reading of *The Confessions of St. Augustine,* Vance digests his experiences, finding in them imaginative food, "the food of the full grown." In the "Confessions," food is often a metaphor for wisdom: "memory is the mind's stomach, as it were, and joy and sadness are like sweet and bitter food. When they are committed to memory, they are as it were passed into the stomach and they can be stored away there."[10] Vance suffers expiatory pneumonia, a last bout with drowning, but recovers, emerging from the ocean of the Mothers under the care of Aaron Brail, the "half educated naturalist" who had wished to become a minister, a half-blind son of Adam who tells Vance about his former fiancée: "I met her when I was observing animals at a circus. She was a lion-tamer" (*GA* 413). Finally matured, Vance considers the feelings of his friend and stifles the impulse to laugh: "Isn't that what they all are?" (*GA* 414).

" 'The food of the full-grown,' he murmured to himself as Brail disappeared among the hemlocks. Yes, it was time to eat of that food; time to grow up; time to fly from his shielded solitude and go down again among the lion-tamers" (*GA* 414). Thinking back to *The Children*'s circus animal allusions and how Bun's mother was a lion-tamer, it becomes evident that the lion-tamers, the civilizers, are the Mothers.

"What he craved for, with a sort of tremulous convalescent hunger, was a sight of the Willows, the old house where his real life had begun" (*GA* 416). As Vance stands at its gate like the gate of Heaven unaware that Halo is within, he remembers Keats's line from "On First Looking into Chapman's Homer": here "he had first travelled in the realms of gold, with Halo guiding him," like Dante's Beatrice (*GA* 417).

Meanwhile Halo is also recovering. She looks back on "the first phase of anguish as mystics do on the dark passages of their spiritual initiation. . . . The decision to live at the Willows had been her final step toward recovery" (*GA* 422). Vance informs her penitently that he has passed through fire, that he is "burnt out, I'm just cinders" (*GA* 429), and that his passion for Floss is now "ashes" (*GA* 431). He tries to explain to Halo, "I read something up there in the woods about God . . . or experience . . . it's the same thing . . . being the food of the full-grown" (*GA* 431, Wharton's ellipses). Now one of the Mothers, Halo's response is to accept Vance as a second child. In a goddesslike gesture that has been criticized as melodramatic, "with a kind of tranquil gravity [Halo] lifted up her arms in the ancient attitude of prayer" (*GA* 432), allowing Vance to perceive her pregnancy and pledging both of them to the higher power of the Mothers, the merger of imaginative and biological creativity. As the structural allusion to Emerson's poem predicts, the real gods, the gods of creativity and love, the Mothers, have arrived.

While *Hudson River Bracketed* features layered allusions, this sequel acts as a kind of summary of all of Edith Wharton's advances in literary allusion: thematic, titular and structural, reverberating, and layered, all clustered under an umbrella theme. The Furies are pacified. The unsoluble dilemmas of *The House of Mirth, The Reef, The Custom of the Country,* and *The Mother's Recompense* have been exchanged for problems that can be managed by wise self-control or deliberate action. The incest theme is absent, but the abandoned child, statutory rape, and suicide are repeated in the background. The thematic bridge between past and present, Europe and America, time and place, in this novel, one that Wharton must have suspected would be her last, is literary allusion. It sums up themes presented in her earlier work and offers advice: live fully and don't be afraid of pain. Now the code, the riddle of the Sphinx's "thousand threads of association" (*GA* 422), can be solved.

# 11 | Messages

Through a thousand voices
  Spoke the universal dame;
"Who telleth one of my meanings
  Is master of all I am."

As EARLY AS 1902 Edith Wharton was hinting about her methods being "depths below depths" and "what fun it will be to puzzle out the allusions."[1] Her motif has been the buried message, the "real stuff" that is "way down, not on the surface," the meanings hidden "underneath the granite outcroppings." The introduction to this study mentioned diaries written in a code of literary allusion and Wharton's deliberate reduction of her writing style to a "more even and unnoticeable texture," arguing that one reason for that style was to hide unprintable themes. The chapters that follow show some of what is buried under the even surface and how Edith Wharton's late work is not merely slick fiction or "prose by the yard" but deliberately just what she said, literature with an "unnoticeable texture."

Writing to Sara Norton about simplifying the surface of prose, Edith Wharton slightly misquotes a phrase from Wordsworth's "Spirit Seal": "Such bareness as 'she neither feels nor sees' is the result of a great deal of writing, of a long & expert process of elimination, selection, concentration of idea & expression. It is not *being simple* so much as being excessively subtle; & the less-practised simplicity is apt to have too loose a 'weave.' "[2] In a letter to an aspiring poet, who has said he fears being too heavily influenced by Wordsworth, Shelley, Moore, and Tennyson, she states the case directly: "The great object of the young writer should be, not to feel these influences, but to seek only the greatest [influences] & to assimilate them so that they become part of his stock-in-trade" (*Letters*, 411). The previous chapters demonstrate that Wharton's excessive subtlety—particularly subtlety of allusion—depends on "a great deal of the deepest kind of culture," requiring exceptional reading and study (*Letters*, 411).

While there is a clearly discernible development in the types and complexities of Wharton's allusions over time, that development cannot be charted chronologically. The structural allusions of *The House of Mirth* create the skeletal frame upon which the literary architect builds a novel about a vain society that kills its most important assets. The "real Lily" is Art destroyed by a combination of vanity and a rigid social structure. Art allusions were not new in 1905—but structural allusions used architecturally to build *The House of Mirth* were. It is probably no accident that major themes of the final novels, *Hudson River Bracketed* and *The Gods Arrive,* were also architectural. The subject brackets Wharton's entire body of work, and because it does, the work must be considered as much a whole as Balzac's is.

Inside this unit, Wharton's original inventions or unique developments of the inventions of others, the thematic and clustered thematic allusions effectively underscore and strongly emphasize themes previously either missed, such as the Greek mythology of the Siren and the Dilemma in *The Reef,* or noticed but not fully explored, such as the psychological incest themes of *The Mother's Recompense.* The mythic allusions of *The Custom of the Country* reveal some Americans as crude, greedy monsters while generic and punning allusions in *The Glimpses of the Moon* elaborate on a rape theme. Topical allusions from *Twilight Sleep* show how the experience of pain (Furies) cannot be solved by ignoring it, masking it, or, like Fred Landers in *The Mother's Recompense,* trying to buy it off. The reverberating and layered allusions of *Hudson River Bracketed* and *The Gods Arrive* reiterate the deplorable attitude toward education that results in America's lack of culture and art. Together with the revelations in *The Children,* these themes are the pieces of an encoded puzzle that, deciphered logically, disclose the nature of Edith Wharton's Furies. Wharton hints of it yet again in *The Gods Arrive* when Halo, having received a message about Vance, "sat and puzzled over it till her eyes ached, as if it had been a cipher of which she had forgotten the key."[3]

The chapter on *The Children* demonstrates in more detail how metaphysical allusions work. An animal conceit used similarly to that of the moon in *The Glimpses of the Moon* functions to compound themes so that the characterization of Martin Boyne by allusions to Faust, Comus, the mad ruler of *Ebb Tide,* and the mad poet of "Maud," succeed in creating a monster even more threatening than the Undine-Lamia. The newest monster is the sum of allusory associations to evils in Boyne's rationalizing personality. Simultaneously, thematic allusions overlap in the reader's imagination so that the children who perform like circus animals become the fairy animals of Comus as well as the animal worshipers of "The Witch of Atlas." The seduction by Comus in Milton's poem combines with the pranks of "The Witch of Atlas" and the chaos of the circus resulting in a fascinating kaleidoscope of images and metaphors for a theme of children endangered because of parental neglect, in need of civilizing by education, each also in need of a unique environment. Wharton's answer to the nature-nurture question she first asks implicitly in *The House of Mirth* is both.

Branching thematic allusions, topical allusions, self- and autoallusions, re-verberating and layered allusions, generic allusions, mythic allusions, and various combinations and permutations like reverberating art allusions reveal not only the author's limitless knowledge but a constantly deepening creativity. My suspicion is that each of Edith Wharton's novels elaborates in some way on one or another facet of an umbrella allusion to Emerson's poem "The Sphinx." While the thesis is not provable unless evidence can be found in the seven novels not included here, and maybe not even then, the idea is too interesting to give up quickly, especially in light of the titular allusion to Emerson in *The Gods Arrive*. Wharton's high opinion of Emerson is manifest in a letter to Robert Brownell quoted by R. W. B. Lewis: "Those two [Whitman and Poe], with Emerson are the best we have—in fact, the all we have." And "it was primarily Emerson's poems that drew her."[4] Further fascinating is that among Emerson's less well known essays is one entitled "Quotation and Originality," in which he argues that "we cannot overstate our debt to the Past"[5] and (quoting Goethe) that literature is an "aggregation of beings taken from the whole of nature" (Emerson, 190). Language, like Nature, is organic, originating with the poetry of humanity, but the mind of a genius will assimilate it and make it new. "Our best thought came from others" (Emerson 187); Shakespeare "was more original than his originals" (Emerson, 182). Emerson also employs the architecture analogy: "Language is a city to the building of which every human being brought a stone" (Emerson, 189-90).

But to insist on the influence of Emerson on Edith Wharton is not to say that even as "the couchant landscape stretched its Sphinx-like paws upon the sea" (*GA* 235), she was an advocate of transcendental romanticism. ("I'm not a vegetarian—never could digest raw landscape").[6] Rather she seems to have considered landscape as one of the foundations of the architecture of American culture to be considered and incorporated into the larger context of civilization. There is some suggestion, though, that she might have agreed with the basic concept of "The Sphinx," that the paradoxes, contradictions, and dilemmas dramatized in her novels are part of some universal whole that could be called Nature or God or a Unifying Force.

A related theme of Emerson's poem is reason— "Reason's 'power to see the whole—all in each.' "[7] Emerson "exploited logical paradox and its literary resolution" (Whitaker 126), and Edith Wharton emulated him that far. Yet Emerson insists in "Circles" and in "Illusions" that "all is riddles, and the key to a riddle is another riddle" (Whitaker 117), which means that trying to apply logic to the "solution" of Edith Wharton's literary allusive novels has *not* solved them—merely revealed more puzzles. In the last analysis she has the final joke; like Nelson Vanderlyn in *The Glimpses of the Moon*, she has "caught me at it." She has caught me with the most wonderful kind of joke, however, because if literature can be merely "solved" like a Conan Doyle mystery, it cannot be great literature. Great literature examines human mysteries that from the beginning have caused mankind to posit God. Like the greatest philosophers, Edith Wharton implicitly asks what kind of God permits children and other innocents to suffer pain. She examines the questions logically, then admits their paradoxes.

In fact, the paradox of literary allusion becomes an actual preoccupation of some of the novels because the emblem of the Furies can be thought of as a psychic, cultural, and artistic symbol, inexorably connected to the ravenous literary appetite that gave birth to these novels and required them to be allusive. Culturally the Furies symbolize the need to make the world better, and artistically they symbolize the desire to do that with order and beauty. Psychologically they are a soul's drive to create a continuum, a bridge, between past and present, physically through children or imaginatively through art. But children can become saints like Terry Wheater or monsters like Undine Spragg, depending on where they are raised and how they are educated. Since allusions both require and promote education, the message of the novels on that level is about the teaching function of allusion itself. Allusions create curiosity, and curiosity leads to education: "The air was electrical, if not with ideas at least with phrases and allusions which led up to them. To Vance the background of education and travel implied by this quick flashing back and forth of names, anecdotes, references to unseen places, unheard-of people, works of art, books, plays, was intoxicating in its manifold suggestions" (*HRB* 402). The allusions themselves are messages that, by and large, have gone unnoticed.

The theme of the unreceived or misunderstood message can be traced through many of the novels, beginning with *The House of Mirth,* in which Lily Bart is sent an intentionally misleading message by Gus Trenor, resulting in her near rape, and continuing in *The Reef,* in which Darrow misinterprets the "unexpected obstacle" of the telegram and causes the avoidable dilemma by throwing the unread explanation into the fire and pocketing Sophy's telegram. The ironic message of *The Mother's Recompense,* "Mrs. Clephane dead," resurrects ghosts of the past, Susy's misinterpretation of Coral's postcard about her husband in *The Glimpses of the Moon* stops her from taking action, whereas Ellen Olenska's husband does contact her: " 'just a message. He never writes. I don't think I've had more than one letter from him.' The allusion brought the color to her cheek" (*AI* 232). An exclamation mark is added to the motif with Halo's "sharp italics" in *Hudson River Bracketed: "It's somebody with a message!"* (*HRB* 52, Wharton's italics). And in *The Gods Arrive,* one of the Mothers, having set aside her umbrella, tells Halo, "What I've come for is to bring you a message . . . a private message . . . " (*GA* 192–93, Wharton's ellipses).

*Hudson River Bracketed* and *The Gods Arrive,* both about the development of the literary artist, feature allusions to allusions: "The books . . . now stole on [Vance] with the magic of low lights, half tints, easy greetings, allusive phrases" (*HRB* 274). "He longed to learn more about this mysterious craft, the instruments of which some passing divinity had carelessly dropped into his hands, leaving him to puzzle out their use." He had "heard that footfall of Destiny which, for Vance, seemed to ring out in the first page of all the great novels, as compelling as the knock of Macbeth's gates, as secret as the opening measures of [Beethoven's] Fifth symphony" (*HRB* 400–401). Contrast the confusion of the modernists to whom allusions were "all a blind labyrinth, a disconnected muddle. . . . " (*HRB* 388, Wharton's ellipses).

Each novel has been a puzzle in itself, but so has the oeuvre. The allusions, Emerson's "thousand voices," more than tighten the weave of Wharton's books. Each one has elaborated in some way a theme of one of the stanzas of Ralph Waldo Emerson's poem: the secret of the Sphinx, the danger to the child, nature, the search for love, God and the soul, and the question of pain that Wharton personified as Furies. Edith Wharton had a "vision of life" as a whole to pass to the next generation. " 'Luckily one can recapture [life] sometimes—in another form. . . . That's exactly your theme, isn't it?' [Halo asked Vance.] He nodded. The allusion sent him back to his work" (*HRB* 343).

For her efforts Wharton felt treated as if she wrote "prose by the yard" (Wharton, *Letters* 428). Frustration (delivered with a hint of Whitman's *Leaves of Grass*) was a natural response: "The scribbled-over sheets lay at [Vance's] feet in a heap—dead leaves indeed! . . . He thought of . . . all the interwoven threads of his life; he felt weak and puzzled as a child" (*GA* 119). All the while, puzzle in hand, "holding the clue to their labyrinth," Wharton stood outside the "mysterious circle" of modernism,[8] outside its "meaningless splinters," that to her offered no enlightenment on what had become for undereducated Americans "dim passages," "mute and unmarked,"[9] of the world's most enduring literature "fading down those far-off perspectives" of time (*MR* 84).

The themes Wharton has supported so elaborately begin to collect and transform. They themselves are metaphysical conceits molded into a cluster of thematic mythic allusions neatly prepared for by *The Custom of the Country*. With major or minor emphasis, these are the themes that Edith Wharton's original allusive techniques reveal: neglected children; the need for education; invaders, intruders, and monsters; incest and sexual perversions or homosexuality (then generally considered a perversion); rape; pain; drugs; poison; sleep/death; suicide; the dilemma; and, finally, the bridge (for which images of knitting and weaving are often substituted).

Whereas the themes revealed by the literary allusions are pieces of a jigsaw puzzle, the allusions to the Sphinx and the Furies are the frames that hold the pieces together. When assembled, the puzzle becomes another mythic allusion, a story at least in part autobiographical. It cannot be emphasized enough, however, that extreme caution needs to be applied here. We can never prove how much of this "autobiographical myth" is literally true and how much is invented or exaggerated for fictional purposes. Furthermore, there are direct contradictions to some of the details in the Lewis and Wolff biographies and in *A Backward Glance*. This reading must be tentative; biographers will investigate facts. Nevertheless, this "autobiographical mythic allusion," Wharton's architecture of an *idea* of her life, provides the material from which, when reduced, the message of the code emerges unmistakably. Assembled from the thematic puzzle pieces, this is the "autobiographical myth":

As a child Edith Wharton was neglected by her vain mother. That neglect had several serious consequences: she nearly died from typhoid, a disease caused by impure or "poisoned" water. More disastrous was a lack of sexual education that left her vulnerable to abuse. "Abuse," though, is a new term for what Wharton herself may have called "rape." She was probably an incest victim and was possibly also sexually abused by monstrous invaders and intruders—pedophiles—because she was not protected.[10] Her lack of education about "life" and her mother's apparent preference for her brothers further misled her into a physically loveless marriage to an unintelligent man. She was left to educate herself through her reading and choice of friends.

The consequence of childhood physical and educational neglect was the great pain she suffered from "neurasthenia," a mental illness something like severe clinical depression, life threatening because it often leads to suicide. Symptoms of depression can include loss of appetite and either insomnia or its reverse—too much sleep.[11] Lily Bart constantly "oversleeps herself" (*HM* 303). For Wharton in particular those symptoms also included enervation, suffocation, choking, and nausea.

Depression, nausea, and a sense of suffocation are now also recognized as the psychosomatic symptoms of sexual abuse.[12] Like the Furies of Aeschylus, "afflicted she had borne what could not be borne" (ll. 790–91). But that topic was unprintable, even unspeakable, in Edith Wharton's era. Unfortunately, sexual abuse was just one of the destructive riddles the Sphinx was forced to keep secret. Chances are also strong that when she suffered from the physical pain and insomnia that resulted from this most confusing kind of familial "love," she was treated with addictive substances like Lily's chloral, and perhaps narcotics like opium or morphine, which were not carefully controlled in those days. Edith Wharton's personal recovery depended on her own "descent to the Mothers." Her "drowning" illnesses led metaphorically to a rebirth that found her "baptized" in the fertile waters of literary creativity. Once recovered, and with literary career launched, she faced the Dilemma. Pursued by Furies that demanded she try to avenge the wrongs she had suffered, vestiges of Victorianism prevented her from writing about them publicly. One need only note the social earthquake caused by Ellen Olenska's divorce to realize that if Wharton overtly dramatized sexual evils in fiction (as she did in the secret "Beatrice Palmato" erotica), her work would be unpublishable. Recall her difficulty placing *The Gods Arrive* because of Halo's unremorseful out-of-wedlock pregnancy. In addition, if she revealed her story directly, she would cause "sterile pain" to innocent people, people not directly involved, and would probably also face ostracism. Undoubtedly also, her sense of spirituality included a realization that exposing the guilty would simply place her on their level. Yet warnings were imperative.

The Sphinx solved her dilemma, paradoxically by speaking and remaining silent at the same time. She secretly created her techniques of literary allusion, probably with the help of Walter Berry,[13] while more overtly she attempted to persuade Americans to improve education of all kinds, including "life stuff." As mentioned in the discussion of *The Reef*, "life" was a euphemism for sex in Wharton's era, for "the facts of life," a significance that explains some of the subject matter of the abandoned "Life and I." It also explains Sophy Viner's face, which wore "the hard stamp of experience" (*RF* 23) because of a too familiar and enthusiastic acquaintance with "life"—her "plunge into the wide bright sea of life surrounding the island of her captivity." Thanks to the "intervention of the ladies who had directed her education" (*RF* 24), Sophy had been "drawn into the turbid current of Mrs. Murrett's career" (*RF* 25). Mrs. Murrett seems to have been the madam for an exclusive call-girl ring.

Both Sphinx and Furies myths involve a strong wish to murder a father. Most scholars who have felt that Wharton was an incest victim have assumed, on the basis of her silence about him and the hand imagery of the "Beatrice Palmato" fragment about father-daughter incest, that the perpetrator was her father.[14] By Freudian theory (with which Wharton was familiar), if she was abused by her father, she would have wished him dead and possibly also the mother who failed to protect her.

Now return to the myths. Even after Oedipus solves the riddle of the Sphinx, he kills his father and marries his mother. Chronus's son resorts to castration instead, accidentally causing conception of the three daughters of Time, the Furies or Eumenides, who turned on him to become avengers of familial crimes. In Aeschylus's *The Eumenides*, Orestes is pursued by the Furies for the murder of his mother, but he is rescued by the goddess Athena, inventor of musical instruments and poetry, who vindicates him and placates the Furies. Edith Wharton hunted the Furies with her writing and vanquished them: "And we are hunted by the prey we chase" (Wharton, "The Eumenides").[15] Her allusions reveal a woman who, if she was neglected by her mother and incestuously abused by her father, had guilty wishes that he would die, and he did die when she was only nineteen (Lewis 19). Her wish had become a reality. Guilt must have been overwhelming. Psychologically she would have felt responsible for her father's death; like Lily Bart, she had subconsciously "murdered" her father, so the Furies had a right to their pursuit—while she must remain silent.

If the "autobiographical myth" just described is approximately true, Wharton's anger with her selfish parents is understandable. Neglect by a socially ambitious mother is a theme of the first chapter of *The House of Mirth,* and abandonment by a vain, promiscuous mother, a theme of the unpublished "Disintegration." For Lily Bart the Furies were a Puritan conscience nagging her about her own selfishness, a "crime" against her parents that indirectly caused their deaths. In *The Children,* parents too involved in affairs and divorces allow their offspring to walk innocently into the dangerous hands of Martin Boyne. In *The Glimpses of the Moon* Clarissa (named after Richardson's famous rape victim) neglected for the same reason, more luckily falls to Susy's care, but even Susy comes close to neglecting the child because of distractions with Nick. In *Twilight Sleep,* both Pauline Manford and her daughter-in-law allow anxiety and boredom to interfere with parenthood, and in *Hudson River Bracketed,* Vance's parents are too busy installing sterile appliances in their new home to notice either the needs of their son or the misbehavior of a grandfather seducing Floss Delaney, an underaged girl. Direct parental abandonment occurs in *The Custom of the Country* when Undine (whose child is treated as a commodity) leaves her son, and Mrs. Tillotson Wing, Val's mother in "Disintegration," seems a precursor of Undine since she is characterized by similar images of light, glitter, dazzle, and flash. In *Summer,* Charity is abandoned by her indigent outlaw mother, and in *The Mother's Recompense,* Kate abandons her three-year-old daughter, Anne, to the Clephanes. In each case either the neglected children or their happiness is placed in danger, usually by suicide, antisocial behavior, rape, incest, or child abuse.

But as the Sphinx, Wharton was guarding more secrets than the riddle of her sexual experience. She speaks of reading book after book "in a secret ecstasy of communion. I say 'secret,' for I cannot remember ever speaking to any one of these enraptured sessions" (*BG* 69–70).[16] There is another type of allusion in the Sphinx's work that, like Poe's purloined letter, is a secret in plain sight—allusions to family names.

There can be little doubt that character names represent a deliberate pattern from which Wharton intentionally diverted readers with her famous comments about them in *A Backward Glance.* "My characters always appear with their names." The first part of the next sentence is a red herring: "Sometimes these names seem to me affected, sometimes almost ridiculous, but I am obliged to own that they are never fundamentally unsuitable. And the proof that they are not, that they really belong to the people, is the difficulty I have in trying to substitute other names" (*BG* 201). The names in fact often do belong to the people. "Mr. Jones," for instance, is hardly an affected, ridiculous name. Sphinx-like Wharton continues in a deliberate evasion comprised of an "excessively subtle" change of topic from names of characters based on people she knows such as Joneses to names of characters she invents such as

Ormerod: "These names are hardly ever what I call 'real names,' that is, the current patronymics one would find in an address-book or a telephone directory; and it is their excessive oddness which often makes me try to change them." Without a cue she then returns to characters based on people she knows: "I often wonder how the novelist whose people arrive without names manages to establish relations with them!" (*BG* 201).

Of course. The characters who arrive without names are not relations; those who arrive with names are. As to invented character names, many of them have been discussed in the preceding chapters, but consider Sophie Viner from "soph," wise (in the ways of life), and "vine," a clinging vine. Most of Wharton's character names can easily be deciphered with the help of the *Oxford English Dictionary, Bartlett's,* or the Bible. Recall the odd name of the seductive tutor in *The Children,* Ormerod, named after a shellfish described in the *Oxford English Dictionary* as "the lowest form of life." And in the same novel the children make a great deal of Mr. Dobree's mysterious first name, which turns out to be "Azariah," Hebrew for "Yaweh has helped."

Those characters who "arrive with names" *are* relations—relatives. It seems more and more clear that the "safe" and "guarded" little girl "life" described in *A Backward Glance* is a deliberate yet revealing misdirection. Consider again the episode cited in the introduction: The five- or six-year-old Edith was "allowed to perch" on the knee of an unidentified man named "Mr. Bedlow"—Low Bed. He was one of the monstrous invaders, one of the "gentlemen" who behaved "so much like the gods of Olympus," who, according to the myths, committed every possible atrocity.

Wharton uses her maiden name in the ghost story, "Mr. Jones," for instance, a tale that has been interpreted as about incest. Her mother, Lucretia, was married to George Frederic Jones. The couple's two eldest children were Fred, sixteen years older than Edith, and Henry (called "Harry"), thirteen years older. The Lucretia Borgia allusion in *Twilight Sleep* represents a mother poisoning her family by neglect; in addition, in Shelley's *The Cenci,* Beatrice's stepmother's name is also Lucretia.

There is still more evidence. In *The Mother's Recompense,* Fred, the man Kate couldn't marry because he was too brotherly, is the name of Edith Wharton's eldest brother, a man to whom she would not speak most of her adult life, a fact that her biographers mention then drop for lack of explanation. The implication that Fred, who was in college when Edith was a child, sexually abused his sister is unavoidable, especially since psychologists say that such abuse often runs in families.[17] Val's father, the Mr. Clephane of "Disintegration," is named Henry. "Clephane" is probably a combination of "cleft" (to split) and profane. The observing friend to whom the child looks with "racking intelligence" is named George (as is George Darrow, subject to the Siren lure of affairs). Abandoned by her mother, four- or five-year-old Val wants to take care of her equally abandoned father. He agrees to the natural but impossible request with a kiss. The name of her supposedly protective nurse, Mary Noonan ("Noony"), contains several negatives: no, noone, none. (Recall Nona of *Twilight Sleep*.) She is subtly and easily removed from that office by the authority of her employer. The little child's excitement includes the illusion that she can preside at table as her mother had and eat meringues like the grown-ups. Her father comments, speaking of women, " 'They're all alike!' . . . in supposed allusion to meringués; then his hand clasped [Val's]. . . . 'Well, come on then'. . . . It must have been . . . meringués . . . that [gave] her intuition of her father's need of her. . . . 'entertaining' him . . . was somehow distinctly connected with her mother's being away" ("Disintegration" 5,6). Edith Wharton claims to have been haunted by "tribal animals." "I was ready to affirm, there was a Wolf under my bed," she notes in *A Backward Glance*, then describes carrying her book and stool to any room in which Doyley or her mother might be in order to avoid "being exposed to meeting the family Totem" when alone (*BG* 28). Remember that the "tribe" of *The Age of Innocence* is family. Rumors of Edith Wharton's illegitimate paternity, probably irrelevant in themselves, arose from gossip about Lucretia's affairs. Included in the implications of the passage above is the possibility that George Frederic Jones took out his anger toward his wife by abusing his daughter and having affairs himself.

A child forced to perform oral sex might well suffer from choking, a sense of suffocation, and nausea. Analogies of meringues (to ejaculate) and an illness caused by typhoid, the disease Edith contracted as a child from drinking contaminated water, may explain why poisoned water is the source of the terrible invasions of *The Custom of the Country* and, indirectly, Vance's suicide attempt in *Hudson River Bracketed*.

By the same logic, there are even more surprising implications to derive from Wharton's use of family names. One of her ghost stories, "Afterward," features a character named Ned who, according to my analysis of the story, is bisexual.[18] "Ned" is a nickname for Edward, Teddy Wharton's name. Henry James's pun that Edith's marriage was an "inconceivable thing" suddenly becomes three-dimensional in this context and that of the Prince in *The Glimpses of the Moon*, about whom there was a rumor of "the improbability of [his] founding a family" (*GM* 241).

Little is known about how Teddy Wharton came into Edith Jones's life except that she says that "he was an *intimate* friend of my brother's" (*BG* 90, italics mine) and calls her husband, a man thirteen years her senior, "boyish" (*BG* 326). Since in the misdirective manner of *A Backward Glance*, she says little else about Teddy Wharton, these may very well be two hints of homosexuality. A thirty-three-year-old bachelor when he was married, Teddy had not previously been engaged or involved with women as far as biographers have mentioned. The brother who seems to have been Teddy's particular friend was Harry. In "Life & I" (1924), Wharton describes the friends of her brother Harry as "handsome gay young men some ten or twelve years older than I."[19] A homosexual relationship between Teddy and Harry might explain why Edith Wharton was exceptionally sympathetic to Harry's wife, Minnie, during and after her divorce from Harry and why she was so disapproving of Harry's second marriage, facts also unexplained by biographers.

Had Mrs. George Frederic Jones feared a gay intimacy?[20] In August 1883, Lucretia Jones gave a dinner in Edward Wharton's honor elaborate enough to make the social columns of *Town Topics* (Lewis 51). This occasion might have been the model for May's dinner to expel Ellen Olenska from New York, a dinner intended to banish Teddy from Harry's life. Even if so, about a year later Teddy reappeared and suddenly married Edith Jones in odd circumstances, with no mention of the bride's name on the invitation, so that the emphasis fell on the marriage of Edward Wharton to Lucretia's *daughter* with the implication that Edith had been the attraction all along.

Edith would eventually make a remark that has puzzled biographers by its apparent exaggeration about how "the failure of [her] mother to supply her with even the rudiments of sexual education did more than anything to falsify and misdirect [her] whole life" (Lewis 53–54). But if Teddy Wharton was a closet bisexual or a closet homosexual, that statement would not be hyperbole. Supposedly the Wharton marriage was not consummated for three weeks because of her ignorance, and after three or four years there was "a cessation of their sexual life together" (Lewis 53–54).[21] Perhaps there never was a sex life. That a cold wife is usually the cause of a sexless marriage is itself a one-sided idea. The concept of the repressed or frigid woman is a social stereotype that needs to be tested case by case, and in Wharton's situation is contradicted by several descriptions of youthful sexual response in "Life & I." Yet, of course, she might have repressed her sexuality after her marriage, she might have learned to control it, or her constant illnesses might have interfered with it.

The stories of Teddy's misbehavior with women, if reliable, do not necessarily contradict the idea of his bisexuality. And if Edith Jones's mother did fail to provide appropriate sex education to protect her child physically at home—from her father, brother(s), and "friends"—and caused her to marry a homosexual or bisexual man, then Lucretia did misdirect and poison Edith's life. A small portion of such burdens might drive almost anyone close to suicide, and significantly, the instruments of suicide in Wharton's novels are either poisonous or phallic: Lily's chloral, the poisoning mother and the gun of *Twilight Sleep,* guns in *The Custom of the Country* and *Hudson River Bracketed,* the projecting limb of the deadly elm in *Ethan Frome,* a streetcar in *The Mother's Recompense,* and a train in *The Gods Arrive.*

Suicide is one of the many themes that emerges from the literary allusions of Edith Wharton's novels that, repeated and combined as they are, contain a message. The technique of the solution is simply to reduce the evidence to its lowest common denominator: child neglect. The evils of the autobiographical myth result from lack of protection. Because of neglect, children are ignorant about sex, life, and literature. Because of their ignorance they not only inherit a culture bereft of the arts but they are also easy prey to monstrous invaders of their bodies, incestuous relatives, pedophiles, rapists, and, later, inappropriate spouses. The result is severe physical and psychological pain that leads to medical intervention and/or self-medication with potentially addictive substances—pain killers or sleeping potions. Neglect, ignorance, invasion, severe pain, depression, and addictive drugs eventually lead to suicide attempts.

The themes of the neglected literary as well as sexual educations of Paul Marvell and Vance Weston indicate Wharton's frustration with American parents' tendency to allow their children to grow up unsupervised, unpursued by intellectual Furies, without a "ravenous desire to learn more and more—to learn, all at once, everything that could be known on every subject— . . . stimulated by . . . allusions and references" (*GA* 45). Having overcome these obstacles to arrive at artistry herself, Wharton was faced with a puzzling dilemma. For readers to receive her message, they needed to be able to recognize literary allusions, but most had not read the works to which she alluded. Learning became a positive Fury, as Edith Wharton noted in a letter: "To have the interests is such an immense, ineffable pull over the people who haven't, that the rest hardly counts. To have as few numb tracts in one's consciousness as possible—that seems to me, so far, the most desirable thing in life, even though the Furies do dance in hob-nailed shoes on the sensitive tracts at a rate that sometimes make one wish for any form of anaesthesia" (Wharton, *Letters* 177). But as we have seen, her advice to writers was that they will never do their best until they write for the "other self with whom the creative artist is always in mysterious correspondence, and who, happily, has an objective existence somewhere, and will some day receive the message sent to him, though the sender may never know it."[22]

Wharton must have known that her ability to convert pain into creativity was rare and that most parentally neglected children would suffer "sterile pain": "I can only say that none of the children I knew had the clue to my labyrinth."[23]

Edith Wharton, as literary mother to "Vance," wanted to teach America how to turn the pain of the Furies into something positive. "It was dreadful the way old memories of pain fed their parasitic growth on new ones, and dead agonies woke and grew rosy when the Furies called . . . " (*GA* 400, Wharton's ellipses). This is the lesson Grandmother Scrimser, the most important of the Mothers, teaches Vance. In experiencing the "long tunnel of darkness" and the "narrow passage" of his grandmother's death, Vance makes another labyrinthine descent to the Mothers, which seems always an experience around death. The first time, when he tried to commit suicide, Vance "felt the arms of life, the ancient mother, reaching out to him, winding about him, crushing him fast again to her great careless bosom" (*HRB* 31). Vance receives a final message: "Pain—perhaps we haven't made enough of it" (*GA* 404). Wharton examines the subject from several sides. Grandmother Scrimser's message recalls Dr. Arklow's variation in *The Mother's Recompense,* who advises Kate to avoid inflicting "sterile pain," and Pauline's attempts to refuse all pain in *Twilight Sleep.*

Memory is an insistent motif in both *Hudson River Bracketed* and *The Gods Arrive.* Vance recalls "the smallest incidents of youth." It was like "watching some obscure creative process, the whirl and buzz of the cosmic wheels." He begins to grapple with the Mothers, with imaginative generativity. "The whole question of woman was the age-long obstacle to peace of spirit and fruitfulness of mind" (*GA* 407). In his grandmother's apparent paradox—optimism and acceptance of pain—he finds merged "a deep central peace" (*GA* 410). The "last words of his grandmother's might turn out to be the clue to his labyrinth" (*GA* 404).

"Out spoke the great mother, / Beholding his fear" (*The Sphinx,* stanza 8, ll. 57–58). " 'Maybe we haven't made enough of pain—been too afraid of it. Don't be afraid of it,' she whispered. Apparently it was her final message" (*GA* 402). "Grab Life including its carelessness, its randomness, its pain, because Life is Experience—God . . . or experience . . . it's the same thing. . . . " (*GA* 431, Wharton's ellipses). " 'Maybe we haven't made enough of pain—' that had been her final discovery" (*GA* 410). Why? Because pleasure is not the absence of pain but its opposite, so that the more pain one allows, correspondingly more pleasure is possible:

And under pain pleasure,—
  Under pleasure pain lies
[Emerson, "The Sphinx," stanza 13]

Apparently this was Wharton's general message, but a more personal message also awaits. Wharton optimistically felt that Americans would in time solve the puzzles and receive the implied message. Manford insists, "There's something still to be done with her . . . give me time . . . time . . . (Wharton's ellipses). Boyne echoes the refrain: "Don't pile up any more puzzles! Give me time—give me time!" Eventually the objective "other self" would surely solve the puzzle—or at least part of it.

The poignant personal message is implicit in another allusion, the epigram to the unpublished novel "Disintegration" from Mignon's Song in Goethe's *Wilhelm Meister:* "Was hat man dir, du armes Kind, getan?" ("What's this, poor child, they've done to thee?") Edith Wharton's reply is Susy Branch (her name echoing "rich many-branching words" of allusions [*HRB* 98]), guiding the Fulmer children ("full sea") in *The Glimpses of the Moon.* She educates the children to love books, the literary progeny of culture. She encourages their natural "fury of intellectual hunger" (*HRB* 114) because the pain of her efforts will be rewarded by her pleasure in their development.

In *Hudson River Bracketed,* when Vance becomes too absorbed in Miss Lorburn's library to dust and sort the books as he had promised, valuable volumes are stolen, a scene that shows Americans at risk of losing their (small enough) literary heritage through neglect. In that novel Halo's mother virtually sells her to Tarrant, and Vance's mother ignores him. But as ineffectual as she is, Mrs. Tracy tries to protect Laura Lou, and though Vance's grandmother is available with her message, he doesn't take her seriously. As shown in *The Children,* "the child is only half a person" to Wharton (*CH* 9). Besides being protected, offspring need to be trained so that they don't grow into "tribal animals." Historically the person who has had this responsibility is their mother, and Judith tells Boyne that Bun's "mother was a lion-tamer" (*CH* 14). The mother of the children in the structural allusion to Margaret Kennedy's novel is also a lion-tamer, and in *The Gods Arrive,* Vance is healed in the woods by Aaron Brail who had married a lion tamer. Vance decides to "go down again among the lion-tamers" (*GA* 413-14). Mythically the reason the Mother has responsibility for culture is that she is half lion herself—recall the cat imagery associated with Zeena and Mattie in *Ethan Frome,* with Kitty Landers in *Twilight Sleep,* and with Edith's youthful nickname, Pussy. It is also noteworthy that Vance is Mrs. Pulsifer's "young lion" (*HRB* 373). And the Sphinx, whom Emerson calls the "great mother" is half lion with the poetic wings of an eagle who can tame lions, perhaps even Furies—psychological, literary, generational. Edith Wharton's personal message is simply this: "Protect the children."

Was Edith Wharton abused by her father and eldest brothers? Was she at one time addicted to drugs and suicidal? Was Teddy Wharton bisexual? We don't know. But the allusions are powerful, and the biographical truth, whatever it was, does not diminish the author's magnificent literary accomplishments, most particularly her anticipation of modern social problems: drugs, broken families, disintegration of education, abuse, even violence (in *The Children*). In light of those, her traditional position in American literature as an unbending Victorian trotting unimaginatively in the shadow of Henry James demands final interment.

The revelation of the Morton Fullerton affair and the discovery of the "Beatrice Palmato" erotica have removed the stigma of Victorian prudishness, yet Wharton's apparent disregard of the Gertrude Stein salon (contradicted in *The Glimpses of the Moon*), her biting satire of modernists like James Joyce in *Hudson River Bracketed* and of cubist painters in *Twilight Sleep,* as well as disdainful remarks about T. S. Eliot, Virginia Woolf, and even Henry James's late work, seem to exclude her from modernism (Lewis 442, 433). But those authors had fragmented allusive surfaces often combined with stream-of-consciousness that has made much of their work so difficult to penetrate that it has perplexed people without teaching them. Wharton put forth her own vision:

> What was the alternative [modernists] proposed? A microscopic analysis of the minute in man, as if the highest imaginative art consisted in decomposing him into his constituent atoms. . . . *The new technique might be right,* but their application of it substituted pathology for invention. Man was man by virtue of the integration of his atoms, not of their dispersal. It was not when you had taken him apart that you could realize him, but when you had built him up. The fishers in the turbid stream-of-consciousness had reduced their fictitious characters to a bundle of loosely tied instincts and habits, borne along blindly on the current of existence. Why not reverse the process, reduce the universe to its component dust, and set man whole and dominant above the ruins? [GA 112–13, italics mine]

While Wharton believed in tradition and cultural continuity, her goal to bridge the world, the generations, and put together the thousand-and-one pieces of the past was similar to the goal of the allusive modernists, who wished to do the same, though often they also wished to wipe out the past and start over. But Wharton's allusive puzzles create a technical bridge that spans the literary historical gap between Henry James and many of the modernists, between Europe and America, between sexes, and between grandparents, and between parents and children. Edith Wharton had already made human beings dominant by alluding to their greatest works in words and pictures in her novels and stories. Today her fiction remains democratically accessible to almost every reader because of the simple surface of Wharton's prose.

In the process, Wharton put forth a modernist theory of her own: don't take humanity apart; put it together. Possibly a female version of Walter Berry, Halo is a natural critic who begins to see "how the bits of the puzzle fitted into each other" (GA 106). She listens to layers of allusions as Vance reads his work, "weighing every phrase, every syllable, the meaning of which she knew he had only half-guessed, while to her it lay bare to the roots" (GA 154). While Vance believes that "all the big geniuses have managed to express themselves in new ways with the old material" (GA 182), it takes him longer to learn: "Vance sat trying to piece together the fragments of his adventure. Everything about it was still so confused and out of focus that he could only put his recollections together in broken bits, brooding over each, and waiting for the missing ones to fit themselves in little by little, and make a picture" (GA 378). Putting the puzzle together, making man whole and dominant, Wharton connected the "mind of the past" to the "goddesses of destiny." She used a framework of an "Olympian story world," with its quite accessible sphinxes, riddles, furies, dilemmas, sirens, and labyrinths, to embue her entire body of work with at least these messages: a human message to make more of pain, and a social message to protect children. Whether she is called a modernist or a bridge between Victorians and modernists, no American writer of her generation can match the genius of Edith Wharton's achievements.

# Notes

## Introduction

1. Edith Wharton, *The Glimpses of the Moon* (New York: Scribner's, 1922), 63.

2. Edith Wharton, *A Backward Glance* (New York: Scribner's, 1934), 33. Subsequent citations in the text refer to this edition.

3. Edith Wharton, *Hudson River Bracketed* (1929; repr., New York: Scribner's, 1985), 320. Subsequent citations in the text refer to this edition.

4. Edith Wharton, *The Custom of the Country* (1913; repr., New York: Scribner's, 1985), 320. Subsequent citations in the text refer to this edition.

5. Edith Wharton, *Ethan Frome* (1911; repr., New York: Scribner's, 1970).

6. Edith Wharton, *The Mother's Recompense* (1925; repr., New York: Scribner's, 1986). Subsequent citations in the text refer to this edition.

7. Edith Wharton, *Summer* (1918; repr., New York: Harper & Row, 1979), 200.

8. Edith Wharton, *The Age of Innocence* (1920; repr., New York: Scribner's, 1970). Subsequent citations in the text refer to this edition.

9. John Hitt, "The Professor," *Lingua Franca* 3:5 (July/August 1993): 25.

10. Horace Walpole, *The Castle of Otronto and Hieroglyphic Tales,* ed. Robert Mack (1764, 1785; repr., London: J. M. Dent, 1993).

11. Edith Wharton, *The Reef* (1912; repr., New York: Scribner's, 1965), 168.

12. Roger Asselineau, "Edith Wharton—She Thought in French and Wrote in English," in *Wretched Exotic: Essays on Edith Wharton in Europe,* ed. Katherine Joslin and Alan Price (New York: Peter Lang, 1993), 357. Interestingly, Asselineau states that the French version contains no clichés.

13. In Edith Wharton's Diary for 1906, Beinecke Rare Book and Manuscript Library, Yale University, New Haven, Conn.

14. Percy Lubbock, *Portrait of Edith Wharton* (New York: D. Appleton-Century, 1947), 185.

15. For a fine discussion of Edith Wharton's travels, see Mary Suzanne Schriber, Introduction to *A Motor-Flight Through France* by Edith Wharton (1908; repr., Urbana: Northern Illinois University Press, 1991).

16. Nicky Mariano, *Forty Years with Berenson* (New York: Alfred A. Knopf, 1966).

17. Edith Wharton, *Italian Backgrounds* (New York: Scribner's, 1905), 85–106.

18. William R. Tyler, "Personal Memories of Edith Wharton," *Proceedings of the Massachusetts Historical Society* 85 (1973): 91–104.

19. Edith Wharton, *The House of Mirth* (New York: Scribner's, 1905), 156.

20. Edith Wharton, *The Children* (New York: D. Appleton, 1928), 27.

21. Edith Wharton, *Twilight Sleep* (New York: D. Appleton, 1927), 167.

22. R. W. B. Lewis, *Edith Wharton: A Biography* (New York: Harper & Row, 1975), 192.

23. Edith Wharton, "A Cycle of Reviewing," *Spectator* 141 (1928): 45.

24. Edith Wharton, Preface, *The Ghost Stories of Edith Wharton* (New York: Scribner's, 1973), 2.

25. Edith Wharton, *The Writing of Fiction* (New York: Scribner's, 1925), 21.

26. For a contrary view, see R. W. B. Lewis, *Edith Wharton: A Biography* (New York: Harper & Row, 1975), 430.

27. Aeschylus, *The Eumenides*, in *Greek Tragedies*, ed. David Grene and Richard Lattimore, vol. 3 (Chicago: University of Chicago Press, 1960), 34, 39. Subsequent citations in the text refer to this edition.

28. Edith Wharton, "In Argonne," *Scribner's Magazine* 57 (1915): 653.

29. Edith Wharton, "The Great American Novel," *Yale Review* n.s. 16 (July 1922): 646–56; Ralph Waldo Emerson, "The Sphinx," in *Selections from Ralph Waldo Emerson*, ed. Stephen E. Whicher (New York: Houghton Mifflin, 1960), 420–24.

30. Ralph Waldo Emerson, "The Sphinx," in *Selections from Ralph Waldo Emerson*, ed. Stephen E. Whicher (New York: Houghton Mifflin, 1960), 420–24.

31. See Barbara A. White, *Edith Wharton: A Study of the Short Fiction* (New York: Twayne, 1991), and Gloria Erlich, *The Sexual Education of Edith Wharton* (Berkeley: University of California Press, 1992).

32. Edith Wharton, "The Eumenides," *Artemis to Actaeon and Other Verse* (New York: Scribner's, 1909).

## 1. *The House of Mirth*

1. Edith Wharton, *The House of Mirth* (New York: Scribner's, 1905). Citations in the text refer to this edition.

2. Alex Preminger, ed., *The Encyclopedia of Poetry and Poetics* (Princeton, N.J.: Princeton University Press, 1965). This seems to be the only work that mentions structural allusions.

3. For a different reading of Selden as a "negative hero," see Linda Wagner-Martin, *The House of Mirth: A Novel of Admonition* (Boston: Twayne, 1990).

4. Edith Wharton, *The Letters of Edith Wharton*, ed. R. W. B. Lewis and Nancy Lewis (New York: Scribner's, 1988), 94–95.

5. R. Y. B. Scott, ed., *The Anchor Bible*, vol. 18, *Proverbs, Ecclesiastes* (New York: Doubleday, 1965), 191.

6. The Lewises note that "Margaret Sangster (1838–1912) was an extremely popular American poet, one of whose main themes was the proper performance of religious duties" (Wharton, *Letters*, 95n).

7. Jonathan Edwards, "Sinners in the Hands of an Angry God," in Cleanth Brooks et al., *American Literature: The Makers and the Making*, vol. 1 (New York: St. Martin's Press, 1973), 97–104.

8. See Chapter 8 on *The Mother's Recompense*.

9. C. S. Collinson, "*The Whirlpool* and *The House of Mirth*," *Gissing Newsletter* 16 (1980): 14. Collinson notes that Henry James wrote a review of *The Whirlpool* in *Harper's*, 31 July 1897. Edith Wharton read nearly everything James wrote.

10. Jacob Korg, *George Gissing: A Critical Biography* (Seattle: University of Washington Press, 1979), 208.

11. Elaine Showalter, "The Death of the Lady (Novelist): Wharton's *House of Mirth*," *Representations* 9 (Winter 1985): 133–49.

12. Wayne W. Westbrook, "*The House of Mirth* and the Insurance Scandal of 1905," *American Notes and Queries* 14 (1976): 134.

13. See Susan Koprince, "The Meaning of Bellomount [*sic*] in *The House of Mirth*," *Edith Wharton Newsletter* 2 (1985): 1, 5, 8.

14. According to the Maggs booksellers' list, Edith Wharton owned a copy of *Table Talk* by John Selden published in London about 1900.

15. Barbara White suggests an allusion to Tennyson's "Elaine" episode in *The Idylls of the King*. See Barbara A. White, *Edith Wharton: A Study of the Short Fiction* (Boston: Twayne, 1991), 169.

16. R. W. B. Lewis, *Edith Wharton: A Biography* (New York: Harper & Row, 1975), 155.

17. See Ellis K. Waterhouse, *Reynolds* (London: Kegan Paul, Trench Trubner, 1941), plate 177, and Charles Robert Leslie and Tom Taylor, *The Life and Times of Sir Joshua Reynolds,* vol. 2 (London: John Murray, 1865), 155. At the time when Edith Wharton might have seen the portrait of Mrs. Lloyd, it was in the private collections of the Rothschilds, at whose home Wharton was an occasional guest.

18. See Jay Martin, *Harvests of Change: American Literature, 1865–1914* (Englewood Cliffs, N.J.: Prentice-Hall, 1967).

19. Wharton's familiarity with Ingersoll is evident from her direct allusions to him in *Twilight Sleep*.

## 2. *The Reef*

1. Edith Wharton, *The Reef* (1912; repr., New York: Scribner's, 1965). Subsequent references to this edition appear in the text.

2. Anonymous, review of *The Reef* by Edith Wharton, *Nation* 95 (12 December 1912): 564.

3. H. D. F. Kitto, *The Greeks* (Baltimore: Penguin, 1967), 25–26.

4. Elizabeth Ammons, "Fairy-Tale Love and *The Reef*," *American Literature* 47 (1976): 620.

5. John Keats, *Selected Poems and Letters by John Keats,* ed. Douglas Bush (Boston: Houghton Mifflin, 1959), 274.

6. Walter Jackson Bate, ed., *Keats: A Collection of Critical Essays* (Englewood Cliffs, N.J.: Prentice-Hall, 1964), 113.

7. James W. Tuttleton, "Mocking Fate: Romantic Idealism in Edith Wharton's *The Reef*," *Studies in the Novel* 19 (1987): 459–74.

8. Homer, *The Odyssey,* trans. W. H. D. Rouse (New York: New American Library, 1937), 139–40.

9. Edith Wharton, *The Letters of Edith Wharton,* ed. R. W. B. Lewis and Nancy Lewis (New York: Scribner's, 1988), 440.

10. R. W. B. Lewis, *Edith Wharton: A Biography* (New York: Harper & Row, 1975), 327.

11. Jean Racine, *The Complete Plays of Jean Racine,* vol. 2, trans. Samuel Solomon (New York: Random House, 1957).

12. Henry James, *The American Scene* (1906; repr. Bloomington: Indiana University Press, 1968), 66.

13. See Jean Gooder, "Unlocking Edith Wharton: An Introduction to *The Reef*," *Cambridge Quarterly* 15 (1986): 33–52, and Elizabeth Ammons, *Edith Wharton's Argument with America* (Athens: University of Georgia Press, 1980), 81.

14. *The Collins Robert French Dictionary* (London: Collins Publishers, 1986), 331.

15. Robert L. Herbert, *Neo-Impressionism* (Princeton: D. Van Nostrand, 1968), 14.

## 3. *The Custom of the Country*

1. Edith Wharton, *The Custom of the Country* (New York: Scribner's, 1913). Subsequent citations in the text refer to this edition.

2. Edith Wharton, *The Letters of Edith Wharton*, ed. R. W. B. Lewis and Nancy Lewis (New York: Scribner's, 1988), 146.

3. Cynthia Griffin Wolff, *A Feast of Words: The Triumph of Edith Wharton* (New York: Oxford University Press, 1978), 230–58. Adeline Tintner refutes this argument for the source of the title, finding it instead in the work of Henry James. See Adeline R. Tintner, "A Source from *Roderick Hudson* for the title of *The Custom of the Country*," *American Notes and Queries* 1 (1977), note 34.

4. Wharton, *Letters*, 263. The book in question is a collection of short stories by Mary Crawford Fraser (Mrs. Hugh Fraser) entitled *The Custom of the Country: Tales of New Japan* (1899; repr., New York: Books for Libraries Press, 1969). There seems to be no connection between this volume and Wharton's novel. I have not been able to trace "The Wake."

5. Wolff, 251. Ellen Phillips Dupree believes that Elmer Moffatt's name "suggests that Wharton was conscious of Howells' influence as she wrote *The Custom of the Country*" (*American Literature* 56 [1984]: 270). The facts that William Dean Howells's Dryfoos family hails from Moffitt, Indiana, and that another character is Indiana Frusk, indicate that Wharton intended to point, perhaps ironically, to the Puritan content of *The Hazard of New Fortunes*.

6. Brian Gibbons, *Jacobean City Comedy* (London: Rupert Hart-David, 1968), 30.

7. Regarding "adjective hunts," see Edith Wharton, *A Backward Glance* (New York: Scribner's, 1934), 116. Subsequent citations in the text refer to this edition.

8. Richard H. Lawson, *Edith Wharton and German Literature* (Bonn: Bouvier Verlag Herbert Grundmann, 1974). Also see Richard H. Lawson, *Edith Wharton* (New York: Frederick Ungar, 1977), and Richard H. Lawson, "Thematic Similarities in Edith Wharton and Thomas Mann," *Twentieth Century Literature* 23 (1977): 289–98.

9. Wayne Andersen, *Gauguin's Paradise Lost* (New York: Viking, 1971), 108.

10. Thomas L. McHaney, "Fouqué's Undine and Edith Wharton's *Custom of the Country*," *Review de Littérature Comparée* 45 (1975): 181–86.

11. Michael Levey, *Rococo to Revolution: Major Trends in Eighteenth Century Painting* (New York: Frederick A. Praeger, 1966), 100–11.

12. E. M. W. Tillyard, *The Elizabethan World Picture* (New York: Vintage, n.d.), 65.

13. Thomas Bulfinch, *Bulfinch's Mythology* (New York: Collier, 1971), 176.

14. Bulfinch, 297.

15. Michel Montaigne, *Michel Montaigne: Oeuvres complètes*, ed. Albert Thibaudet and Maurice Rat (Paris: Gallimard, 1962). Another essay, "Of Custom, and That An Established Law is Not Lightly to be Changed" (Book 1, Chapter 23) is an intraauthorial allusion that discusses how "men buy women of their neighbours" and "Husbands may repudiate their wives without showing any cause, but the women may not do so for any cause whatever" (108), also how women "dare not marry till first they have made the king a tender of their virginity if he please to accept it" (109). This appears to support the theme of Beaumont and Fletcher's play, *The Custom of the Country*.

16. Michel Montaigne, *Montaigne*, trans. E. J. Trechmann (London: Oxford University Press, 1942), 5.

17. Bulfinch, 297.

18. The painting with which Paul empathizes does appear to be a Van Dyck as suggested by Peter Conn in *The Divided Mind: Ideology and Imagination in America, 1898–*

*1917* (New York: Cambridge University Press, 1983), 188. Wharton's description does not supply enough information for us to determine which of several Van Dyck "boy with dog" paintings might be meant.

## 4. *The Age of Innocence*

1. Edith Wharton, *The Age of Innocence* 1920 (New York: Scribner's, 1970). Subsequent citations in the text refer to this edition.

2. Linda W. Wagner, "A Note on Wharton's Use of *Faust*," *Edith Wharton Newsletter* 3 (1986): 1, 8; James W. Gargano, "Tableaux of Renunciation: Wharton's Use of *The Shaughran* in *The Age of Innocence*," *Studies in American Fiction* 15 (1987): 1–11; Edwin M. Mosley, "*The Age of Innocence*: Edith Wharton's Weak *Faust*," *College English* 21 (1959): 156–80.

3. Edith Wharton, *A Backward Glance* (New York: Scribner's 1934), 68.

4. Fitz-Greene Halleck, *The Poetical Writings of Fitz-Greene Halleck with Extracts from those of Joseph Rodman Drake* (New York: D. Appleton, 1869), 228–30.

5. Washington Irving, "The Three Beautiful Princesses," in *The Alhambra* (New York: G. P. Putnam, n.d.). See the discussion of this allusion in Chapter 7.

6. Alan Price, "Edith Wharton's *The Age of Innocence*," *Yale University Library Gazette* 55 (1980): 26.

7. Honoré de Balzac, "Innocence," in *Contes drolatiques* (New York: Random House, n.d.), 528.

8. Margaret Drabble, ed., *The Oxford Companion to English Literature* (New York: Oxford University Press, 1985), 192.

9. See also the allusion to *The Confessions of St. Augustine* in Chapter 10, in *The Gods Arrive*.

10. Balzac, 526.

11. Ibid.

12. Edgar Allan Poe, *The Narrative of Arthur Gordon Pym* (New York: Hill & Wang, 1960).

13. Vernon Lee, *Euphorion: Being Studies of the Antique and the Mediaeval in the Renaissance* vol. 2 (London: T. Fisher Unwin, 1884). Vernon Lee argues that the poetry grew out of conditions in which great numbers of knights and soldiers were garrisoned where the wife of the ruling nobleman and her servants were the only women permitted.

14. "Ollen," a red deer, *The Compact Edition of the Oxford English Dictionary* (New York: Oxford University Press, 1985). This detail may further allude to a painting of Thomas Townshend and Colonel Acland by Sir Joshua Reynolds called *The Archers* (1770). Recently, David Holbrook speculated that May's archery scene was taken from George Eliot's *Daniel Deronda*. See David Holbrook, *Edith Wharton and the Unsatisfactory Man* (New York: St. Martin's Press, 1991), 130.

## 5. *The Glimpses of the Moon*

1. Edith Wharton, *The Glimpses of the Moon* (New York: D. Appleton, 1922), 21. Subsequent citations in the text refer to this edition.

2. R. W. B. Lewis, *Edith Wharton: A Biography* (New York: Harper & Row, 1975), 445.

3. Cynthia Griffin Wolff, *A Feast of Words: The Triumph of Edith Wharton* (New York: Oxford University Press, 1977).

4. Edith Wharton, *The Letters of Edith Wharton,* ed. R. W. B. Lewis and Nancy Lewis (New York: Scribner's, 1988), 446.

5. Wharton, 418.

6. William Waters and Emily Waters, trans., *The Vespasiano Memoirs* (London: George Routledge & Sons, 1926), 256.

7. James Thomas Flexner, *History of American Painting, vol. 2: The Light of Distant Skies, 1760–1835* (New York: Dover, 1969), 145–46. A reproduction of the Van Dyck "Antiope" can be viewed in Erik Larson, ed., *L'opera completa di Van Dyck 1613–1626* (Milano: Rizzoli Editore, 1980).

8. Helen Killoran, "An Unnoticed Source for *The Great Gatsby:* The Influence of Edith Wharton's *The Glimpses of the Moon,*" *Canadian Review of American Studies* 21:2 (Fall 1990): 223–24.

9. The word "queer" as slang for male homosexuality came into general use in the 1920s. See Eric Partridge, *A Dictionary of Slang and Unconventional English,* ed. Paul Beale (London: Routledge & Kegan, 1984), 947.

10. Though Wharton did not visit Gertrude Stein, and Picasso's portrait of Stein was not exhibited publicly until the 1930s, Wharton surely heard of it from her good friend Bernard Berenson, who did frequent the Stein salon. See James R. Mellow, *Charmed Circle: Gertrude Stein & Company* (New York: Frederick A. Praeger, 1974), 52–116.

11. Ad de Vries, *Dictionary of Symbols and Images* (Amsterdam: N. Holland Publishing, 1972).

12. Catherine B. Avery, ed., *The New Century Italian Renaissance Encyclopedia* (New York: Appleton-Century-Crofts, 1972), 709.

13. Sheridan Le Fanu, *In a Glass Darkly* (London: Lehmann, 1947). Subsequent references appear in the text. Wharton mentions Le Fanu in her preface to *The Ghost Stories of Edith Wharton* (New York: Scribner's, 1973), 3.

14. Michael H. Begnal, *Joseph Sheridan Le Fanu* (Lewisburg, Pa.: Bucknell University Press, 1977), 44.

15. Walter Pater, *Marius the Epicurean* (London: J. M. Dent, 1966), 17.

16. Walter Pater, *The Renaissance* (London: Macmillan, 1873). This passage is also the source for the title of Edith Wharton's short story, "The Fulness of Life."

17. Ibid.

18. David Cecil, *A Portrait of Jane Austen* (New York: Hill & Wang), 67.

19. This image seems to come from Yeats's "The Song of Wandering Aengus" (1897): "The silver apples of the moon / The golden apples of the sun." Yeats was one of Wharton's favorite poets. (See Lewis, 347.)

20. Filed among Wharton's miscellaneous papers at the Beinecke Library, Yale University, is a newspaper clipping from the *Herald* (n.d.) entitled "Nuptual Contract Causes Amazement" about a marriage agreement similar to Nick's and Susy's. The article features a photograph of a young woman wearing a cloche, a hat style popular in the early 1920s.

## 6. *The Mother's Recompense*

1. Edith Wharton, *The Mother's Recompense* (1925; repr., New York: Scribner's, 1986). Subsequent references appear in the text.

2. Grace Aguilar, *The Mother's Recompense* (New York: D. Appleton, 1893), 60.

3. Aguilar, 170.

4. Aguilar, 12.

5. Edith Wharton, *The Letters of Edith Wharton,* ed. R. W. B. Lewis and Nancy Lewis (New York: Scribner's, 1988), 483.

6. Stuart Curran, *Shelley's Cenci: Scorpions Ringed with Fire* (New Jersey: Princeton University Press, 1970).

7. Mary Shelley, *Frankenstein* (New York: New American Library, 1983), 96.

8. M. H. Abrams, *Natural Supernaturalism* (New York: W. W. Norton, 1977), 299.

9. Leo Tolstoy, *Anna Karenina,* trans. George Bibian (New York: W. W. Norton, 1977), 299.

10. Tolstoy, 490.

11. Michiko Katutani, review of *The Mother's Recompense* by Edith Wharton, *New York Times,* October 25, 1986.

12. Cynthia Griffin Wolff, *A Feast of Words: The Triumph of Edith Wharton* (New York: Oxford University Press, 1977), 372.

13. Stella's *Brooklyn Bridge* is located at the Yale University Art Gallery, New Haven, Connecticut.

## 7. *Twilight Sleep*

1. Edith Wharton, *Twilight Sleep* (1925; repr., New York: D. Appleton, 1927). Subsequent references appear in the text.

2. Edmund Wilson, "Twilight Sleep," review of *Twilight Sleep* by Edith Wharton, *New Republic* 51 (1927): 78.

3. R. W. B. Lewis, *Edith Wharton: A Biography* (New York: Harper & Row, 1975), 474.

4. Johann Wolfgang von Goethe, *Faust I & II,* trans. Charles E. Passage (New York: Macmillan, 1987), 388–89.

5. Gauss and Kroenig, *Twilight Sleep, American Journal of Clinical Medicine* (n.p., 1915). The rest of the title reads: "and How to Induce it as Practised by Gauss and Kroenig at Freiberg, Germany; including a series of master articles on painless labor and how to prepare for it." The journal does not provide first names or initials, publisher, or volume number.

6. Though in Greek theater "Iphigenia" was performed among the tragedies, in genre it is closer to romance, according to Wittner Bynner, trans., *Iphigenia in Tauris,* in *Greek Tragedies* vol. 2, ed. David Grene and Richmond Lattimore (Chicago: University of Chicago Press, 1960), 113.

7. Washington Irving, *The Alhambra* (London: Macmillan, 1832), 297.

8. A possible source for the Dawnside episode is an article in the *New York Times,* 23 June 1925, 22:3. "Mountain View will be subject to strict police supervision according to Chief of Police Hamilton of Wayne Township. As a result of numerous complaints received lately of 'wild and drunken parties' in the bungalow colony, a raiding party was formed. . . . Fifty bungalows were visited early Sunday morning. Forty unchaperoned girls found in the company of men in bungalows were put on buses and ordered out of town." Mountain View is in Connecticut, as is Cedarledge and presumably also Dawnside. "They say the police don't want to move because so many people we know are mixed up in it; but London's back is up, and he swears he won't rest till he gets the case before the Grand Jury" (*TW* 46).

9. Col. R. G. Ingersoll, "Is Suicide a Sin?" in *Lectures of Col. R. G. Ingersoll: Latest* (Chicago: Rhodes & McClure, 1900), 851.

10. Col. R. G. Ingersoll, "Why I Am an Agnostic," in *Ingersoll's Greatest Lectures* (New York: Freethought Press Association, 1944), 23.

11. Havelock Ellis, *The Task of Social Hygiene* (Boston: Houghton Mifflin, 1912), vi. Subsequent references appear in the text. Ellis says in part: "All social hygiene, in its fullest sense, is but an increasingly complex and extended method of purification—the purification of the conditions of life by sound legislation, the purification of our own minds by better knowledge, the purification of our hearts by a growing sense of responsibility, the purifica-

tion of the race itself by an enlightened eugenics, consciously aiding Nature in her manifest effort to embody a new ideal of life."

12. Amalasuntha (A.D. 498–535) was daughter of Theodoric, king of the Ostrogoths. "She devoted herself with special solicitude to the education of [her son] . . . , but the young heir to the throne threw off the restraints imposed by his mother [and] plunged into debauchery." *The Encyclopaedia Britannica*, 1962 ed., s.v. "Amalasuntha."

13. A thorough search of *Vogue* issues of 1924, 1925, and 1926 reveals no such article, though *Vogue* did sometimes feature art. A possible source for the country estate at Cedarledge is an article in *Vogue*, "The Estate of Harris Hammond, Esq.," 15 October 1926, p. 68. The grounds and architecture of the estate match Wharton's description of Cedarledge. Significantly, as at Cedarledge, a painting by Raeburn hangs on the dining room wall.

14. Maria Bellonci, *The Life and Times of Lucrezia Borgia* (New York: Harcourt Brace, 1953), 120. A "very clever discovery, a masterpiece of wickedness, able to deal out death after a calculated lapse of time," the poison may have been an arsenic acid "capable of producing intermittent fevers manifested in two forms; one, and the commonest, a gastric fever, the other a cerebro-spinal fever" (217).

15. Virginia Surtees, *The Drawings and Paintings of Dante Gabriel Rossetti, 1828–1882* (Oxford: Clarendon Press, 1971), 77–78.

16. Wilson, 35.

## 8. *The Children*

1. Edith Wharton, *The Children* (New York: D. Appleton, 1928), 287. Subsequent citations in the text refer to this edition.

2. Cynthia Griffin Wolff, *A Feast of Words: The Triumph of Edith Wharton* (New York: Oxford University Press, 1977).

3. Katherine Ann Lewis, "Satire and Irony in the Later Novels of Edith Wharton." *Dissertation Abstracts International* 29 (1968): 608A (Stanford University).

4. Margaret McDowell, *Edith Wharton* (Boston: Twayne, 1976), 120.

5. Margaret Kennedy, *The Constant Nymph* (New York: Doubleday, Page, 1925).

6. Kennedy, 3.

7. Kennedy, 26.

8. A possible source for this episode is *A Collection of Original Poetry* composed by "Edward Boyne, a blind man" (Toronto: Model, n.d.). Most of this sentimental verse, published about 1900, is, appropriately, addressed to Boyne's children.

9. Harold Bloom, *The Visionary Company* (Ithaca: Cornell University Press, 1971), 236.

10. Edith Wharton, *In Morocco* (1920; repr., New York: Hippocrene, 1984). Subsequent references appear in the text. Edith Wharton had "long enjoyed making secretive use of her own previous writings in new compositions" (R. W. B. Lewis, *Edith Wharton: A Biography* [New York: Harper & Row, 1975], 503).

11. Wharton was nearly raped one night in her Morocco hotel room, but her screams frightened away the perpetrator. Edith Wharton, *The Letters of Edith Wharton*, ed. R. W. B. Lewis and Nancy Lewis (New York: Scribner's, 1988), 318.

12. Robert Lewis Stevenson and Lloyd Osbourne, *The Ebb Tide* (Chicago: Stone & Kimball, 1893), 15–16. Three beach bums, one of them a former ship's captain, pirate a rig from the South Pacific. Because the captain drinks, the ship loses course, pulling into port at an uncharted island depopulated by smallpox and ruled by a madman who thinks he is God.

13. Stevenson and Osbourne, 200.

14. Ibid.

## 9. *Hudson River Bracketed*

1. Edith Wharton, *Hudson River Bracketed* (1929; repr., New York: Scribner's, 1985), and Edith Wharton, *The Gods Arrive* (New York: D. Appleton, 1932). Subsequent references appear in the text.

2. Blake Nevius, *Edith Wharton: A Study of Her Fiction* (Berkeley: University of California Press, 1953), 226.

3. Margaret McDowell, *Edith Wharton* (Boston: Twayne, 1976), 130–31.

4. Information about the history of higher education has been derived from the following sources: Frederick Rudolph, *The American College and University: A History* (New York: Alfred A. Knopf, 1962); John Dewey, *Democracy and Education* (New York: Macmillan, 1916); John Dewey, *Experience and Nature* (New York: Macmillan, 1924); Irving K. Babbitt, *Literature and the American College* (1908); Arthur N. Applebee, *Tradition and Reform in the Teaching of English: A History* (Urbana: National Council of Teachers of English, 1974); Steven L. Tanner, "Humanitas and Higher Education," review of *Literature and the American College* by Irving Babbitt, *University Bookman* 27:4 (1987): 20–22; and Henry A. Burd "English Literature Courses in the Small College," *English Journal* 3:2 (1914): 99–108.

5. While it is impossible to know which *Sixth Reader* Wharton may have meant, one that seems typical was published in 1904 by a midwestern educator, L. H. Jones, "President of the Michigan State Normal College, formerly Superintendent of Schools in Indianapolis, Indiana, and Cleveland, Ohio."

6. Ralph Waldo Emerson, "Experience," in *Complete Works* (Boston: Houghton Mifflin, 1883), 263.

7. Andrew Jackson Downing, *A Facsimile Edition of a Treatise on the Theory and Practice of Landscape Gardening* (1858; repr., New York: Funk & Wagnalls, 1967), 338–90.

8. Andrew Jackson Downing, *Victorian Cottage Residences* (1850; repr., New York: Dover, 1981). The school is often called "Hudson River Gothic," but the term "Hudson River Bracketed" is also in current use. See Downing, *Treatise*, 353.

9. John K. Howat, *The Hudson River and Its Painters* (New York: American Legacy Press, 1983), 137. This book includes a color photograph of the Rondel from an anonymous private collection.

10. William Cullan Bryant, *The Poetical Works of William Cullen Bryant* (New York: Russell & Russell, 1967).

11. Matthew Arnold, "Literature and Science," in *Victorian Literature: Prose*, ed. G. B. Tennyson and Donald J. Gray (New York: Macmillan, 1976), 961.

12. Ralph Waldo Emerson, "Experience," in *Complete Works* (Boston: Houghton Mifflin, 1883), 263.

13. Stephen C. Brennan and Stephen R. Yarbrough, *Irving Babbitt* (Boston: Twayne, 1987), 105.

14. John Keats, *Selected Poems and Letters*, ed. Douglas Bush (Boston: Houghton Mifflin, 1959), 298.

15. James R. Thompson, *Thomas Lovell Beddoes* (Boston: Twayne, 1985), 52.

16. Edith Wharton, *The Letters of Edith Wharton*, ed. R. W. B. Lewis and Nancy Lewis (New York: Scribner's, 1988), 411.

## 10. *The Gods Arrive*

1. Edith Wharton, *The Gods Arrive* (New York: D. Appleton, 1932). All references are to this edition. The novel by Annie E. Holdsworth, *The Gods Arrive* (London: W. Heinemann, 1897), a strong thematic allusion, features a liberated woman writer.

2. Edith Wharton, *Hudson River Bracketed* (1929; repr., New York: Scribner's, 1985). All references are to this edition.

3. Sara Elizabeth Sheppard (E. Berger), *Charles Auchester* (1853; repr. New York: E. P. Dutton, 1928).

4. Sheppard, 119. Clara is a Jenny Lind figure.

5. Ralph Waldo Emerson, "Quotation and Originality," in *Complete Works* (Boston: Houghton Mifflin, 1883).

6. No painting entitled *Poet and Muse* was included in the lists of Poussin's works. The *Inspiration of the Poet* seems to be the title Wharton meant.

7. "Ineffectual angels" is an allusion to Matthew Arnold's essay on Shelley.

8. Harold Jantz, *The Mothers in Faust: The Myth of Time and Creativity* (Baltimore: Johns Hopkins University Press, 1969), 37.

9. The phrase "free as air" is an allusion to Alexander Pope's "Eloisa to Abelard."

10. John K. Ryan, trans., *The Confessions of St. Augustine* (New York: Image Books, 1960), 243.

## 11. *Messages*

1. Edith Wharton, "Disintegration," Beinecke Rare Book and Manuscript Library, Yale University, 34. Reprinted by permission of the author's estate and the Watkins/Loomis Agency.

2. Edith Wharton, *The Letters of Edith Wharton,* ed. R. W. B. Lewis and Nancy Lewis (New York: Scribner's, 1988), 106.

3. Edith Wharton, *The Gods Arrive* (New York: Scribner's, 1932), 318.

4. R. W. B. Lewis, *Edith Wharton: A Biography* (New York: Harper & Row, 1975), 236. Subsequent references appear in the text.

5. Ralph Waldo Emerson, "Quotation and Originality," in *Complete Works* (Boston: Houghton Mifflin, 1883), 193. Subsequent references appear in the text.

6. Edith Wharton, *Hudson River Bracketed* (1929; repr., New York: Scribner's, 1985), 72. Subsequent references appear in the text.

7. Thomas R. Whitaker, "The Riddle of Emerson's 'Sphinx,' " in *Ralph Waldo Emerson,* ed. Lewis Leary (Chapel Hill: University of North Carolina Press, 1982), 123.

8. Edith Wharton, *The Mother's Recompense* (1925; repr., New York: Scribner's, 1986), 106. Subsequent references appear in the text.

9. Edith Wharton, *The Reef* (1912; repr., New York: Scribner's, 1965), 314. Subsequent references appear in the text.

10. The subject was implied by the Lewis biography but first raised directly by Adeline Tintner. See "Mothers and Daughters and Incest in the Late Novels of Edith Wharton," *The Lost Tradition: Mothers and Daughters in Literature,* ed. Cathy N. Davidson and E. M. Grouner (New York: F. Ungar, 1980). Recent writers who have discussed the probability that Edith Wharton was an incest victim include Gloria Erlich, *The Sexual Education of Edith Wharton* (Berkeley: University of California Press, 1992); David Holbrook, *Edith Wharton and the Unsatisfactory Man* (New York: St. Martin's Press, 1991); and Barbara A. White, *Edith Wharton: A Study of the Short Fiction* (New York: Twayne, 1991).

11. See Maggie Scarf, *Unfinished Business* (New York: Ballantine, 1988). Scarf's work is a popular but reliable source on the causes and effects of clinical depression in the lives of women at various stages of life.

12. Louise De Salvo, *Virginia Woolf: The Impact of Childhood Sexual Abuse on Her Life and Work* (Boston: Beacon Press, 1989), 10–12, 109. Also see Karen C. Meiselman,

*Incest: A Psychological Study of Causes and Effects with Treatment Recommendations* (San Francisco: Jossey-Bass Publishers, 1979), 195.

13. Edith Wharton, *A Backward Glance* (New York: Scribner's, 1985). Subsequent references appear in the text. Chapter 6 strongly suggests Berry's influence.

14. Erlich, 40ff.

15. Edith Wharton, "The Eumenides," in *Artemis and Acteon and Other Verse* (New York: Scribner's, 1909).

16. Erlich, 34. Erlich notes the autoerotic nature of the imagery.

17. DeSalvo and Meiselman both discuss the intergenerational development of sexual abuse. If a girl's father was abusive, chances are strong that her grandfather and brothers were also.

18. Readings of "Mr. Jones" and "Afterward" are an integral part of my book-length work in progress.

19. Edith Wharton, "Life & I," Beinecke Rare Book and Manuscript Library, Yale University, 44. Reprinted by permission of the author's estate and the Watkins/Loomis Agency.

20. See Chapter 5, note 9.

21. Lewis does not provide the source of this intimate information.

22. Edith Wharton, *The Writing of Fiction* (New York: Scribner's, 1925), 20–21.

23. "Life & I," 14.

# Bibliography

## Primary Sources

*The Age of Innocence.* 1920. New York: Scribner's, 1970.
*Artemis to Actaeon and Other Verse.* New York: Scribner's, 1909.
*A Backward Glance.* New York: Scribner's, 1934.
*The Children.* New York: D. Appleton, 1928.
*The Custom of the Country.* New York: Scribner's, 1913.
"A Cycle of Reviewing." *Spectator* 141 (1928): 44–45.
"Disintegration." Beinecke Rare Book and Manuscript Library, Yale University, New Haven, Conn.
*Ethan Frome.* New York: Scribner's, 1911.
*The Glimpses of the Moon.* New York: D. Appleton, 1922.
*The Gods Arrive.* New York: D. Appleton, 1932.
"The Great American Novel." *Yale Review,* n.s. 16 (July 1922): 646–56.
"Henry James in His Letters." *Quarterly Review* 234 (1920): 188–202.
*The House of Mirth.* New York: Scribner's, 1905.
*Hudson River Bracketed.* 1929. New York: Scribner's, 1985.
*In Morocco.* 1920. Reprint. New York: Hippocrene, 1984.
*Italian Backgrounds.* New York: Scribner's, 1905.
*The Letters of Edith Wharton.* Edited by R. W. B. Lewis and Nancy Lewis. New York: Scribner's, 1988.
"Life and I." 1924. Beinecke Rare Book and Manuscript Library, Yale University, New Haven, Conn.
"A Little Girl's New York." *Harper's Magazine* 176 (March 1938): 356–64.
*The Mother's Recompense.* 1925. Reprint. New York: Scribner's, 1986.
*The Reef.* 1912. Reprint. New York: Scribner's, 1965.
*Twilight Sleep.* 1925. Reprint. New York: D. Appleton, 1927.

## Secondary Sources

Abrams, M. H. *Natural Supernaturalism.* New York: W. W. Norton, 1977.
Aguilar, Grace. *The Mother's Recompense.* New York: D. Appleton, 1893.
Ammons, Elizabeth. *Edith Wharton's Argument with America.* Athens: University of Georgia Press, 1980.
——. "Fairy-Tale Love and *The Reef.*" *American Literature* 47 (1976): 620.
Andersen, Wayne. *Gauguin's Paradise Lost.* New York: Viking, 1971.
Anonymous. "The Estate of Harris Hammond, Esq." *Vogue,* 15 October 1926, p. 68.
——. "Mountain View Will Be Subject to Strict Police Supervision." *New York Times,* 23 June 1925, p. 22:3.

————. Review of *The Reef* by Edith Wharton. *Nation* 95 (12 December 1912): 564.

Applebee, Arthur N. *Tradition and Reform in the Teaching of English: A History.* Urbana, Ill.: National Council of Teachers of English, 1974.

Arnold, Mathew. "Literature and Science." In *Victorian Literature: Prose,* edited by G. B. Tennyson and Donald J. Gray. New York: Macmillan, 1976.

Avery, Catherine B., ed. *The New Century Italian Renaissance Encyclopedia.* New York: Appleton-Century-Crofts, 1972.

Babbitt, Irving K. *Literature and the American College.* Boston: Houghton Mifflin, 1908.

Balzac, Honore de. "Innocence." *Contes drôlatiques.* New York: Random House, n.d.

Bate, Walter Jackson, ed. *Keats: A Collection of Critical Essays.* Englewood Cliffs, N.J.: Prentice-Hall, 1964.

Begnal, Michael H. *Joseph Sheridan Le Fanu.* Lewisburg, Pa.: Bucknell University Press, 1977.

Bellonci, Maria. *The Life and Times of Lucrezia Borgia.* New York: Harcourt Brace, 1953.

Bendixon, Alfred, and Annette Zilversmit, eds. *Edith Wharton: New Critical Essays.* New York: Garland, 1992.

Bloom, Harold. *The Visionary Company.* Ithaca: Cornell University Press, 1971.

Boyne, Edward. *A Collection of Original Poetry.* Toronto: Model, n.d.

Brennan, Stephen C., and Stephen R. Yarbrough. *Irving Babbitt.* Boston: Twayne, 1987.

Bryant, William Cullen. *The Poetical Works of William Cullen Bryant.* New York: Russell & Russell, 1967.

Bulfinch, Thomas. *Bulfinch's Mythology.* New York: Collier, 1971.

Burd, Henry A. "English Literature Courses in the Small College." *English Journal* 3:2 (1914): 99–108.

Cecil, David. *A Portrait of Jane Austen.* New York: Hill & Wang, 1978.

Collinson, C. S. "*The Whirlpool* and *The House of Mirth.*" *Gissing Newsletter* 16 (1980): 12.

Curran, Stuart. *Shelley's Cenci: Scorpions Ringed with Fire.* Princeton, N.J.: Princeton University Press, 1970.

Dahl, Curtis. "Edith Wharton's *The House of Mirth:* Sermon on a Text." *Modern Fiction Studies* 21 (1976): 572–76.

De Salvo, Louise. *Virginia Woolf: The Impact of Childhood Sexual Abuse on Her Life and Work.* Boston: Beacon Press, 1989.

de Vries, Ad. *Dictionary of Symbols and Images.* Amsterdam: N. Holland Publishing, 1972.

Dewey, John. *Democracy and Education.* New York: Macmillan, 1916.

————. *Experience and Nature.* New York: Macmillan, 1924.

Downing, Andrew Jackson. *A Facsimile Edition of a Treatise on the Theory and Practice of Landscape Gardening.* 1858. Reprint. New York: Funk & Wagnalls, 1967.

————. *Victorian Cottage Residences.* 1850. Reprint. New York: Dover, 1981.

Drabble, Margaret, ed. *The Oxford Companion to English Literature.* New York: Oxford University Press, 1985.

Edwards, Jonathan. "Sinners in the Hands of an Angry God." Cleanth Brooks et al., eds. *American Literature: The Makers and the Making.* Vol. 1. New York: St. Martin's Press, 1973.

Ellis, Havelock. *The Task of Social Hygiene.* Boston: Houghton Mifflin, 1912.

Emerson, Ralph Waldo. "Experience." In *The Works of Ralph Waldo Emerson,* edited by James Elliot Cabot. New York: Houghton Mifflin, 1883.

——. *Selections from Ralph Waldo Emerson.* Edited by Stephen E. Whicher. New York: Houghton Mifflin, 1960.

Erlich, Gloria. *The Sexual Education of Edith Wharton.* Berkeley: University of California Press, 1992.

Euripides. *Iphigenia in Tauris.* Translated by Wittner Bynner. In *Greek Tragedies,* vol. 2, edited by David Grene and Richmond Lattimore. Chicago: University of Chicago Press, 1960.

Flexner, James Thomas. *History of American Painting.* Vol. 2. *The Light of Distant Skies (1760–1835).* New York: Dover, 1969.

Fryer, Judith. *Felicitous Space: The Imaginative Structures of Edith Wharton and Willa Cather.* Chapel Hill: University of North Carolina Press, 1986.

——. "Purity and Power in *The Age of Innocence.*" *American Literary Realism* 17 (1985): 165.

Gargano, James W. "Tableaux of Renunciation: Wharton's Use of *The Shaughran* in *The Age of Innocence.*" *Studies in American Fiction* 15 (1987): 1–11.

Gauss and Kroenig. *Twilight Sleep. American Journal of Clinical Medicine* (1915).

Gibbons, Brian. *Jacobean City Comedy.* London: Rupert Hart-David, 1968.

Goethe, Johann Wolfgang von. *Faust.* Trans. Bayer Taylor. Boston: Houghton Mifflin, 1912.

——. *Faust I & II.* Trans. Charles E. Passage. New York: Macmillan, 1987.

Gooder, Jean. "Unlocking Edith Wharton: An Introduction to *The Reef.*" *Cambridge Quarterly* 15 (1986): 33–52.

Goodman, Susan. *Edith Wharton's Women Friends & Rivals.* Hanover, N.H.: University Press of New England, 1990.

Grene, David, and Richard Lattimore, eds. *Greek Tragedies,* vol. 3. Chicago: University of Chicago Press, 1960.

Halleck, Fitz-Greene. *The Poetical Writings of Fitz-Greene Halleck with Extracts from Those of Joseph Rodman Drake.* New York: D. Appleton, 1869.

Herbert, Robert L. *Neo-Impressionism.* Princeton, N.J.: D. Van Nostrand, 1968.

Holbrook, David. *Edith Wharton and the Unsatisfactory Man.* New York: St. Martin's Press, 1991.

Homer. *The Odyssey.* Translated by W. H. D. Rouse. New York: New American Library, 1937.

Howatt, John K. *The Hudson River and Its Painters.* New York: American Legacy Press, 1983.

Howe, Irving. *Edith Wharton: A Collection of Critical Essays.* Englewood Cliffs, N.J.: Prentice-Hall, 1962.

Ingersoll, Col. R. G. "Is Suicide a Sin?" *Lectures of Col. R. G. Ingersoll: Latest.* Chicago: Rhodes & McClure, 1900.

——. "Why I Am an Agnostic." In *Ingersoll's Greatest Lectures.* New York: Freethought Press Association, 1944.

Irving, Washington. "The Three Beautiful Princesses." In *The Alhambra.* New York: G. P. Putnam, n.d.

James, Henry. *The American Scene.* 1906. Reprint. Bloomington: Indiana University Press, 1968.

Jantz, Harold. *The Mothers in "Faust": The Myth of Time and Creativity.* Baltimore: Johns Hopkins University Press, 1969.

Jones, L. H. *The Jones Readers by Grades: Book Six.* Boston: Ginn, 1904.

Katutani, Michiko. Review of *The Mother's Recompense* by Edith Wharton. *New York Times.* 25 October 1986.

Keats, John. *Selected Poems and Letters by John Keats.* Edited by Douglas Bush. Boston: Houghton Mifflin, 1959.

Kennedy, Margaret. *The Constant Nymph.* New York: Doubleday Page, 1925.

Killoran, Helen. "Edith Wharton's Reading in European Languages and Its Influence on Her Work." In *Wretched Exotic: Edith Wharton in Europe,* edited by Alan Price and Katherine Joslin. New York: Peter Lang, 1993.

———. "An Unnoticed Source for *The Great Gatsby:* The Influence of Edith Wharton's *The Glimpses of the Moon.*" *Canadian Review of American Studies* 21:2 (Fall 1990): 223–24.

Koprince, Susan. "The Meaning of Bellomount [*sic*] in *The House of Mirth.*" *Edith Wharton Newsletter* 2 (1985): 1, 5, 8.

Korg, Jacob. *George Gissing: A Critical Biography.* Seattle: University of Washington Press, 1979.

Lauer, Kristin O., and Margaret P. Murray, eds. *Edith Wharton: An Annotated Secondary Bibliography.* New York: Garland, 1991.

Lawson, Richard H. *Edith Wharton.* New York: Frederick Ungar, 1977.

———. *Edith Wharton and German Literature.* Bonn: Bouvier Verlag Herbert Grundmann, 1974.

———. "Thematic Similarities in Edith Wharton and Thomas Mann." *Twentieth Century Literature* 23 (1977): 289–98.

Lee, Vernon. *Euphorion: Being Studies of the Antique and the Mediaeval in the Renaissance.* Vol. 2. London: T. Fisher Unwin, 1884.

Le Fanu, Sheridan. *In a Glass Darkly.* London: Lehmann, 1947.

Leslie, Charles Robert, and Tom Taylor. *The Life and Times of Sir Joshua Reynolds.* Vol. 2. London: John Murray, 1865.

Levey, Michael. *Rococo to Revolution: Major Trends in Eighteenth Century Painting.* New York: Frederick A. Praeger, 1966.

Lewis, Katherine Ann. "Satire and Irony in the Later Novels of Edith Wharton." *Dissertation Abstracts International* 29 (1968): 608A (Stanford University).

Lewis, R. W. B. *Edith Wharton: A Biography.* New York: Fromm International, 1985.

Lindberg, Gary H. *Edith Wharton and the Novel of Manners.* Charlottesville: University Press of Virginia, 1975.

Lovett, Robert Morss. *Edith Wharton.* New York: Robert B. Merrill, 1925.

Lubbock, Percy. *Portrait of Edith Wharton.* New York: D. Appleton Century, 1947.

McDowell, Margaret. *Edith Wharton.* Boston: Twayne, 1976.

McHaney, Thomas L. "Fouqué's Undine and Edith Wharton's *Custom of the Country.*" *Revue de Littérature Comparée* 45 (1975): 181–86.

Mack, Robert, ed. *The Castle of Otronto and Hieroglyphic Tales* by Horace Walpole. London: J. M. Dent, 1993.

Mariano, Nicky. *Forty Years with Berenson.* New York: Alfred A. Knopf, 1966.

Martin, Jay. *Harvests of Change: American Literature, 1865–1914.* Englewood Cliffs, N.J.: Prentice-Hall, 1967.

Meiselman, Karen C. *Incest: A Psychological Study of Causes and Effects with Treatment Recommendations.* San Francisco: Jossey-Bass Publishers, 1979.

Montaigne, Michel. *The Essays of Montaigne.* Translated by E. J. Trenchman. London: Oxford University Press, 1942.

————. *Michel Montaigne: Oeuvres complètes.* Edited by Albert Thibaudet and Maurice Rat. Paris: Gallimard, 1962.

Mosley, Edwin M. "*The Age of Innocence*: Edith Wharton's Weak *Faust.*" *College English* 21 (1959): 156–80.

Nevius, Blake. *Edith Wharton: A Study of Her Fiction.* Berkeley: University of California Press, 1953.

Partridge, Eric. *A Dictionary of Slang and Unconventional English.* Ed. Paul Beale. London: Routledge & Kegan, 1984.

Pater, Walter. *Marius the Epicurean.* London: J. M. Dent, 1966.

————. *The Renaissance.* London: Macmillan, 1873.

Perri, Carmela, et al. "An International Annotated Bibliography of Allusion Studies." *Style* 13 (1979): 178–225.

Poe, Edgar Allan. *The Narrative of Arthur Gordon Pym.* New York: Hill & Wang, 1960.

Preminger, Alex, ed. *The Encyclopedia of Poetry and Poetics.* Princeton, N.J.: Princeton University Press, 1965.

Price, Alan. "Edith Wharton's *The Age of Innocence.*" *Yale University Library Gazette* 55 (1980): 26.

Racine, Jean. *The Complete Plays of Jean Racine.* Vol. 2. Translated by Samuel Solomon. New York: Random House, 1957.

Raphael, Lev. *Edith Wharton's Prisoners of Shame: A New Perspective on Her Neglected Fiction.* New York: St. Martin's Press, 1991.

Rudolph, Frederick. *The American College and University: A History.* New York: Alfred A. Knopf, 1962.

St. Augustine. *The Confessions of St. Augustine.* Translated by John K. Ryan. New York: Image Books, 1960.

Scarf, Maggie. *Unfinished Business.* New York: Ballantine, 1988.

Schriber, Mary Suzanne. *Gender and the Writer's Imagination: From Cooper to Wharton.* Lexington: University Press of Kentucky, 1987.

————. Introduction. *A Motor-Flight Through France* by Edith Wharton. DeKalb: Northern Illinois University Press, 1991.

Scott, R. Y. B., ed. *The Anchor Bible.* New York: Doubleday, 1965.

Shelley, Mary. *Frankenstein.* New York: New American Library, 1983.

Sheppard, Sara Elizabeth. *Charles Auchester.* 1853. Reprint. New York: E. P. Dutton, 1928.

Showalter, Elaine. "The Death of the Lady (Novelist): Wharton's *House of Mirth.*" *Representations* 9 (Winter 1985): 133–49.

Stevenson, Robert Lewis, and Lloyd Osbourne. *The Ebb Tide.* Chicago: Stone & Kimball, 1893.

Surtees, Virginia. *The Drawings and Paintings of Dante Gabriel Rossetti (1828–1882).* Oxford: Clarendon Press, 1971.

Tanner, Steven L. "Humanitas and Higher Education." Review of *Literature and the American College* by Irving Babbitt. *University Bookman* 27:4 (1987): 20–22.

Thompson, James. R. *Thomas Lovell Beddoes.* Boston: Twayne, 1985.

Tillyard, E. M. W. *The Elizabethan World Picture.* New York: Vintage, n.d.

Tintner, Adeline. "Mothers and Daughters and Incest in the Late Novels of Edith Wharton." In *The Lost Tradition: Mothers and Daughters in Literature,* ed. Cathy N. Davidson and E. M. Grouner. New York: F. Ungar, 1980.

Tolstoy, Leo. *Anna Karenina*. Translated by George Bibian. New York: W. W. Norton, 1977.

Tuttleton, James. "Mocking Fate: Romantic Idealism in Edith Wharton's *The Reef*." *Studies in the Novel* 19 (1987): 459–74.

———. *The Novel of Manners in America*. Chapel Hill: University of North Carolina Press, 1972.

———. "The President and the Lady: Edith Wharton and Theodore Roosevelt." *Bulletin of the New York Public Library* 69 (1965): 45–57.

Tyler, William R. "Personal Memories of Edith Wharton." *Proceedings of the Massachusetts Historical Society* 85 (1973): 91–104.

Vita-Finzi, Penelope. *Edith Wharton and the Art of Fiction*. New York: St. Martin's Press, 1990.

Wagner, Linda W. "A Note on Wharton's Use of *Faust*." *Edith Wharton Newsletter* 3 (1986): 1, 8.

Wagner-Martin, Linda. *The House of Mirth: A Novel of Admonition*. Boston: Twayne, 1990.

Waid, Candace. *Letters from the Underworld: Fictions of Women and Writing*. Chapel Hill: University of North Carolina Press, 1991.

Walton, Geoffrey. *Edith Wharton*. Rutherford, N.J.: Fairleigh Dickinson University Press, 1970.

Waterhouse, Ellis K. *Reynolds*. London: Kegan Paul, Trench Trubner, 1941.

Waters, William, and Emily Waters, trans. *The Vespasiano Memoirs*. London: George Routledge & Sons, 1926.

Wershoven, Carol. *The Female Intruder in the Novels of Edith Wharton*. Rutherford, N.J.: Fairleigh Dickinson University Press, 1982.

Westbrook, Wayne W. "*The House of Mirth* and the Insurance Scandal of 1905." *American Notes and Queries* 14 (1976): 134–37.

———. "Lily-Bartering on the New York Social Exchange in *The House of Mirth*." *Ball State University Forum* 20 (1979): 59–64.

Whitaker, Thomas R. "The Riddle of Emerson's 'Sphinx.' " In *Ralph Waldo Emerson*, edited by Lewis Leary. Chapel Hill: University of North Carolina Press, 1982.

White, Barbara A. *Edith Wharton: A Study of the Short Fiction*. New York: Twayne, 1991.

Wilson, Edmund. "Twilight Sleep." Review of *Twilight Sleep* by Edith Wharton. *New Republic* 51 (1927): 78.

Wolff, Cynthia Griffin. *A Feast of Words: The Triumph of Edith Wharton*. New York: Oxford University Press, 1977.

# Index